D0910215

The Masks of Mary Renault

THE MASKS OF Mary Renault

A Literary Biography

Caroline Zilboorg

University of Missouri Press
Columbia and London

University of Missouri Press, Columbia, Missouri 65201
Printed and bound in the United States of America

5 4 3 2 1 05 04 03 02 01

Library of Congress Cataloging-in-Publications Data

Zilboorg, Caroline.
The masks of Mary Renault : a literary biography / Caroline Zilboorg.
p. cm.
Includes bibliographical references and index.
ISBN 0-8262-1322-7 (alk. paper)
1. Renault, Mary. 2. Homosexuality and literature—History—20th century. 3. Women novelists, English—20th century—Biography. 4. Lesbians—Great Britain—Biography. 5. Lesbians—South Africa—Biography I. Title.

PR6035.E55 Z99 2001
823'.912—dc21
[B]

00-066602

⊗™ This paper meets the requirements of the American National Standard for Permanence of Paper for Printed Library Materials, Z39.48, 1984.

Designer: Stephanie Foley
Typesetter: BOOKCOMP, Inc.
Printer and binder: Thomson-Shore, Inc.
Typefaces: Franklin Gothic and Minion

Frontispiece: Mary Renault in Durban, 1955. Photo courtesy of Julie Mullard.

For Austin, Toby, Elodie, and Miranda

contents

preface

In the process of writing this book, I have often been asked how I came to choose my subject. Most people with whom I discuss it recognize Mary Renault as the author of historical novels about the classical world; many confess to remembering a title or two; and some vividly recall *The Last of the Wine*, her first "Greek" novel, published in 1956, or *The King Must Die*, the first of her two books about the mythical Theseus, or her sweeping trilogy about Alexander the Great. I was drawn to her by none of these. Indeed, I dimly recall looking at *The King Must Die* in my school library and deciding that it was about experience so distant from my own that I made another choice.

Then, after a summer of European travel in 1992, my family and I headed to Berlin for eight days in a pension on Knesebeck Strasse. We arrived early on a sunny August afternoon, but we found the doors locked and no one at home. As we strolled about in front of the building, waiting for the proprietor, I perused the display tables under the awning of a nearby bookshop, discovering among the secondhand volumes an alluring paperback copy of *The Charioteer*. The trove of books we had brought with us was nearly completely read, and I was very tempted by this one, even at six Deutschmarks. My children (two boys, then aged thirteen and twelve, and two girls, then nine and seven) needed to use the lavatory, so we wandered into the shop, were directed through and out into a nineteenth-century courtyard, to a small room on the left. I had seen the saleswoman raise her eyebrows at my request, but I was used to that: Any mother with four young children is used to such looks—there seem so many of us. When we returned to the shop, however, my husband beckoned me outside into the street. He was astonished; he had found a book he had long been seeking, Käte Kollwitz's *Tagebucher*, but when he took it up to the counter to pay, he was told that he could not buy it: the shop was for "women only." I should have guessed from its name: Lilith.

Leaving my boys to wait with my husband, I went back in to purchase *The Charioteer,* for I was now fascinated. The cover featured a pastel illustration of a gentle young man with auburn hair. Dressed in a khaki uniform, he looked down and off to the left, while behind him a crutch was propped. The back cover advertised the story as a "moving and sensitive portrayal of a modern homosexual relationship." I had thought Renault only wrote about great men in the ancient world. What was this "modern" novel about the Second World War? And what was a book about a homosexual man doing in a lesbian bookshop? What, in fact, was Mary Renault doing there?

After hours of touring Berlin, I read *The Charioteer* late into the night over the next few days. It is a wonderful novel, and I realized by the end that it was, in complex ways I did not then understand, related to the Greek novels advertised inside as "Other titles by the same author." I had no idea until several months later that this was the last book she would set in twentieth-century England, but I already felt that, when I finished the project I was then working on, I wanted to write something on Mary Renault.

Renault wrote six successful novels with contemporary settings before turning in the 1950s to the historical fiction with meticulously researched classical backgrounds for which she continues to be well known. Renault's writing both obscured her life and allowed her to explore issues vital to her—among them war, peace, heroism, career and vocation, women's roles, sexual expression, and both female and male homosexuality and bisexuality. In this biography I explore Renault's identity as a gifted writer and a sexual woman in a society in which neither of these identities was clear or easy. The shift in her writing from contemporary to Greek situations divides her work in a way that may be useful if simplistic, but certainly the classical settings allowed her to mask material too explosive to deal with directly while simultaneously giving her an "academic" freedom to write about her subjects with both personal and critical safety. Renault's reception also complicates an understanding of her achievement, for she has a special status within the academic community where she is both widely read and little written about; she is "popular" with a sophisticated audience, yet often not taken seriously as a consummate artist. One reason for her reputation is her choice of the genre of historical fiction, generally perceived as a limiting form, neither history nor fiction; another reason must certainly be her femaleness. Renault's interest in sexuality and specifically in homosexuality and bisexuality, in fluid gender roles and identities further contributed to her marginalization—yet these very interests, particularly today, warrant a reevaluation of her work and a rereading of all of her writing.

From the very beginning of her literary career, Renault engaged with questions about what constitutes homosexual identity and the meaning of same-sex love or same-sex sex acts or desire (or, for that matter, the meaning of opposite-sex love or sex acts or desire)—just the sorts of issues now receiving attention from feminist, lesbian, gay, and queer theorists.[1] Renault's own views derive from a predominantly constructionist position, which is at once conservative (that is, shaped by Freudian notions current in the 1930s through the 1950s) and radical, based on her own experiences of both heterosexual and lesbian desire and on her historical and intercultural awareness that same-sex desire and same-sex sex acts have different meanings at different times and in different places. Of course, as Renault seems well aware, heterosexuality is as much a construct as homosexuality, and both are equally dependent on changing cultural models; both categories have histories and are arbitrary and contingent. Renault is, in fact, concerned to demonstrate that heterosexuality as well as homosexuality needs to be "denaturalized"—that is, contextualized and historicized—rather than assumed as natural, while she presents homosexuality as both a more or less stable identity (a minoritizing view) and a general, more or less stable if not often realized tendency (a universalizing view).

Gender is also an important issue for Renault; indeed, her understanding of what she presents in her work as a wide spectrum of sexualities has its source in her awareness of gender and its performative dimensions. Renault's writing offers eloquent evidence for Jagose's observation that many of the insights and hopes associated with queer theory at the end of the twentieth century have long histories,[2] while Renault's subjects and themes have more in common with queer understandings of sexuality than with the progressive homophile movements and thinking of her youth and early maturity or even with the "gay liberationist" movements and theories of the 1970s and 1980s. A critique of gender itself seems implicit in her fiction, while the denaturalization of gender in her attention to human sexualities suggests a stance not merely liberationist but queer.

1. See, for example, Annamarie Jagose's historical survey of these issues in *Queer Theory.*
2. Ibid., 43.

Because she refuses to naturalize the concept of gender, Renault's novels implicitly challenge many of the conclusions—especially those concerning male homosexuality and lesbian feminism—that Adrienne Rich offers in her famous essay "Compulsory Heterosexuality and Lesbian Existence." Rather, Renault's writing reveals affinities with the sort of thinking about sexuality and gender (as well as about power, class, race, and love) that underlies Monique Wittig's work. For example, Wittig's arguments destabilize the presumption of gender central to Rich's analysis and conclude that "In a society in which men do not oppress women, and sexual expression is allowed to follow feelings, the categories of homosexuality and heterosexuality would disappear." Theorists such as Judith Butler and Diana Fuss have criticized such thinking, while Rich, committed to generating political action, has gone so far as to characterize Wittig's position as "a liberal leap across the tasks and struggles of the here and now," words that might well—although not necessarily negatively—apply to the attitudes Renault develops in her contemporary as well as in her historical fiction.[3]

Despite a lifelong partnership with a woman, Renault refused to use the term *lesbian* to characterize either herself or her relationship. Her rejection of this category may have something to do with the pejorative associations the term carried in her youth, but she was also wary of the simplicity of later liberationist labels. Lesbianism in the 1970s and 1980s was frequently theorized as a sexuality of equality untroubled by power differentials. Scholars such as Lillian Federman have tended to assume that lesbianism was as much about political choice and affectional preferences as about physical sex, so that lesbian love was posited as the inverse of masculine sexuality. In this context, Renault's life and work may be seen as particularly problematic. As Elizabeth Däumer has pointed out, bisexual women (or even lesbian women who in other ways and to various extents lead lives different from the "politically correct" model) are frequently seen as "pre-gendered, polymorphously perverse, or simply sexually undecided, uncommitted and hence untrustworthy."[4] Similarly, Joan Nestle has suggested that lesbians who identify as more or less butch or femme may be understood as having internalized a heterosexual necessity for gender differentiation within a sexual relationship. However, Renault's life and work,

3. Radicalesbians, "The Woman-Identified Woman," 163; Adrienne Rich, "Compulsory Heterosexuality and Lesbian Existence," 35; see also Judith Butler, *Gender Trouble: Feminism and the Subversion of Identity,* and Diana Fuss, *Essentially Speaking: Feminism, Nature, and Difference.*

4. Elizabeth D. Däumer, "Queer Ethics; or, The Challenge of Bisexuality to Lesbian Ethics," 92.

as I present them here, dispute such attitudes and offer a sophisticated, even "queer" understanding of the multiplicity of transgressive love and sexuality.

Indeed, as recent theory has begun to question the dominant lesbian feminist assumptions that lesbian sex is couple-based, monogamous, women-identified and political, exceptions to "standard" lesbian sexuality—such as bisexuality, sadomasochism or butch/femme—are no longer seen as necessarily "ideologically suspect assimilations of patriarchal values."[5] Thus Renault's life seems especially interesting now, while her fiction, as my study should suggest, is startlingly contemporary, for it is exactly these issues that she explores, challenging not only patriarchal authority but identity politics and the conventional lesbian feminist model of sexuality.

5. Jagose, *Queer Theory*, 65.

acknowledgments

No biography is possible without the help and support of colleagues, friends, acquaintances, interested strangers, correspondents, librarians, organizations, and fortuitous connections. I have been very lucky.

I have received vital support from the start from others who have worked on Renault in the past, especially from Peter Wolfe and Bernard Dick, who shared with me Renault's correspondence with them, and from David Sweetman, Renault's first biographer, who generously passed on to me all of his working materials (letters, audiotaped interviews, transcripts of recorded material, and notes). His kindness in sharing with me his experiences and understanding, even while still busy finishing his own book, has been invaluable, and he has been consistently helpful and encouraging in person, on the telephone and in correspondence.

Among those who knew Mary Renault personally, I am most grateful to her lifelong companion and executor, Julie Mullard, who has been throughout my work encouraging and extremely helpful with myriad particulars, writing me regularly and frankly from South Africa in response to my numerous letters. Without her shared memories and generosity in granting permission for quotation of unpublished material, this book would not have been possible.

Others who knew Renault were also remarkably kind in sharing with me letters and memories, especially Joyce Challans, Mary's sister, who provided a lovely tea in Devon as well as answers over the years to particular queries, and Colin Spencer, who shared with me his letters from Renault and useful thoughts. I am also grateful to Brian Bamford, current President of the P.E.N. Club of South Africa in Cape Town; to Nadine Gordimer and to John Guest, Mary's friend and editor at Longman's for many years. Among Renault's classmates at St. Hugh's College, Oxford University, I would like particularly to thank Winifred Forth, Phyllis Hartnoll, Joan M. Hussey, Helen Lamb, and Marjorie Wrottesley. I am also grateful to the late A. D. "Daisy" Day, former Matron at the Radcliffe Infirmary, who shared with me her recollections of both Nurse Challans and Nurse Mullard.

A number of people in Oxford have helped me to understand Renault's experiences there, among them Elizabeth Boardman, Archivist, Oxford Health Authority; Susan Pease, Editor, *St. Hugh's Chronicle;* Dr. John Potter and his wife, Kathleen; and Debbie Quare, Librarian at St. Hugh's College. I am additionally grateful to the staff of the Radcliffe Infirmary: C.B.T. Adams, Mrs. Elizabeth Morgan, Dr. Susan Pembrey, Roslyn Sturny, and Les Willis.

Other people in their official and unofficial capacities were also helpful, among them Mary Wilkins of Southmead Health Services, Bristol, and former staff members of the Winford Hospital: Pauline Clarke, Meriel Eyre-Brook, and Stella Saywell. I am grateful as well to Elizabeth Bevan, Librarian, Bath Central Library; Julian Hunt, Local Studies Librarian, Buckinghamshire County Library and Museum; Elizabeth Jeffery, Reference Librarian, Bristol Central Library; Maggie Parham of the Royal Society of Literature; and J. D. Walters, Headmistress of Clifton High School for Girls.

I would also like to thank other people less formally connected to Mary Renault whose interest I have valued: Dieter Bertram, the screenwriter Norman Corwin, the late composer Howard Ferguson, Dirk La Cock, the composer and musicologist Klaus Roy, and Michael Wilson, son of Dr. Robert Rowand Wilson.

Tim Evens, who as a Conscientious Objector served at the Winford Hospital in the early years of the war, has been wonderfully generous in sharing with me his memories, information, photographs, critical judgment, and good sense. He read an early draft of what was initially the first chapter, which later became everything I had to say about *The Charioteer.* The book has profited from his comments and encouragement.

My colleagues at Clare Hall, Cambridge University, have been supportive throughout the years I have been at work on this project. I am particularly grateful to Janet Huskinson, Carole Newlands, Antoinette Quinn, Esther Rothblum, and Henry Sullivan (who read a section of Chapter 1 in typescript). The Clare Hall Women's Group has been unfailingly kind in responding to ideas I shared with them. Special thanks go to Leila Ahmed (who read Chapter 8 in typescript) and to Terri Apter, who as organizer of the Clare Hall Literature Group allowed me my first opportunity to speak on Renault, in 1993.

Other friends and colleagues who have supported me and this project in numerous ways include Wendy Arundale, Mary Beard, Barbara Grier, Carolyn Heilbrun, Mathilda Hills, Janet Howarth, Phyllis Lassner, Allison Meinhold, Sharon Ouditt, Diane Purkiss, Martin Stannard, George Steiner, the late Martin Taylor, and Chad Wilson. My husband, Thomas Nevin, as well as two of my four children, Austin and Elodie Nevin, read various chapters and sections at various stages. Tobias and Miranda Nevin did not read anything, but were an invaluable help through their patience and interest nonetheless.

I am always grateful to those who nourish a project before they or even I know what may come from nascent interest. I am indebted to Jan Parker, who shared with me her copy of *Purposes of Love*, which confirmed my sense of Renault's gifts, as well as to Paud Hegarty of the London bookshop Gay's the Word and to the female staff of the Lilith bookshop in Berlin.

The National Endowment for the Humanities also deserves my thanks for the Fellowship, granted during the 1995–1996 academic year, which allowed me to complete my research and to make substantial progress in the writing of the book.

I am additionally grateful to the following libraries and institutions:

Bath Central Library
The BBC Archive, Reading
The Beinecke Rare Book and Manuscript Library, Yale University
Bristol Central Library
The British Library Sound Archive
Buckinghamshire County Library and Museum
Cambridge University Library
Churchill College Archives, Cambridge
Clifton School for Girls, Bristol
Friends House, London
Grasselli Library at John Carroll University
Greater London Record Office and History Library
The Harry Ransom Humanities Research Center, University of Texas
The Imperial War Museum
Lincoln Library, Lake Erie College
Local Studies Library, Stratford, London
Mugar Library, Boston University
The National Institute for Nursing, Oxford
Oxford Heath Authority Archives

Oxford Polytechnic, Department of Health Care Studies
The Radcliffe Infirmary Archives
The Royal Society of Literature, London
St. Hugh's College Library, Oxford
St. Mary's Hospital, London
University of California Library, Los Angeles
University of Cape Town Library, Rondebosch
The Wellcome Institute for the Study of the History of Medicine, London

I would also like to thank the following people and institutions for permission to read and to quote from unpublished or copyrighted material:

Julie Mullard for permission to quote from Mary Renault's work and from her unpublished correspondence as well as from her own correspondence with me; also for permission to use photos from her collection.

Anthea Morton-Saner, Renault's literary agent at Curtis Brown, for permission to quote from Mary Renault's published work.

The Beinecke Rare Book and Manuscript Library for permission to quote from Mary Renault's correspondence with Bryher (Winifred Ellerman).

Barbara Williams for permission to read Mary Renault's correspondence with her husband, Jay Williams, and the Mugar Library, Boston University, and for permission to quote from these letters.

Pauline Clark, Tim Evens, and Meriel Eyre-Brook for permission to quote from personal correspondence with me; Tim Evens for permission to use two photographs from his collection.

St. Hugh's College Library for permission to quote from Mary Renault's correspondence with Kathleen Abbott.

Joan Hussey for her permission to quote from her letters to me.

Bernard Dick and Peter Wolfe for their permission to quote from Mary Renault's letters to them.

Elsa Worrall for permission to quote from her husband Clifford Worrall's unpublished autobiography.

Colin Spencer for his permission to quote from Mary Renault's letters to him and from his letters to me.

The audiotapes and typescripts of David Sweetman's interviews with Mary Renault and Julie Mullard are at St. Hugh's College Library, as are his extensive notes made while researching his biography. Transcripts of interviews between

Renault and Sue MacGregor and between Renault and Cyril Watling are also at St. Hugh's, as are all letters from Mary Renault to various correspondents, unless otherwise noted. Copies of correspondence from Renault shared with me by the recipients, among them Bernard Dick and Peter Wolfe, remain in my possession, while the originals remain with the recipients. Copies and originals of correspondence between Renault and Colin Spencer are in Spencer's possession, while Elsa Worrell owns the original of Clifford Worrell's autobiography. All personal correspondence with me is in my possession.

The Masks of Mary Renault

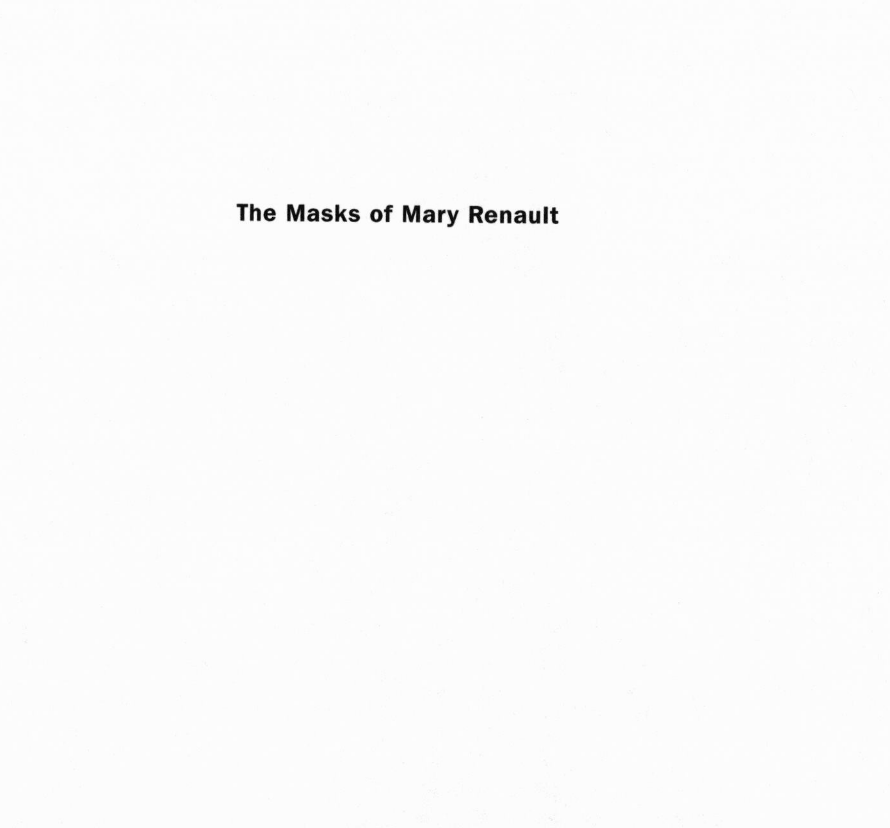

one

Formative Years
1905–1928

Among Mary Renault's papers, there is only one letter to a child. Although she never wanted children any more than she wanted marriage, Renault vividly remembered what girlhood was like, and the letter to young Oriane Messina is both charming and revealing:

> Your school uniform is very pretty. When my mother was at Kensington High School uniforms had not started. When she was in one of the middle forms, she wanted to be smart so she made up a bustle, though her mother said she was too young to wear it. A bustle was like a cushion you tied on over your bottom, to make your skirt stick out at the back, which was very fashionable at the time, for grownup people. My mother's was home-made and she put it on just before she went out, when no-one was looking. Only she didn't tie it on tight enough, so it fell off, and the next thing she knew, a little boy was running after her waving it and saying, "Clemmie, you've dropped your bustle!" She never tried one after that till she was grown up, and then they were out of fashion, so she never wore a bustle in the end.[1]

This amusing anecdote suggests the author's sensitivity to the interests and language of a young child, but Renault's humor and simple syntax obscure the tale's significant implications. This story, confided to Renault by her mother and then passed on gratuitously by Renault to Oriane, seems a cautionary

1. Renault to Oriane Messina, daughter of Ruth and Cedric Messina, June 30, 1976. Unless otherwise indicated (see p. xix), all letters from Renault to various correspondents are at St. Hugh's College Library, Oxford.

woman's tale about conformity and difference, femaleness and sexuality, about what is hidden that is suddenly revealed as irregular—to the male, who draws attention to it; to the female, who is shamed. As a result, she never has the chance to claim this feminine distinction, this concealed difference, this pronounced self-assertion, this independently fashioned identity.

Born Eileen Mary Challans in London in 1905, Mary Renault, called "Molly" at home, seldom aligned herself with her traditional mother; throughout her childhood in London's East End, where her father was a physician in general practice, she always thought of herself as a writer. Her parents' marriage was an unhappy one, and after the birth of her sister Joyce in 1911, Frank and Clementine Challans led increasingly separate lives. Renault saw her childhood as defined in many ways by this awkward union. She wrote to the English author Colin Spencer that she was particularly interested in corresponding with him because of shared affinities she sensed from having read his autobiographical novels. She, too, had had a stormy childhood in large measure as a result of her parents' unhappy lives. Despite a flirtation with "a rather charming waster without a brain in his head," her mother had been "carefully segregated" until meeting her father. Renault commented with characteristic insight and acerbity,

> That they were engaged for *four years* without finding out that they were totally incompatible mentally (naturally they did not have the chance to discover the sexual aspect) is one of those things you would not believe if you read it in a book. My father was a militant realist, my mother liked everything nice. *He* thought (though often mistakenly) that he was a logical person; my mother thought logic was some sort of materialistic philosophy which should be stubbornly resisted. He had a bitter tongue, and could always win an argument; she of course revenged herself by making it personal, and he could beat her at that too. I can never remember, though I was born within a year of their marriage, a time when they seemed to me even to like each other.[2]

In constructing here a brief autobiography, Renault places herself within a literary context: she infers Spencer's unhappy past from his novels; she recreates for him in a letter a vivid, almost novelistic account of the atmosphere surrounding her own childhood, which "you would not believe if you read

2. Renault to Colin Spencer, September 20, 1967.

it in a book." Renault also sees herself as developing within the context of her parents' relationship, a triangle that she will repeatedly explore in her fiction through the creation of stormy childhoods made believable through Freudian psychology, an analysis of gender and political power, and the use of factual evidence. She is reading her own life for Spencer, aware that it is a reality shaped by experiences unbelievable in literature while simultaneously giving it literary expression and credibility in a letter. Writing, in other words, communicates through a transformation of reality that is a strategic distortion without which one could not communicate the truth of experience.

The idea of the hidden and the revealed becomes central for Renault both as a motif that suggests how her own writing works (in what it hides, in what it reveals) and as a motif within her work. She continues perceptively in this important letter to Spencer: "Do you know that I still, quite often, find myself going out of my way through several open doors in the house, rather than open a closed one? . . . I realise now that I do it for no practical reason whatever. It is because of those closed doors at home behind which a frightful row was going on." What is hidden, even forbidden, to the self by the self, is not the unknown but in fact the known, the "frightful row" behind the closed doors, the parental discord, which is wrong and which excludes the child, which begot the child but provides no place for her except the shut-out spaces of exterior corridors and empty rooms.

Renault came to see herself as a pawn in her parents' unhappiness as her mother "confided" in her and as each parent elicited her loyalty. Never one to indulge in self-pity, she concluded with characteristic generosity:

> Of course there were faults on both sides but neither wanted me to admit this. I think either of them could have been reasonably contented with someone else. It is odd to think that if my mother, who had no intellectual interests at all, had married her old sweetheart, who apparently had none either, she would probably have kept him off the bottle and had several nice extroverted non-intellectual children, and I would have been one of those unrealised genetic potentialities which exists in their countless millions of millions wherever there are people. Human identity is a great mystery.[3]

Renault confesses here her own not-so-nice, introverted, and intellectual personality, attributable to genetic chance as well as to her early home

3. Ibid.

environment. She is, as it were, as much Elsie in *The Friendly Young Ladies* (1944) as she is her older sister Leo. In this, Renault's third novel, the focus is finally on the bisexual "friendly young ladies"—it is Helen, the former nurse turned illustrator, and the work's protagonist, the conflicted writer Leo, who are the title figures—but the novel begins as Elsie's story, the story of an infantilized young woman who is the victim of her parents' bad marriage. Like Renault, Elsie is trying to escape from home and all that it represents, and the metaphor is domestic geography. The novel begins: "Very quietly and carefully, hardly moving her thin young neck and round shoulders, Elsie looked round the room, first at the french windows into the garden, then at the door, measuring distances. Her calculations were instinctive, like those of a mouse; she had been making them since she could crawl. There was hardly any need to look this time; the way to the door lay flat across her father's line of vision." Elsie tries to negotiate an exit while her parents argue, but she lacks her older sister's bravura, is noticed and drawn by her parents into the altercation, feels "Guilt and shame," sees herself as "inferior and inadequate," and escapes into the damp Cornish chill only when her father tells her she can go.[4]

Renault was never the mouse that Elsie is; she was never the naive and unreflective child whom she depicts in this book—but Elsie's desire to escape from the physical confines of home and from the parental arguments that the house represents is certainly Renault's own struggle from earliest childhood (perhaps "since she could crawl") to separate herself from her parents, to assert her unique intellectual and private self on her own terms, to escape unseen, unacknowledged, unrevealed, without opening a closed door. Reflecting more generally on having grown up in London, a metaphor here for her life within the confines of her family and, by extension, within the confines of both gender and conventional heterosexuality, she wrote eloquently to the American author Jay Williams: "I was born there and spent most of my childhood in it, and I can't remember a time when I didn't want out—as soon, whenever it was, as I discovered that out existed."[5]

In 1911, the same year her sister was born, "Molly" began her formal education at Romford House School, a small, private, coeducational institution in Forest Gate, not far from her home, and soon after discovered the world of

4. Mary Renault, *The Friendly Young Ladies,* 5, 6, 9. All further references to this novel (hereafter cited as *FYL*) will be included parenthetically in the text.

5. Renault to Jay Williams, February 21, 1975.

literature. Her father encouraged her reading, sharing with her the books in his library, among them the standard Victorian and Edwardian fare, including all of Dickens and Kipling. Molly spent most of the Great War with her mother and sister in London, but from its start in August, 1914, Frank Challans was eager to enlist. It seems likely that he was stirred by the wave of patriotism that swept the country, but it is possible that he was also eager to escape a cloying marriage. Rejected initially because of poor eyesight, by 1915, with the decimation of "Kitchener's Army," the military was eager for recruits. Dr. Challans joined the Royal Army Medical Corps and was posted to India, where he remained until demobilized in early 1919.

In 1916, at the age of eleven, Molly was a star pupil, coming in first in class examinations and receiving a copy of *Kingsley's Heroes* as a prize. To escape the danger of bombing raids, in June of 1917 Molly and Joyce were sent to Whiteleaf, a Buckinghamshire village, where they stayed for nearly a year and attended the local village school. When they returned to London, Joyce went happily back to her former classmates. Molly, however, would remain in a kind of limbo; she returned to Romford House School but seems to have devoted herself to independent reading while the choice of a secondary school was deferred until after the war. When she and Joyce became ill with flu in 1918, her father did not inform them of the severity of the epidemic, but Renault recalled his stories of attending patients in houses "where the door stood open with a note pinned on it saying DOCTOR COME UPSTAIRS, because there was nobody fit to open the door."[6] Finally, in 1920, at her Aunt Bertha's urging, Molly was sent away from home to Clifton School for Girls in Bristol.

At fifteen, Molly was the oldest girl in her year. She took the standard variety of subjects, excelling particularly in French and doing well in English (both literature and writing), geography, science, and Latin. In history her performance was adequate; in math only "fair." Here, as at home, Molly appears to have gone her own way, finding, like many adolescents, that what was really important seemed to be experienced outside the classroom, and for the first time she developed friendships with other girls.[7]

6. Renault to Bryher, January 9, 1972. Bryher was the name taken by Winifred Ellerman (1894–1983), the British writer and philanthropist who was the companion of American writer H. D. (Hilda Doolittle).

7. I am indebted to David Sweetman for many factual details about Renault's early life; see his *Mary Renault: A Biography,* 7–19. I am grateful to J. D. Walters, headmistress of Clifton High School for Girls, for sharing with me Renault's records, on which I draw for information about her formal education there.

Before leaving home, she had thought of herself as a tomboy and had joined in boys' rather than in girls' games, recalling years later that "I used to climb trees and all that sort of nonsense." In fact, she wanted to be "a cowboy": "I trained for that very rigourously: I practiced with my lasso, which I made out of a clothes line—and then I confided this ambition to my mother, who told me that if I went out West, I would have to darn cowboys' socks and cook, so I forgot about that. And then I wanted to be a boy scout, and my mother said, 'Well, you can't be a boy scout, but you can be a girl guide.'" Yet when Molly visited a session, the girl guides seemed petty, competitive, and juvenile, so she was put off and never joined. The fantasy of being not a literal boy but "a cowboy," a dashing young male hero of the sort she had read about in Kipling and in other "boys' adventure stories," captured her imagination while it contrasted starkly with the reality offered to her by her mother. Revealing her early resistance to conventional gender roles, Renault admitted, "I always identified with the boys and I always thought the girls are always somehow tagging on. . . ."[8]

At Clifton, however, Molly became one of a group of six or seven girls and found a female friend, a best friend, in Beryl Lewis, a day student with whose family Renault lived after her first year. Julie Mullard, Renault's partner, reflecting on the information and feelings Mary had shared with her, has emphasized Beryl's importance in Mary's life during their school days: It was Mary's first experience of a close friendship, and Beryl's integrity and affection must have seemed marvelous to her. Holiday visits to her schoolmate's loving family offered a sharp contrast to the unhappiness of Mary's own home, while her friendship with Beryl was helpfully undemanding. Julie has also pointed out that, although conventional herself, Beryl accepted unconventionality in others. Yet young Molly was not especially unconventional; her greatest distinction was probably her energy and intellectual promise combined with a marked lack of mental rigor. She tended to be a leader, but also a girl who enjoyed the solitude and independence necessary for extensive reading. Sexually she was naive, ignorant of all but the biological facts, and certainly as physically inexperienced as most young women of her class and age would then have been. If she was already certain that she did not want to marry,

8. These quotations and reflections are taken from the uncut transcript of Sweetman's interviews with Renault on January 26–30, 1982. These conversations, severely truncated, formed the basis for the televised BBC *Omnibus* program and are hereafter cited as "*Omnibus* interview."

she had formed her conviction on the basis of her parents' union, the only marriage she knew, and not on the basis of any possible alternative partnership or transgressive desires. In contrast, Beryl, who would go on to train as a secretary, "knew exactly where she was going: to marriage and a family."[9]

Encouraged by her teachers, Renault entered Oxford after completing the qualifying exams at Clifton. It was a dramatic step for a woman of her time to go off to a university, but nowhere near so unusual an event as it had been for the previous college generation, which included Vera Brittain, Dorothy Sayers, and Winifred Holtby, women whose experiences were defined by the Great War and the struggle not only for the vote but for the right to receive university degrees, a battle waged and won at Oxford by the time Renault arrived at St. Hugh's College in October 1925. At twenty, she was again chronologically older than most women in her year, but she was in many ways intellectually and emotionally younger; she was still Molly Challans and not yet "Mary Renault." Looking back at this period, she characterized herself to a university classmate, Kathleen Abbott, as "an exceptionally late developer" and "completely adolescent." To fellow writer Jay Williams, she reiterated, " . . . looking back I realise that all the time I was at Oxford I was a sixth-former in mental age, and had to start all over again later, educating myself when I was at a stage to take it in."[10]

Her education, despite the demands of a challenging program at Clifton High School, had been haphazard and undisciplined, preparing her neither for a specific career nor for the kind of learning she was expected to do at a university. Joan Hussey, a St. Hugh's classmate who went on to become a historian at the University of London, commented on the impression Renault made: "Molly Challans stands out in my memory as an uncommonly vivacious, lively individual with a bush of black hair, standing on edge simply sparkling and indeed positively sizzling with energy, with boundless and frequently changing enthusiasms, determined, but not then possessed of the capacity for sustained application, somewhat undisciplined, experimental, very right wing and pro-colonial and imperial, attracted to the less usual. . . ." Hussey added perceptively: "I myself was turning into a dedicated medievalist and had been taught from early years how to work and I came from a satisfying home circle with brothers overlapping with me at Oxford. I don't think Molly Challans had any of these advantages and she never fitted into what I would

9. Mullard to Sweetman, December 19, 1989.
10. Renault to Kathleen Abbott, September 15, 1964; Renault to Williams, May 18, 1966.

call normal academic life and this, combined with her passionate desire to express herself in writing, led her to run before she could walk."[11]

While Renault invariably defined herself in terms of her own independent intellectual life—her research in classical history was consistently a private and individual effort—she always felt grateful for having had a formal education, for having experienced the structured and rigid pattern of learning outside the home, which until her generation was often reserved solely for boys and men. Responding to Williams's reservations about institutionalized education, she declared:

> I am sure that psychologically we were often grossly mishandled (when have children not been since the world began?) But it taught me French, and some German and some Latin, as a result of which though I never learned Italian I can have a good guess at it; and it grounded me in Greek myth so that I have known something about it since I was twelve years old; the kind of core to which curiosity and further knowledge sticks. . . . But for my school library, where when senior we were allowed to browse, I would not have read Plato at eighteen, which is I suppose about the age Plato would have wanted one to start on him. I wouldn't have discovered Malory; I might even love *The Once and Future King* instead of puking. I wouldn't have lived with Shakespeare and the Border Ballads and Campion and Lovelace and Byron. My father's library, though good of its kind, covered hardly anything but from about 1880–1924. The only exception I remember was an early Culpeper from which I learned where babies come from. No, honestly I think I'm quite glad I went to school, though of course I suffered agonies like everyone else.[12]

Renault's feelings about formal education remained a curious mixture. She very much valued the intellectual matter that was taught or purported to be taught in schools, while she felt deeply skeptical about the women in authority who, in her experience, were relegated to teaching girls and young women. She did not question their competence—their knowledge or skills—but was invariably disappointed in their limited experience of the world and in their inability to communicate to her enthusiasm, excitement, passion for their subjects. Thus she remembered not particular teachers but particular achievements—in this case, in languages—and particular authors, discovered

11. Joan M. Hussey, letter to author, July 18, 1993.
12. Renault to Williams, January 13, 1968.

not so much in the classroom apparently as in the school library. The exception is "an early Culpeper," a technical and explicit medical text from her father's library by an eighteenth-century herbalist, which like her own later nursing career would be at odds with her formal education.

Renault had exorbitant expectations of her schools and teachers, whom she tended to romanticize well into her thirties. For her, educational institutions and individual women were initially idealized as the counterpart to home with its domestic tensions and intellectual vacuity. Thus when one of the dons invited her to dine at high table at St. Hugh's while she was training in the 1930s as a nurse at the Radcliffe Infirmary just down the road, she was disconcerted to find the experience dull:

> I went thinking hopefully how nice it would be after the rather down-to-earth conversation of the hospital dining-room to breathe a more rarified air. It was quite a shock to me, having vaguely supposed I think that we should talk books and plays over the coffee, to find just as much small-talk as I had been hearing, only without the racy personalities and fundamental life-and-death considerations which keep hospital talk at least from being dull. Men do seem able to acquire the noble virtues of scholarship without being engulfed in that damp mist of gray good taste. Well, perhaps women do by now, I wouldn't know.[13]

Academic life, Renault fantasized, would provide the "out" she had sought for as long as she could remember, and she resented what she felt were its failures: superficiality, tedium, and finally the "damp mist of gray good taste," which must have recalled for her her mother's insistence on what was "nice" in contrast to her father's emphasis on what was logical and real. Renault never regretted having rejected an academic career as a scholar-teacher, a career for which a degree in English at Oxford would logically have qualified her. She felt saved from what she saw as the fate of the St. Hugh's don and others like her by both her nursing and her writing, and could be quite bitter in her mockery of individual scholars, particularly women in her own fields of literature, history, and classical studies. Thus she imagined "Poor Jane Harrison [the pioneering classical anthropologist] stifling among the antimacassars and dreaming of nights on the bare mountain. I wonder how she would have felt if she could have been transported in a time machine to look on at a real orgy. My bet is that

13. Renault to Abbott, undated, probably written in December 1958.

she would have rushed behind a bush and been very sick."[14] Renault finally saw academic life for women as pathetically insulating, although not necessarily so but only because of social conventions, which she always hoped would change. Her own experiences at Oxford had been stimulating and great fun, but she felt that a career in academe after graduation would have been deadening.

She had fond memories of her three years at St. Hugh's, although the most wonderful bits occurred outside the classroom and were marginalized experiences. To Kathleen Abbott, she wrote of Oxford in the early spring: "No doubt they are sailing on Port Meadow and once again 'the river is in high flood and all the weirs are drawn.' Do you remember how we paddled among the pollard willows? I suppose it was rather mad of us, but wasn't it a lovely day?" She also recalled "long arguments . . . about Milton and Byron," the latter a writer whom, with Malory, she would admire all her life.[15] Her friendships with other young women were also important to her, and Kathleen was her closest companion. She and Renault got to know each other when, in their second year at St. Hugh's, they each had a room in the same college house on Woodstock Road some distance from the college itself. Placed together in tutorials, Renault, Abbott recalled, was the bolder student, and generally "the leader and pranker." Both young women were keen on acting, and Renault took on starring roles. When she excelled as François Villon in a play about his life, a notice in one of the men's college reviews amused them both by praising Renault as "an extremely beautiful girl." Abbott remarked, "She had in fact very much of a Rossetti look. I believe it was through her that I first fell in love with the Greek world, at least we were drawn together by our love of it, as we were, too, in fact, over the 'romantic' middle ages." But a shared interest in the ancient world really developed later, after both women had left Oxford; during the years together at St. Hugh's, it was medieval France, animated for Renault through various sorts of dramatic performance, that captured their imaginations. Abbott admits that in college "Mary showed no particular interest in the Greeks. She was much more excited by the legends and stories of the medieval times (via Malory, etc.) In fact, this was a kind of romantic passion. She collected swords and had them hanging in her room, and she wrote poems expressing this love. She loved acting and always chose the plays." Performance finally became the defining element of Renault's circle: "The little group who acted together were all friends from the beginning; they

14. Renault to Abbott, September 16, 1962.
15. Renault to Abbott, February 25, 1963, and May 14, 1960.

had cocoa together in each others' rooms in college in the evenings, and later in Woodstock Road they met frequently to discuss, among other things, the plays they acted. Mary was the main instigator of all this; she was generally popular and a leader."[16]

The nature of these friendships, however, was conventional and while affectionate was in no way intimate. Just as Julie Mullard was careful to stress Beryl Lewis's traditional heterosexuality, Frances Aubrey-Smith, the cousin with whom Kathleen Abbott lived later in life, insisted that "There was no suggestion of homosexual relations between any of them. . . . Mary's and Kathleen's friendship was a perfectly normal one based on the enthusiasms which they shared. Much later, when Kathleen read one of Mary's first books, she was quite surprised at the tone generally; Mary seemed to have changed in outlook."[17] It would seem that Mary's sexuality was primarily or exclusively heterosexual during her college years, but the important point is that her sexuality was conventional at this time in that it was private and probably as yet unexamined. Certainly it remained unexpressed except in traditional social terms—she shared the national passion for the Prince of Wales, for example. This conventionality is not really surprising, given contemporary attitudes towards sex in general and women's sexuality in specific. In England in the 1920s, there was no accessible and appealing lesbian or bisexual identity that Renault could have claimed, even if she had wanted to, no transgressive identity of which she was aware that accurately reflected the vivacious, good-humored, and generally conventional young woman she seemed to be both to her contemporaries and to herself. Julie confirms Frances Aubrey-Smith's impression: Kathleen Abbott "was surprised at some of the experiences which Mary included in her novels and was particularly surprised at her interest in homosexuality. She never seemed interested in the subject at college, and girls' boarding schools did not seem to foster the same sort of relationships as boys' schools." Indeed, like most other young women at Oxford, Renault had "men friends," although no one in particular.[18]

More than community or specific friendships, Renault seems to have valued the physical independence she encountered for the first time at the university. This freedom was a new and thrilling if often solitary experience. For instance,

16. I quote here from notes (dated November 6 and 13, 1990) dictated by Kathleen Abbott to her cousin Frances Aubrey-Smith, who sent them to David Sweetman, and from notes made by Abbott for Sweetman in November 1990.

17. Frances Aubrey-Smith to Sweetman, November 13, 1990.

18. Mullard to Sweetman, July 7, 1988.

she once cycled on her own in a single day as far as the Malvern hills. Tired but self-satisfied, she spent the night in a hotel that looked "like some obscure wing of Balmoral," while the next day she climbed in the surrounding countryside. She recalled that "the view was lovely but it hadn't rained for ages and the grass was baked to a thin coating of dry hay, very slippery to the foot." Indeed, she was an experienced walker and sought out such challenges, commenting, "I used to do a lot of solitary rambling at that age."[19]

More generally, however, she recognized that Oxford had offered her the peace and quiet she needed for intellectual work, but felt that "once you cease to be an undergraduate it offers little in the way of stimulus; people have to get that from outside in their own way." When a new principal was appointed to St. Hugh's in the 1960s, Renault was glad to hear that she was an archaeologist. "Such a good job for mixing and getting around," she wrote to Kathleen, "and I am sure that after coping with fellaheen, Greek peasants and so on and mixing with men on the dig, it would be impossible to be so desiccated about human relationships as Miss Gwyer [the former principal] always seemed to be. I cannot . . . imagine bringing her any personal problem; I can't even imagine bringing her an intellectual one."[20]

Ironically, "out" (as well as the self-recognition and sexual revelation that this word implies) would not come through her experiences at school and at the university but only years later through her nursing and through her writing. Her nursing would allow her the factual, direct, and gritty experience of physical reality that she valued as early as her discovery of Culpeper; her writing, with its roots in childhood fantasies, adolescent dramatics, and private reading, would offer her the masks, the strategies, and the voice she required for self-expression. Thus, Renault confided to a friend, "While I was at Oxford—and much more so after I'd left it and looked in on it from a less sheltered environment—I was much struck by the frequency with which works of literature, and facts of history, which sinful and suffering human beings had created with blood and tears, were expounded by scholars who, with the most meticulously detailed knowledge of the externals, had not the remotest clue as to what any of it was all about."[21]

Throughout her life Renault felt a mixture of envy and resentment toward scholars. She was convinced on the basis of her own experiences that while

19. Renault to Williams, September 12, 1959.
20. Renault to Abbott, January 5, 1964.
21. Renault to Williams, January 31, 1958.

teachers in institutions had privileged access to great books and history and to the specialized knowledge required to understand what they read and taught, they too often failed to communicate the excitement and reality of literature and the past. She was harshly critical of the merely academic, confiding years later to Kathleen that " . . . the more I read of history, the more I realise how little the lifelong, academic historian ever relates his discipline to real life and the history that goes on around him, real human drives and reactions." Indeed, she felt she had learned more about history by living in South Africa than she could have learned in fifty years at a university.[22]

In *North Face* (1949), the last novel Renault wrote before leaving England, she explicitly examines the female scholar in the character of Miss Searle, a well-bred woman "scarcely, if at all, past her thirties," a university don whose specialty is Chaucer.[23] She is paired and contrasted throughout the book with Miss Fisher, a nurse of the same age but of quite a different personality and class. Initially, it seems that the plot will stem from the contrasts between these two women and their potential relationship as they meet while staying in the same Devon boarding house during a summer holiday. Early in the novel, Renault brings the two women together:

> Miss Fisher's ball of wool rolled off her lap, and over to Miss Searle's feet. She reached for it as Miss Searle stooped politely. For a moment their hands met on the ball: the hand of a scholar, meticulous, with fineness but no strength in the bone, taut blue veins under the thin skin at the back, nails rubbed, brittle and flecked here and there with white; the other broad-palmed and short-fingered, with the aggressive smooth cleanliness that comes of much scrubbing with antiseptic followed by much compensating cream, with nails filed short and round, their holiday varnish spruce. (*NF,* 15)

The differences between the don and the nurse are unbridgeable, however, and Renault uses the contrast to suggest two female types rather than to develop individual characters who will drive her novel. With some sympathy for each woman, Renault finally shows us the vacuity at the center of their lives: They are defined by their professions in ways that are limiting rather than personally enriching, with Miss Fisher perhaps having the better excuse in that

22. Renault to Abbott, July 27, 1969.

23. Mary Renault, *North Face,* 11. All further references to this novel (hereafter cited as *NF*) will be included parenthetically in the text.

she actually helps people. The problem is, in part, one of different perceptions. For example, "What Miss Searle felt to be mental and conversational decency, Miss Fisher saw as an iron curtain of spinsterly repression" (*NF,* 15), while for her part Miss Searle finds Miss Fisher coarse and insensitive. Specifically, Miss Searle resents Miss Fisher's interest in (hetero)sexuality, feeling "almost physically embarrassed by women whose manner altered in the presence of men" (25).

Even experiences that might join them (Miss Fisher's helpfulness in looking after Miss Searle's cold; Miss Searle's attempt to introduce Miss Fisher to literature) become humorous scenes rather than moments of empathy or friendship. Thus, for instance, when Miss Fisher picks up Miss Searle's copy of *The Canterbury Tales,* she is at first impressed: "The archaisms within made her see Miss Searle with new eyes. A brain like that was enough to choke off any man; Miss Fisher's envy was for the first time mixed with a protective feeling." However, she soon comes upon "The Miller's Tale," which she reads "incredulously," then discovers a glossary and concludes dismissively: "*Well* . . . Doesn't that show you? I've met *that* sort before" (*NF,* 30). When Miss Fisher returns the volume, Miss Searle suspects "a stifled intellectual curiosity, to which all that was best of the pedagogue in her responded" (31). She tells Miss Fisher, " 'Both technically and humanly, it's almost inexhaustible. The vitality, the fascinating touches of realism. . . . It seems unbelievable that for centuries his verse was thought to be irregular and crude. Because of the changing sound-laws, of course—' " Miss Fisher thinks perceptively: "She hasn't noticed it's about *people*" (32).

These irreconcilable differences finally make it impossible for the two women to communicate, and their interchanges are soon reduced to rather nasty gossip about the budding romance of the major characters, Neil Langton and Ellen Shorland, who take over the novel. Renault's analysis of Miss Searle is meticulous, but as a personality she is necessarily static and finally dull because what is basically intellectual sterility is closely related to her physical unease and sexual repression.

Neil is also a teacher, but he fares better on several counts. To begin with, he is a man, and while sexually numbed by recent experiences, he has had two highly emotionally charged relationships, a homoerotic friendship with a fellow mountain climber, Sammy Randall, and an insubstantial but sexual marriage with the undependable and sentimental school nurse, Susan. The novel will in part be an account of his sexual reawakening. A classicist by training, Neil has never taught at a university but at a boys' boarding school, where he was much liked by students and staff, but unfulfilled by the experience of the classroom. Traumatized by the death of his small daughter, Sally, and Susan's irresponsibility and adultery, he has left teaching and now the London flat in which for a period he isolated himself in urban anonymity. He is currently struggling to restore himself through physical exertion (rock climbing) and a change in profession. Forcing himself towards creativity, he is translating Virgil when the novel opens, proving "some sort of concentration to be within the grip of his will" (*NF,* 39), and by the novel's end he has admitted to himself and to Ellen that he is really called to write. Responsible for much of the actual material in Sammy's popular and highly regarded books on climbing, he finally commits himself to writing under his own name.

Neil's literary sensitivity and creativity, his worldly experience, physical skills, and respect for nature make him a sharp contrast to Miss Searle. When Neil and Ellen fail to return to the boarding house one night, having gone on an excursion together and missed the last bus back, Miss Searle can only stare blankly out of the window into the dark, which she sees as "almost medieval." Renault comments: "It did not occur to her that her own mind was contributing anything to her associations, except by way of criticism. Her attitude to its literary contents had been for years that of a curator. . . . She was used to the classified specimens in her mind, on their proper shelves. She could enumerate their beauties. It was a long time since any of them had stirred in their places: she had quite forgotten they were alive" (*NF,* 201).

Renault makes quite explicit that it is sexuality and love that are shut out by such "scholarship." Having taken an aspirin for her persistent cold, Miss Searle tries to settle down to sleep. She moves her head out of the moonlight that falls upon her pillow, and "vague associations" bring to her mind a passage from Milton in which Dido longs for Aeneas. Her only response to the poetry is linguistic ("extraordinary how frequently, even by the literate, the 'in' was misquoted 'on' "), and she decides, "one had only oneself to blame for being unable to sleep, if one were foolish enough to take one's work to bed with one" (*NF,* 206). This solitary woman alone in her bed suggests all that Renault rejected in her own education when she criticized her female teachers and the world of the classroom.

In contrast was the independent learning that Renault came to on her own. Recalling a particular teacher at St. Hugh's, Renault reflected that "it shocks me sometimes to think how Seaton never taught us to follow up references, to go after supplementary sources, burrow out obscure but fascinating sidelines, or do any of those things that make a subject alive. I had to find out all that sort of thing for myself years later in another subject, where I could only do it in a very limited way, not being a classical scholar."[24] Renault regretted not having learned ancient Greek, as she surely would have had she been a boy, but she took all the more pride in her independent achievements because they were accomplished in spite of her gender and because she had arrived at them later in life when she had found her own direction beyond those offered to her by the establishment, by her society, and by the institutions that granted her degrees and certificates. She could, as it were, afford to be philosophical from a position of security beyond the confines of conventional English society, and she always strove to speak honestly about her education, keeping in mind her own academic meandering and dreamy, undisciplined youth, for which she never blamed her teachers but which she always accepted as a given part of her herself as a "late developer" the source of whose prolonged adolescence she did not consciously examine. Thus she wrote candidly and placidly to the American scholar Bernard Dick that she did Latin at school but no Greek, for few girls' schools taught Greek and very few women at the time went on to read classics at a university. While she herself read English, her main historical interest during her years at St. Hugh's was the Middle Ages. She had wanted to take on Old French as a "special" subject, but her tutor had discouraged it because of her weakness in the compulsory Anglo-Saxon. "Unfortunately", Renault admitted, "my interest in sound changes was minimal and after all I turned in a very poor paper; I might just as well have had fun with the Romances and Froissart. I still think the Morte D'arthur is one of the greatest and most beautiful of the world's masterpieces; but on the whole my interest in the middle ages has otherwise evaporated." Instead, she followed the traditional and rather rigid curriculum in the single subject Oxford required, with the result that all her Greek was "self-taught". She confessed to Dick, "I get my sources in the Loeb, and know the little I do from following both texts.[25]

Deprived of a classical education by chance and of a scholarly education by virtue of an adolescent lack of discipline only overcome later in life, Renault took particular delight in independent learning and private discoveries. Writing in 1977 to Audrey Stephens, a St. Hugh's classmate, Renault reminisced: "Do you remember how on one occasion I decided for some mad reason to do the set Latin translation into hexameters? Miss Ritchie said she could have put

24. Renault to Abbott, September 15, 1964.
25. Renault to Bernard Dick, July 9, 1970.

up with its having been the French prose I translated by mistake, if only the qualities had been right. It's nice of you to like the Greek books, autodidact as I am." Responding to Kathleen Abbott's account of the inauguration of a new library at St. Hugh's, Renault wrote, "I have affectionate memories of the old one which is inextricably twined with the books I read there, especially those outside the syllabus like Plato." Similarly, she warmly remembered a time at Clifton High School when she found "the Phaedrus in the library and how excited I was suddenly to realise whence Traherne had got his poem." Even at Romford House School, she recalled herself as a solitary although in no way an unhappy student who claimed intellectual and aesthetic experience independently and on her own terms:

> I *still* love Lays of Ancient Rome. It was one of the first grownup poems I took to on my own account, I knew both Horatius and most of Regillus by heart when I was ten or twelve and used to recite it at the top of my voice, in fact I think I must have been even younger, because I remember some adult being very put about by my asking what the deed of shame was that false Sextus had done. They told me he insulted a lady so dreadfully that she killed herself, and I kept wondering whatever he said to her. I remember a specially favourite bit of mine was in Regillus where the Great Twin Brethren appear. And where Horatius jumps in to swim home.[26]

Renault's accounts of her education reveal a marginality that is presented as consciously chosen and characteristic: her joy in reading "outside the syllabus," in bending the rules, in venturing into unknown territory, into the forbidden or at least the uncharted—what Laurie Odell in *The Charioteer* (1953) will think of as "white on the map."[27]

If much of Renault's education was a private experience, her fascination with drama, with performance, made it also a public event. Asserting ownership of Roman myths by memorizing "Horatius and most of Regillus" on her own, she also recited them loudly, much to the chagrin of "some adult." When she made the private public (by revealing to others her reading; her joy in language; her discovery of historical or factual material; the sexual, whether understood or merely intimated), Renault was censored, given incomplete or

26. Renault to Audrey Stephens, March 19, 1977; Renault to Abbott, September 15, 1964, and September 6, 1968.

27. Mary Renault, *The Charioteer*, 1. All further references to this novel (hereafter cited as *TC*) will be included parenthetically in the text.

misleading information, made to feel danger (male or female sexual expression results in a woman's suicide) and confusion. The counterpart to Renault's individual, undisciplined, and impressionistic education, which seems to have consisted almost entirely of reading, including both fiction and history, with an emphasis on language (poetry, memorization, foreign languages), was drama, a matter finally of confident performance that depended on the utterance of words, either the memorized texts of others or self-generated words—writing.

Renault's rather grim portrait of her "stormy childhood" is mitigated by her discovery of literature on the one hand and her sense of the dramatic on the other. The private domain of literature opened to Renault the more public, fantasy world of theater. To Williams she wrote of "the happy days when I would climb with two pistols on top of a wardrobe or whatever, and utter through clenched teeth, 'One more step, Mr. Hands, and I'll blow your brains out.' "[28] This sort of play consisted at first of Renault's assuming the male role of the cowboy in a mythologized Wild West, consciously performing what she had read in popular novels of the period. Later, she would relinquish this juvenile material for the medieval world, which captured her creative imagination well into early adulthood. Her first novel was in fact a lengthy historical fiction. She remembered: "When I was up at the university I started a very terrible novel about the middle ages. Of course it was terrible because I hadn't done any research . . . and really it was a romance."[29] Although she initially attempted to publish it, she later destroyed the manuscript, turning her attention to her own immediate experience and replacing a fantasized past with the autobiographical and contemporary hospital world in *Purposes of Love* in 1939. She would not return to the genre of the historical novel until *The Last of the Wine* in 1956, but acting, another mode of exploring as well as masking reality, whose roots for Renault go back at least as far as the cowboy on the wardrobe, would continue to absorb her and appears either as a motif or an explicit subject in all of her work.

The line from the medieval romance to her classical novels was clearly evident to Renault herself. Offering an account of her development as a writer, she wrote to Williams that she had been "very much taken up with the Middle Ages" until the 1950s, when she had gotten "so involved with Greece." The significant link between medieval Europe and ancient Greece was not period,

28. Renault to Williams, March 24, 1964.
29. Renault, *Omnibus* interview.

of course, but the fact of a historical setting with the consequent necessity for responsible scholarship, something Renault lacked in her twenties and sensed she lacked and an element that came to define her mature writing. To Sue MacGregor, Renault confessed that her first novel had been about "knights bashing about in some kind of never-never land." At Oxford, she had known what research was, but "I seemed to think you could spin this thing out of your head without ever doing any. . . . I never really got down to a sound job of actually getting my facts right." Julie recalled Renault's response to this juvenile first effort. After rereading it, she declared, " 'What nonsense. I have done no research, it's all just come out of my head, I haven't thought: what did they wear, how did they think, how did they eat, how did they drink? . . . This is nothing; it's just a sort of fantasy of mine.' " Renault thought, " 'Thank God no one ever saw that thing on which I had done no research. Only now, years later, do I realise the immense amount of homework one must do before one puts pen to paper.' " These are the reasons, according to Julie, that Renault was "difficult" about ever showing it to anyone and that she finally decided to destroy it in the 1930s.[30]

Renault never regretted her destruction of this first novel so reflective of her university experience. Looking back on her career, she wrote to Bernard Dick about her decision to turn instead to fiction about contemporary life. After the first abortive attempt, she declared that she had never planned to write another historical novel. Associating her initial effort with her adolescence, she described it as derivative, "bred entirely from other people's historical novels with a smattering of Froissart and Malory." At the time, she had not had "the slightest notion of how background material is got up, or the narrative checked for anachronisms," and concluded that "A kindly Providence directed that this work should be rejected by the few editors it was submitted to. The characters were pure romantic pasteboard. It is now safely cremated."[31]

Throughout her mature life Renault would work to prove herself as the scholar she had failed to become while at Oxford. Through her fiction, she would eventually communicate as both scholar and teacher, the two vocations she had consciously rejected through lack of maturity, intellectual preparation, and conventional aptitude. Thus even within months of her

30. Renault to Williams, April 7, 1958; transcript of Sue MacGregor's interview with Renault for the BBC radio program *Kaleidoscope;* transcript of one of David Sweetman's interviews with Julie Mullard, tape 6, side A.

31. Renault to Dick, August 3, 1969.

death Renault revealed herself to her friend John Guest as the dramatic teacher she longed for but never found at Oxford, the careful but dynamic academic who examines a work with both accuracy and sensitivity. Delighted with a new electronic typewriter that allowed her to revise text much more easily than earlier models, she was very tempted to play about with it, "just for the sake of it." In fact, she soon found herself "dashing off the whole of Mark Antony's speech over the body of Caesar, which has stuck in my head ever since school, in order to see where I had gone wrong and do the corrections." She concluded that at least, "I now know the speech *right.*" The exercise in quoting from memory and then checking her version against the printed the text of *Julius Caesar* led her to reflect, "Don't you often think that the Mark Antony in that play is an entirely different man from the one in *Antony and Cleopatra?* Much cleverer, for one thing. One somehow doesn't see him letting her stand in his way. People often say that Caesar himself doesn't come over like a soldier, which is true." She added that she suspected the reason for the characterization was that at the back of Shakespeare's mind was "old Queen Elizabeth, " and suggested, "For Pompey, perhaps read Essex," then caught herself up short in her cross-gendered, even homosexual reading, commenting, "Really, how I do run on."[32] We can easily see here the English student and professor in Renault, the scholar who reads and rereads a text for the beauty of its memorable language, for its drama and insights both into the ostensible subject and into the context out of which the text itself comes—in this case, the social and political life of late Elizabethan England.

Using the same standards of scholarly discipline, Renault could also be sharply critical. For instance, in a letter written late in life, she castigated an academic who had sent her a treatise on Alexander as an alcoholic. She criticized his methods (his arbitrary assumptions and selective use of evidence), and then pointed out that using his "combination of suppressing contradictory evidence, and drawing . . . conclusions from inadequate premises," one could "demonstrate nearly anything." She offered in turn her own *ex tempore* and outrageous reading of the life of Jesus, which revealed him as a drunkard, and concluded: "I trust this [illustration] has not shocked you. I would only like to point out that in terms of documentation, provided of course that your system is applied, it is better than anything you have on Alexander." Interviewed by Cyril Watling about her philosophy of life, Renault summed up her position forcefully in a response she probably wrote

32. Renault to John Guest, August 3, 1983.

out ahead of time: "A lot of trouble would be saved if people would learn the nature of evidence."[33]

Intellectual responsibility as both an artistic method and a subject in her writing persisted as an issue in all of Renault's work. Most obviously, in the context of her own early experiences, she was fascinated with the concept of a proper apprenticeship and the ideal teacher. In all of her Greek novels, she pays careful attention to the childhood and education of her protagonists. Socrates, whom in her interview with Watling she would call her "patron saint," is an important character in *The Last of the Wine,* in which he serves as a teacher as well as a role model for her protagonist Alexias and his friends Lysis and the young Plato; Plato, a character peripheral in this first Greek novel, appears again as a more central character and a teacher in his own right in *The Mask of Apollo* (1966), Renault's fourth classical fiction. In her fifth book about the ancient world, *Fire from Heaven* (1970), Renault examines the youth of Alexander the Great, stressing not only his relationship with his parents but his education by Aristotle, whose influence both through his principles and through his political machinations continues to shape his pupil's life in the second volume of the Alexander trilogy, *The Persian Boy* (1972). Similarly, Renault develops fictional teachers in her two novels about Theseus. In *The King Must Die* (1958), Theseus is at once his own teacher (like Renault, Theseus is for the most part an "autodidact" who must learn, often painfully, through his own experience) and a teacher-leader of others, in this case of the young male and female companions whom he accompanies to Crete where their "school" is the bull court. In *The Bull from the Sea* (1962), Chiron, the centaur physician, is a gifted teacher who links the lives of Theseus, his friend Pirithoos, and Achilles, who enters as the protagonist's spiritual heir at the novel's end. In *The Praise Singer* (1979), Simonides is empowered by his teacher, the fictional bard Kleobis, who takes him from his brutal childhood on Kos and teaches him not only Homer but the discipline of creation and the moral principles necessary both to politics and to a worthy life, without which, Renault stresses, no truly beautiful art can result. In his own turn, Simonides becomes the teacher for his nephew Bacchylides, who links the oral with the written tradition. Their relationship exemplifies Renault's ideal. The childless Simonides muses in old age that time and careful instruction

33. Renault to "Dr. O'Brien," July 15, 1981; Renault, interview by Cyril Watling, *What Life Has Taught Me,* SABC radio program, 1965[?]. I am grateful to David Sweetman for sharing with me a transcript of this interview given to him by Julie Mullard.

have "turned Bacchylides from a charming son to a gifted pupil. Which was just as it ought to be; for he was not my son, and not in search of a father. If I'd really begotten him, maybe we'd have fallen out; a father's expectations can fret a boy like a chain. But we had freely chosen one another, each for his own good; our bond was close, but easy. Maybe that's why he has always cared for me as a son."[34]

Renault would never teach in a school or university nor serve as a mentor for a younger writer nor become a mother, a variant teacher who at the very least may instruct the child in society's expectations. Her communication of her experiences, knowledge, and values would always occur through her work. Ironically, she remained in awe of the clearly identifiable teacher while often failing to see her own didactic role in conveying information and moral attitudes to a readership larger than any more individual instructor's lifetime of filled classrooms. Characteristically amused and a bit abashed, she wrote towards the end of her life to her friends Ruth and Cedric Messina about David Sweetman's request to interview her for BBC television. Reluctant to appear on film, Renault admitted feeling inadequate: "I don't think I am a rewarding prospect in one of these things where they do you against your background." She was particularly embarrassed because he "asked me if I lectured anywhere, so that they could film me doing it!" She finally confessed, "I tried to explain I am just a writer."[35]

34. Mary Renault, *The Praise Singer,* 243–44. All further references to this novel (hereafter cited as *PS*) will be included parenthetically in the text.

35. Renault to Ruth and Cedric Messina, January 13, 1980.

two

Casting About 1928–1933

In June of 1928, when Mary left Oxford with a third in English (a degree granted on the basis of a low pass), she took her unfinished novel with her and went home. Her parents had moved in 1926 from London to Bristol, where Dr. Challans had taken up a position as the city's deputy health inspector, and it was to their comfortable house that Mary returned. Here, she was begrudged a room of her own, formerly the guest room, and an allowance of twenty pounds a year—not exactly the congenial atmosphere and independence that Virginia Woolf would insist on as necessary to the female writer when she addressed the students of Newnham and Girton Colleges in Cambridge that very autumn. Having decided not to teach, Mary found herself in a quandary: Either she would need to live in her parents' house, where she could try to write under oppressive conditions, or she could find a simple job to supplement her allowance and live away from home in cheap lodgings, where she might find the peace and solitude she needed. She soon chose to move out.

The series of jobs Mary held in the late twenties and early thirties barely supported her and provided little intellectual stimulation. She worked for a time in Clark's boot and shoe factory, then as a civil service counter clerk, and briefly for a chocolate company, where as a minor technician she weighed samples of silver wrapping paper. Julie would later describe these years as a "gray period," a time of private, extended youth without a clear direction. It was also a period of frustrating personal poverty and relative isolation. Having decided to live on her own, Mary had no desire to be a frequent visitor at her parents' home; they did not approve of her struggle for independence and were unwelcoming on the rare occasions when she did visit. Her university friends had either remained in Oxford, gone on to promising teaching careers, or married and started families of their own. She had no circle of friends from her London childhood, and her jobs did not bring her into contact with the sorts of people who might have anchored her in a friendly or romantic relationship. Probably through her interest in theater, she did meet a rather dashing young man whose social life revolved around an amateur dramatics group in Bath. The local paper, which regularly reviewed the performances put on by Citizen House, cites him only as "R. D. Caesar," but his picture appeared on several occasions: A tall, dark, muscular young man of apparently great energy and versatility, he acted in a wide variety of plays, sometimes serving as their director as well.

Citizen House was an exciting center of activity in Bath during the late twenties and early thirties, and with Caesar, who had a car of his own and no job to demand his attention, Renault spent much of her free time there. Founded in 1913 and originally run as an educational and social center, Citizen House had developed into a drama institute during the First World War. Situated elegantly in Chandos Buildings, it contained thousands of costumes, many of them carefully collected and dating back to the eighteenth century. The heyday of Citizen House conveniently coincided with Renault's years in Bristol—it was badly damaged in a large fire in 1936, continued to put on plays in a diminished capacity until 1944, then became merely a costume hire concern until its collection was finally sold in 1958. During the summer of 1929, however, it put on a series of one-act plays and sponsored a "Summer School of Dramatic Production" that August, offering twenty plays both in its own Little Theatre and outdoors in Bath's public parks. These two weeks of intense activity boasted experienced directors from London and an "international enrollment" of over a hundred participants, including professionals. "Mr. Caesar" directed a variety entertainment entitled *Hit or Miss* and himself acted in one of its skits. Among the productions was *The Love Potion,* a farcical romance set in medieval Florence—just the sort of piece that would have appealed to Renault's wit and imagination. There were also more serious and scholarly elements to the summer school: Professor Horrox, dean of arts at Exeter University, delivered a talk on Greek drama and oversaw the production of a classical play. There was even a musical comedy, *The Cyclops,* performed at Institution Gardens, in which "R. D. Caesar" starred as Odysseus.

Citizen House provided accommodations for all of the summer school participants, and it seems likely that Mary and Caesar during these weeks and at other times frequently stayed overnight here as they participated in late rehearsals and evening performances. The summer school proved very popular and became a regular feature of the dramatic year. In 1930, Caesar starred as John Fleming in *The Ghostly Ball* amid a busy schedule that included scenes from *King Lear,* the whole of *Midsummer Night's Dream,* and a performance of Aristophanes' *The Frogs* in Bath's famous Pump Room. The local paper began to refer to regular performers as "members" of Citizen House, and it seems likely, too, that both Caesar and Renault had this status as constantly involved participants. While Caesar's name often appears in reviews, Mary does not achieve this local credit until the annual Christmas mystery play in 1930: Caesar took the part of one of the kings, while the part of the angel Gabriel was taken by "Miss Challans." *Bethlehem* was repeatedly performed throughout December until Christmas Eve, suggesting not only residence in Bath but little time either for her unfulfilling jobs or her writing.[1]

If her years on her own did little to anchor Renault in a profession or to establish her identity as a writer either in her own eyes or publicly, they did provide her with this friendship and nourish her lifelong interest in the theater. Her experience with acting went at least as far back as her cowboy fantasies as a little girl. Beyond reciting poetry at school and at home, she had been an avid participant in organized productions at Clifton High School and St. Hugh's, and the world of animated make-believe seems to have been an ongoing part of her friendships with Beryl Lewis and Kathleen Abbott. Oxford during the twenties gave her ample opportunity to attend local plays sponsored not only by individual colleges and traveling groups but by the Oxford University Dramatic Society, whose reputation as an exclusive (and exclusively male) club gave it a special status and panache.

In his history of the society, Humphrey Carpenter notes that "By the mid 1920s the OUDS were . . . a formidable social body, not a little alarming to those Oxford undergraduates whose family background and education [not to mention gender] placed them apart from the elegant and well-off young men who provided the backbone of the society." The OUDS during this period regularly put on first-rate productions, especially of Shakespeare, as well as a wide range of farcical spoofs, and offered the university community the sort of dashing, larger-than-life figures so appealing to the young Mary Renault. Carpenter cites the popular and talented Gyles Isham, the society's

1. Information about Citizen House and these performances is taken from the *Bath and Wiltshire Chronicle and Herald,* July 20, 1929, 14; August 17, 1929, 1, 10, 12; August 9, 1930, 14; August 16, 1930, 26; and December 6, 1930, 15.

president in 1925, the year Mary arrived at St. Hugh's, as the "golden boy of the 1920s." Isham was lauded in local reviews as "gracious and graceful," "wonderful," a "genius," and his great popularity lead to wide discussion of his "talents, character, and appearance." It seems impossible that Renault was unaware of such an exciting actor, and unlikely that she would not also have seen performances by the young Emlyn Williams, another senior member of the OUDS in the autumn of 1925. His performance in *Henry IV, Part 2* in February 1926 earned him rave reviews in the London press, which routinely noticed OUDS productions. Williams became so involved with the OUDS that his academic work for a time fell entirely by the wayside (evidently a fairly common phenomenon among serious university actors) and he suffered an emotional breakdown—drama at Oxford was a passionate and consuming affair. While Carpenter indicates that the society "was better at discovering comic talent than serious acting," all of their plays drew large audiences.[2]

Renault's own interest in acting generally and particularly in the OUDS, its productions, reputation, politics, and role in university life, is particularly clear in her two contemporary novels that feature acting and the literal putting on of plays: in *Kind Are Her Answers* (1940), her second novel, she makes explicit use of experiences at Citizen House, while in *Return to Night* (1947), her fourth novel, she draws on the world of university and amateur theater in the development of Julian Fleming, her central male character. In both of these works Renault examines performance as process and product in order to suggest the instability of identity and gender roles, but denying the unity and stability of identity is not the same thing as denying the body, and Renault emphasizes throughout these texts her simultaneous awareness of the body as an incontrovertible presence at once socially constructed and physically, medically, and sexually real. That is, she explores the notion of gender performativity while insisting on the reality of the material body.[3]

Entire sections of *Kind Are Her Answers* take place in the local theater in which the young Christie is employed during most of the book. Childish, selfish, and eager to please, Christie is invariably playing at life, both in her position as part-time companion to her dying aunt and in her relationship

2. Humphrey Carpenter, *OUDS: A Centenary History of the Oxford University Dramatic Society,* 70, 80–81, 82, 102. I am indebted to Carpenter's detailed history for information about individual actors and performances during this period.

3. See Susan Bordo, *Unbearable Weight: Feminism, Western Culture, and the Body,* 228, and Judith Butler, *Bodies That Matter: On the Discursive Limits of "Sex",* 2.

with a married doctor, Kit Anderson, the romantic center of the novel. The sequences set in Christie's theater provide vivid evidence of what Renault's experience must have been like. We are made privy to the machinations involved in the annual nativity play, in which the rather sexually indiscriminate Christie is ironically cast as the "Christmas Madonna," a part she plays exquisitely well, being "loving and amazed and unsuspecting of grief."[4] We also see inside the world of the theater's summer school, which despite his lack of talent and interest Kit joins in order to be near Christie. Renault's attitude towards acting in this novel is essentially humorous and clever. She mocks her characters, who are not above playing out various conventional romantic roles in their offstage relationships, and details the tiffs and backstage tensions that she must have come to know well through her participation in performances at Citizen House. Typically, she even has the summer school put on as one of its secondary offerings Justin Huntly McCarthy's *If I Were King,* the very play in which she herself had appeared as François Villon in a college production during Michaelmas Term, 1927.

Specific evidence of Renault's awareness of the OUDS comes not only in Julian Fleming's background (he had been a stellar performer in OUDS plays in the 1930s) but in his very name, a private joke that could be shared exclusively by the few readers familiar with the life of the society during Renault's own years at St. Hugh's. Peter Fleming, who went on to become a popular travel and adventure writer, was a student at Christ Church when he made his OUDS debut in *King Lear* during Michaelmas term, 1926; he was elected president of the society in early 1928. He also played Antonio, "a part which gave some scope to his Bull Drummond personality," in a 1927 performance of *The Tempest,* in which another promising young star, Julian Hall, was prevented at the last minute from playing the part of Prospero when he was seriously injured in a car crash.[5]

The cleverness indicated in Julian Fleming's composite name is characteristic of Renault's wit and of her attitude towards making use of her experiences. His surname, in also echoing the part of John Fleming played by Caesar in 1930, is a very exclusive allusion. Her novels are in no way transparent autobiography for public consumption, but she constantly draws—for details as well as for subjects and themes—on her own private life. Her art is itself, in

4. Mary Renault, *Kind Are Her Answers,* 215. All further references to this novel (hereafter cited as *Kind*) will be included parenthetically in the text.

5. Carpenter, *OUDS,* 111–12.

other words, a performance in which she masks personal material, transforms it as if with make-up, and, through the shifting and splitting, recasts gender and traditional roles. More specifically, her fascination with acting leads her to use it as a literal subject not only in her contemporary fiction but in her historical novels (there is an actual actor or performer in nearly all of her Greek works, and both *The Mask of Apollo* and *The Praise Singer* feature such protagonists). But she also uses acting symbolically, and the playing of parts, dressing up, the putting on of masks, the motif of hiding or veiling as a device for also revealing become significant elements in her narratives, an important part of her fictional method in which even romantic love stories or historical novels raise complex issues of identity and morality beyond the apparent limits of the work. *Return to Night* provides an obvious illustration of Renault's strategies while suggesting further the complicated nature of the author's attraction to acting as both fact and idea.

This novel has two central characters: Hilary Mansell, a thirty-four-year-old brain surgeon, trained at Oxford, but now working in general practice in the Cotswolds, who falls in love with the wealthy Oxford-educated Julian Fleming, who at twenty-three looks nineteen. The story is set during the tense prewar period of 1938 and 1939, at a time when Renault herself, like Hilary, had been thirty-four and had also recently left hospital medicine for private work in a rural situation. In turn, Julian, whose first name also suggests that of Julie Mullard, is three years younger than Julie would have been at the time, but the same age as Julie was when she and Mary first fell in love.

In characteristic fashion, Renault shifts genders (Julie becomes Julian) and professions (Hilary is not a nurse but a physician, specifically trained in the treatment of head injuries, Renault's specialty during the war). The author also splits experience. Julian's birth is irregular, like Julie's, but his education (an Oxford degree in English, despite his having been tempted to study medicine) is Mary's, as is his difficulty in following his vocation. He has always felt called to be an actor and is especially gifted, but he is unable to commit himself to acting as a profession. For Mary, it was lack of money and experience (in writing, in life, perhaps even in self-confidence because of her parents' discouragement) that inhibited her development as an author. Julian is also inhibited by money (he has plenty and need not work) and by his own psychology: His mother has convinced him that acting (like nursing in the 1930s) is a low profession and that to realize his talents on the stage would be a personal admission and public declaration of his own effeminacy and potential homosexuality. Hilary's sexual identity is also in question. That is, as an unmarried female doctor she is seen by her community as masculine, not a real woman. Thus Julie's and Mary's sexuality is split between the effeminate and inexperienced Julian and the socially masculinized and more experienced Hilary, whose previous affair with the chauvinistic David confirms (for her, for the reader) her heterosexual desires as well as her rejection of conventional gender relations. Like Mary, Hilary will become the sexual initiator in her relationship with Julian, but both will assume a variety of roles with each other (predominant among them those of doctor and patient and mother and child).

These autobiographical echoes in no way reduce the novel to coded confession; rather, they (and many other such parallels) help the author to convey a vivid and authentic reality enriched by firsthand knowledge while indicating Renault's rewriting, reworking, and recasting of her own experience for a wide readership. The fiction becomes a way for the writer to make the personal significant, to make the private public. In turn, these biographical elements provide insight into Renault's life while emphasizing its relation to her art.

The central characters' roles in *Return to Night* are often in a delicate balance and shift uneasily and quickly back and forth, calling into question both of the characters' independent identities and the boundaries of their personalities, their autonomy and authority. For example, while Hilary is the objective doctor who must diagnose and treat Julian early in the novel when he is brought into the local hospital as an unconscious patient with a serious head injury, she is moved beyond her theoretically dispassionate and ungendered professional role when she responds aesthetically and erotically to the beauty of Julian's naked body prepared for examination. Her position is made particularly unstable as she has previously seen Julian by chance while he was exercising his horse, from which he has now been thrown. At dawn, after a long night of hospital work, she had rested in a field and, unseen herself and waking suddenly, she had observed a mounted figure emerge into "the lake of sunlight in the clearing . . . a rider sitting loosely and at ease." Renault emphasizes the dramatic unreality of the situation for Hilary: "The light, the setting, the hour seemed a theatrical extravagance." Hilary reflects that Julian himself appears more a product of art than of nature, and she concludes that "It was fantastic that anyone unselfconscious and alone should look so faultlessly arranged."[6] In the hospital, again unseen by him as he now lies

6. Mary Renault, *Return to Night,* 10, 11. All further references to this novel (hereafter cited as *RN*) will be included parenthetically in the text.

unconscious, Hilary must shift her position from emotionally responsive but physically uninvolved secret observer (a member of the audience, as it were) to active but dispassionate participant (a fellow actor). By his very male physical presence, Julian shifts the balance of power between them.

Renault emphasizes Julian's potential to determine their relationship during an important interchange just as he is regaining consciousness. As the examining physician, Hilary questions him in order to discover the nature of his injury, the degree of his disorientation. At first Julian drifts in and out of awareness, and when Hilary adjusts the bandage on his head, he presumes they are both actors: " 'What the hell are you playing at, . . . mucking about? . . . Don't shift that, you fool, I'm on in two minutes.' " Next, he sees her as a lover: " 'It's you. . . . I lost you. . . . I'll hold you, can I?' " (*RN*, 23). Julian grasps her hand, then sleeps, then quotes Shakespeare's Caliban: " 'Art thou afeared? Be not afeared, the isle is full of noises, sounds, and sweet airs, that give delight and hurt not. Sometimes . . . sometimes. . . ." Hilary spontaneously fills in the line Julian cannot remember, thus entering his fantasy by responding to him as a fellow player, a prompter assuming the actor's own role: " 'And I awake, and cry to sleep again' " (24).[7] As Julian becomes more rational, Hilary asks him his name and goes through the usual roster of questions (" 'How are you feeling now?' " " 'Do you know where you are?' ") But when she comes to what turns out to be one of the novel's crucial questions—" 'Do you know who I am?' "—Julian, confused and unsure, but aware of his own acting abilities, cannot answer except by evasion, dramatic and playful pretense. With the suggestion of a smile, Julian quips, " 'Yes, of course.' " Hilary pushes him: " 'Tell me,' " she repeats, "with patient clear insistence, 'who you think I am?' " When Julian, evincing both doubt and distress, cannot identify her, she declares " 'I'm a doctor' " (26), a simple statement that, however true, is mitigated by the intimate feelings involved in Hilary's response to him. As if to define her role in physical rather than loaded emotional terms, Renault has Julian begin to drift off once more, then become briefly and insistently alert: " 'Look out. I'm going to be sick.' " Hilary's response is immediate and appropriate as she reacts with trained efficiency, but her sensitivity to his body is at once professional and personal: " 'Here.' She caught up the enamel

7. Both Julian and Hilary are quoting somewhat freely from Caliban's speech to Trinculo and Stefano in *The Tempest*, 3.2.138–46. In Shakespeare's play, Caliban is both reassuring his audience about the island's safety and recounting an occasional wonderful dream that is sweeter than the reality one discovers when one wakes.

bowl from the locker and steadied his head. Movement and disturbance made things worse, and he was very sick indeed. She took his weight on her shoulder, protected his injured arm, and felt under her hand the loose, boyish softness of his black hair" (27). Renault stresses the complexity of shifting roles here as the ironically "patient" doctor struggles unsuccessfully to establish Julian's identity and her own as separately fixed while in fact both are fluid and interdependent.

Julian will repeatedly recast their parts throughout the novel as he is attracted to Hilary and pursues her for complicated reasons: She has overheard his revealing mumblings while he was unconscious and thus possesses knowledge about him of which he senses he is not himself consciously aware; further, he feels he has perhaps confessed personal details that he wants to deny or at least keep private (he wants to know what she knows). Julian also sees Hilary as a savior, the doctor who has arranged the right treatment and preserved his life and mind; the wise and vigilant mother who, displacing his own mother at his bedside, has intervened at just the right moment with the requisite care. Julian finally responds to Hilary sexually, the first time he has felt this way toward a woman, and he turns up uninvited at her home, takes her with him on country drives and out to eat, and at one of the novel's climactic moments, enters her bedroom in the middle of the night and soon after her bed. In each case it is his physical presence as well as the increasingly complex emotional dynamics of their relationship that makes it impossible for Hilary to maintain her position as Julian's doctor. His physical presence in her life also threatens her public position in the community as well as her more private position of conventional respectability in her landlady's house.

But while it is Julian who seeks Hilary out, defining their relationship by his pursuit, it is she, despite her own incomplete self-awareness, who knows more—about life in general, about Julian's personal life, about the body (including specifically his body), and about sexuality and lovemaking. His desire to know what she knows places him in the role of student while she plays the teacher, confirms him as the novice while Hilary is the initiator.

These positions persist throughout the book, but the roles are periodically reversed when Julian asserts a traditional maleness. For example, when he races his red sports car at dangerous speeds across the countryside, Hilary as his passenger is forced into the position of a passive victim in his assertion of physical power. Similarly, she is relegated, despite her anger and voiced objections, to the role of "damsel-in-distress" when Julian responds with offensive aggression to a drunken lout who rudely teases them while they walk together in a local park. This awkward incident results in a messy fight between the two men. The drunk is bloodied and gets sick; Julian "wins" but is badly roughed up, especially about the face, whose bruises provide visual, material evidence of his irrational and conventional chauvinism. His injuries ironically undermine his role as hero as they subsequently require Hilary's medical attention, rendering Julian her patient once more, but during the altercation itself, she can only stand by as the frustrated, unwilling, and impotent observer of the men's rivalry.

Hilary is similarly reduced to a dependent follower when Julian shows her a large local cave which he has often explored and knows well. Hilary is peculiarly disoriented by the bats and damp stalactites, the dark passages and huge inner room. She feels threatened, claustrophobic, uncomfortable with Julian's fascination with this natural curiosity, which is also a uterine space of unmediated desire. Visiting the cave represents for Julian a return to the womb, entering a space that will allow a reconstitution of their relationship and, in fact, his own rebirth, a rewriting of the identity forced upon him by his biological mother and a reclaiming of himself by himself. This complicated psychological process, into which he leads Hilary twice in the novel, occasions another role reversal. In a primeval darkness that finally threatens Hilary to the point of hysteria, Julian becomes the child who redefines Hilary as the mother.

Their first visit together to the cave Julian has often visited alone culminates in a crucial moment of sexual initiation. Physically close, their hands touching, the two sit in the complete darkness. Julian begins to recite poetry that stirs them both. Hilary "was aware of nothing clearly, except the necessity of seeing his face; and scarcely knowing what she did, she put out her hands to serve her instead of eyes. They touched his hair and his forehead . . ." (*RN,* 161). Soon he can no longer continue speaking:

> She slipped her arm about his rigid shoulders and felt, without hearing, the violently controlled breath which she had never recognised, till now, except as the index of scarcely endurable pain. . . . She bent her mouth to his hair—it felt soft and warm, like a child's—but found no response except a sense of tension drawn so far beyond the natural breaking-point that she dared venture no more. . . . [S]he lifted a hanging fold of her loose coat and gathered it round him.
>
> He caught in his breath (the small movement seemed to pass, like a shudder, all through him) and the arm with which he had gripped her waist fell loosely round her. Silently in her arms his hard immobility changed to a death-like relaxation. His head fell back against her shoulder.

> She experienced a moment of intense sweetness and exaltation, followed by guilt and remorse, like the guilt of murder. Blindly, between expiation and helpless love, she stooped and began to kiss his forehead and brows and closed eyes. (162–63)

This experience, in which Hilary's orgasm quickly follows Julian's, confirms the two as lovers. At one level, this scene depicts the loss of Julian's virginity. Hilary's "loose coat" with its "hanging fold" is graphically vaginal as she wraps it around Julian's "rigid shoulders." His rigidity is itself clearly phallic as Renault writes of his body's "tension" and "his hard immobility" that becomes "death-like relaxation" at the moment of ejaculation. But while Julian's and Hilary's orgasms are literal and real (there is no doubting his "shudder" or her "moment of intense sweetness and exaltation"), intercourse has only occurred symbolically at this point in the novel. Actually, as their relationship is charged with Julian's and Hilary's incestuous desires, their real physical responses to each other have occurred independently. Julian's orgasm, which occurs at the moment he is enfolded in Hilary's coat, is a kind of premature ejaculation—symbolically, he climaxes at the moment of entering her body; literally, he comes even before he is inside her. Insomuch as his feelings for her are those of a son for a mother, insomuch as the cave is a fantastic, dreamlike space, a projection of Julian's unconscious desires, what is literally premature ejaculation becomes here also a kind of wet-dream, a form of masturbation (Julian has told Hilary earlier " 'I know this place like the back of my hand' " [159]), evidence of an adolescent sexuality. For her part, Hilary's pleasure is complicated by her sense of guilt. She recognizes that she is excited by her maternal feelings for Julian as well as by her desire for an adult male lover, a part Julian is not here playing, a part he is as yet unready for.

The second scene in the cave is even more upsetting. Again, the space is sexualized and a symbolic intercourse occurs. By this point, however, Julian and Hilary have been literal lovers for some time. Their first actual intercourse with each other, involving Julian's real loss of his virginity, is a satisfying experience for both of them, but neither feels the intensity created by the guilt of their experiences in the cave. Hilary's bedroom may be "a dim green cavern," but it is also a theatrical space of self-consciousness and some humor. When Julian finally climbs the stairs, as both have planned, and appears in her doorway, he stands "easily and well," although Renault cannot help adding perceptively, "a little too well, a little better than life, as if he were gathering himself together for an entrance from the wings" (*RN*, 219). Hilary also feels "the acute stage-fright" (218) of sexual anticipation as she awaits Julian's scripted entry (into her room, into her body).

Following this actual initiation, the two characters struggle to create a mature union of equals, hoping for a marriage that will confirm both in their professional as well as personal lives. Whatever psychological progress they manage to achieve, however, is extremely tenuous. In the climactic scene in the cave at the novel's conclusion, their developing relationship is unwritten and rewritten; the incestuous element, which had been partially resolved for each of them, again surfaces undeniably, finally shaping their future irrevocably. The second cave scene concludes when Julian curls himself into Hilary's lap and kisses her breasts. Despite the heavy Freudian elements in these important sequences, the unease they generate (for Hilary, for the reader) works effectively to convey the depth and complexity of Julian's psychic distress and the attendant difficulties for Hilary if she accepts his passive-aggressive definition of her role. As the mother she has only apparent power; she sacrifices her potential status as an independent woman with her own sexuality for a eroticized female role dependent on Julian's status as infant, a status necessarily limited as he becomes empowered by the rebirth occasioned by his claiming her as the mother.

Another of the novel's persistent motifs is Julian's psychological difficulty with his own identity even beyond his relation to Hilary. This process of self-acceptance is related in part to his efforts to realize his calling as an actor. His professional conflict, with its source in his unhealthy relationship with his possessive and manipulating mother, is figured in his struggle to recast himself as someone else and to deny his material body (as beautiful and erotic, as an object of others' desires, as adult and male and human). Renault explores Julian's distress symbolically in the series of tensions that lead up to and culminate in the final scene in the cave. She also, however, uses acting, literal role-playing on a stage, as a way of portraying Julian's personal as well as professional problems.

Once physically recovered from his injury, Julian reappears in the novel when he returns to the hospital in the autumn of 1938 in an effort to sort out exactly what happened to him. His concussion has caused him to forget most of the experience, so he is in search of factual as well as psychological knowledge. Julian is also, however, hiding from reality, from himself, a process Renault represents through his playing of extraordinary parts. Thus Hilary next meets him in a hospital corridor where he is entertaining two ill children by impersonating a monkey:

> Squatting on the last few steps of the staircase, in a doubled-up simian crouch, was a man whose face it was at first difficult to see, since it was partially obscured by his knees. He was scratching his armpit, reproducing vividly a monkey's sporadic but earnest concentration. When he moved she glimpsed a prognathous-looking jaw and a hideously grimacing mouth beneath a mournful stare. . . .
>
> He got up. His face, after a few minor adjustments such as the removal of the tongue from inside the lower lip, had resolved itself into one at which she stared with unbelieving recognition. It had been like a trick done with mirrors. (*RN,* 54–55)

Julian indeed revels in such transgressive roles both on and off a literal stage, roles that, with and without make-up, permit him to distort his facial features, to conceal his age, attractiveness, youth, even his gender and very humanity. At the hospital's annual Christmas party, when everyone is being rather silly as Dr. Dundas, dressed as Santa, entertains the group and kisses one of the nurses, a little girl urges Julian, " 'Go on, Monkey. *You* kiss a lady' " (*RN,* 75). No longer pretending to be simian, Julian nevertheless can only approach Hilary in the exaggerated role of a courtier: "With a long, swift, graceful stride, he crossed the floor to her, made an eighteenth-century bow, said 'Madam your servant,' and handed her out under the chandelier. He kissed her, briskly, cheerfully, and inaccurately, and bowed again, and let her go. It went very well; almost as well as Dr. Dundas" (76). Julian's grace is affected and the exchange merely a show in which the impression he creates for his audience is more important than the accuracy of his kiss.

When Julian later comes to Hilary's office looking for a skeleton to use as a stage prop in a play he is producing for the local dramatic society, he confesses to his extensive acting experience at school and in the OUDS. Hilary responds, " 'Really? I might even have seen you, then. No, I suppose not; the only one I've seen in the last four years was *The Tempest,* one of the summer ones. You weren't in that.' " Julian is delighted that she has not recognized his role and teases, " 'Don't you remember me?' ": "She cast her mind back: the Ferdinand, fair and much too small; the Prospero, broad, and the voice too deep; Trinculo, definitely not. Perhaps she might have missed him in a minor part. She said, apologetically, 'I came in too late for a programme; and there were so many beards.' " But it was not the conventional trappings of adult maleness, the "beards," that obscured Julian's identity. He responds gleefully " 'Not on me.' " He then reenacts his part: "He leaned forward, and suddenly dropped his arms so that they hung beside his knees. His face, thrust out, took on a mournful and malevolent stare. It recalled for her the face he had made for Betty and Christine; but this time it expressed, with startling vividness, the tragic lostness which one glimpses sometimes in the eyes of a monkey sitting quiet in the corner of its cage" (*RN,* 87–88). When Julian begins to quote his lines, Hilary suddenly remembers "the gross and forlorn voice whose sullenness had been so curiously moving," and exclaims, " 'Don't try to tell me that Caliban was you.' " Julian is delighted, eagerly confessing the details of the extensive make-up that so successfully masked his identity. His other OUDS roles were similarly exotic: " 'I was the First Madman in *Malfi.* That was *great* fun. I had a sort of cheese-coloured face, paralysed down one side. . . . [A]nd I was Oberon the year after. . . . I was after Bottom, really . . .' " (88–89). Such distorted parts please Julian, but in showing off to Hilary press photos and rave reviews, he unintentionally lets her see a picture of him as the young Prince Hal. Julian is embarrassed to admit that he has ever played a serious role so close to his offstage self. Acting for Julian has in fact become an opportunity to hide himself, to mask the sincerity of his professional aspirations and the range of his talents, to conceal especially his human maleness and conflicted bisexuality. Renault later becomes even more explicit. When Julian must take over in his local production for a suddenly absent actor, he is frantic when he cannot disguise himself because the part " 'will mean making-up practically straight.' " He finally confesses, " 'Actually, I never feel myself on the stage unless I look different' " (106).

Acting becomes in the novel a coded sexual revelation, a substitution for sexual activity, make-believe that allows the displacement of one's actual (sexual) identity. Thus just after the play, Hilary finds herself alone with Julian:

> " . . . they had fun with it in the end. I certainly did. Didn't you?"
>
> "M-mm." He stretched, and linked his hands behind his head. "You can call it that. It's a funny thing, it never feels at all that way while it's going on. Even if nothing goes wrong, and you feel more or less on top of things, I wouldn't say . . . no, you can't call it enjoyment, not at the time. More like walking a tight-rope, really. I suppose that sounds a fatuous thing to say after a romp like to-night; but you can't help feeling it. And yet, when it's all over . . . I wonder . . . I suppose you wouldn't have a spare cigarette about you? (*RN,* 118, Renault's ellipses)

Like partners in bed after lovemaking, Hilary and Julian here share with each other their perceptions of the experience, "it," in a brief period of intense intimacy. Acting thus serves Renault as a metaphor for sexuality, specifically for gendered—in this case, male—sexuality and more precisely for homosexuality, bisexuality, or any sexuality that crosses boundaries (for instance of age or class or race). Julian tries to repress, suppress, mask his desire for acting, his calling as a professional actor, but he cannot. When Hilary asks, " 'But is there anything else at all you want to do except this?' " Julian only responds " 'No.' " He delights in "talking shop," confesses " ' . . . it's absolute hell to keep it in.' " When Julian uses amputation, a medical condition, as a metaphor for not acting (for hiding his own sexuality, for repressing desire, for a kind of Freudian castration), Hilary counters, " 'Except that the leg's still there.' " Just like one's material body, forbidden desire, one's own sexuality, no matter how masked or repressed, is "still there." Julian admits, " 'That's worse, in a way' " (121–22).

As Julian discusses both his professional and, somewhat obliquely, his sexual crisis in this important scene, Hilary confesses to him the difficulties in her own decision to enter medicine. She parallels her becoming a physician, taking on an unconventional role, one even traditionally forbidden to a woman, with his desire to act, his (bi)sexuality. Medicine and bisexuality in this novel thus also serve autobiographically, through the complex process of encoding I suggest here, for Renault's desire to write, for her own sexuality and literary vocation with which, through the prism of this novel, we can see her struggling in the late 1920s and early 1930s. Hilary details her professional and sexual conflict:

> . . . getting my people to let me train took more than a year. . . . I spent years wanting to be the sort of person they needed me to have been, but it wasn't any use. . . . If I'd wanted to get married . . . or teach, they'd have made no trouble, I knew. But medicine [or writing, sexual independence, even lesbian sexuality, for Renault herself] was more than they could swallow; they belonged to the generation that [only] talked about the New Woman. . . .
>
> My father thought that besides being unwomanly it [for Hilary, being a doctor; for Renault herself, writing and having an unconventional sexual life] was perfectly pointless, being a job in which no woman ever gets to the top. And my mother thought it so immodest that she couldn't believe I knew what it meant. . . . This is the point: that even the best people [that is, good parents, admirable representatives of traditional society] don't always know what it is they're asking for. If they did, they wouldn't ask it. They thought I only needed weaning from this silly idea, to give them

> a nice home-loving girl about the place. I knew that all they'd get would be a slowly decaying corpse. . . . So in the end, I went. (*RN*, 124)

For his part, Julian tries to explain his mother's objections to his professional aspirations, which compound his own doubts about his acting potential. She "thinks I'd go to the bad in some way. . . . It's impossible even to begin to talk with her about it. . . . I honestly think it would kill her, or crack her up in some way, if I went on the stage. You'll say that isn't reasonable; perhaps it isn't. You can't say, can you, why some people get better from a disease and some people die" (*RN*, 125). In this significant scene, acting, the practice of medicine, writing as a profession, sexuality, homosexuality, and disease all come to double for one another at various levels of the discourse. Thus Renault writes later in the novel that for Julian acting "had always had the guilty sweetness of a forbidden indulgence." Julian feels his dead father would also have objected to his acting, as if to say, " 'All this emotion. . . . Not quite the thing. Not what I expect in a son of mine. A brisk walk and a cold bath . . .' "(134–35)—the scoutmaster's conventional antidote for sexual passion.

This 1947 novel is in many ways Renault's most erotic, her most explicit treatment of the complexities of both male and female sexual desire, and it should come as no surprise that contemporary reviewers found it confusing. With some exasperation, Thomas Sagrue concluded, "Miss Renault writes with competence and beauty, but what does she mean?"[8] *Return to Night* is also Renault's last novel with a female protagonist. Although she returns throughout her later work to the fact and idea of acting, her treatment of acting as a coded experience will in no other novel result in such a complex series of meanings. While in 1947 Renault had arrived at a much more sophisticated understanding of sexuality than she certainly had in the 1930s, and while this postwar novel reflects in many ways her subsequent medical training and professional experience both as a nurse and as an accomplished author, *Return to Night* offers a fascinating gloss on her earlier life. It allows us to see through Hilary and through Julian what must have been to a degree her own earlier struggle to leave home with its conventional social expectations and repressive notions of what it meant to be a woman. The novel further suggests the deep personal conflicts involved in Renault's forging of her own independent professional and sexual identity. The book casts light as well on

8. Thomas Sagrue, *New York Herald Tribune Weekly Book Review*, April 20, 1947, 16.

an issue that was probably a salient feature of her inner life during this period of "casting about": the extent to which self is a matter of relationship and interdependence, and the extent to which it is a unique matter of solitary and painful definition. Her experiences at Citizen House would provide her with an insider's knowledge of the world of amateur drama on which she would draw so vividly for the rest of her career. Evidence of her friendships during this time is scant, but it seems likely that the tensions we find in both Julian and Hilary are rooted at least in some measure here.

The particular nature and depth of Renault's relationship with Caesar remain vague. Julie described him as "special," that is, a beau, and she indicated that when at one point Mary took him to her parents' home, her mother fussed and flirted with him, much to Renault's embarrassment. Reflecting on the degree of sexual experience the two young women would bring to their own relationship in the 1930s, Julie declared frankly that at the time they met "Mary had never been to bed with anyone," although she felt that Mary and Caesar had been obviously attracted to each other. More specifically, they were close friends who once or twice went on a rock-climbing holiday together. Except to note that Caesar was an only child, lived with his mother, and owned a car, Julie could add few further details, not even his first name. The beginning of the war dispersed the Citizen House group, and Julie equivocated, "Caesar could have been killed in the war. Mary never mentioned him after that. She told me about Caesar when we first met [in 1934]. . . . She was probably still writing to him. I don't know if they did [continue to write or see each other]. She was obviously thinking about him. She'd known him recently. But after that [time] she never mentioned him unless it was something to do with the theatre."[9]

Caesar was clearly an important companion beyond whatever romantic involvement they may have shared: He opened doors for Renault into the world of organized amateur theater and through him she developed a group of social acquaintances whom she joined on hiking and climbing expeditions. These athletic excursions drew her away from the urban poverty of her small bed/sitting room in Bristol and into the neighboring countryside. On weekend and overnight trips, sometimes with several friends, occasionally it would seem with Caesar alone, Renault had many opportunities to develop an intimate relationship, but the erotic and even the personal may have played

9. Mullard, interview by Sweetman, tape 7, side B; Mullard to Sweetman, October 12, 1990; Mullard, interview by Sweetman, tape 8, side A.

only a small role in the dynamics of their friendship. Beyond fostering her interest in acting, Caesar seems to have functioned as a sole friend and even mentor during this "gray period," for as the more experienced athlete as well as actor, he taught Renault skills and offered her specialized information, especially about climbing, which appealed to her developing interest in technology, in particular and precise material realities, in disciplined and responsible activity. This rather scientific knowledge and experience would begin to provide her with the very rigor and order that her formal education and her own approach to it had lacked.

In her later writing, rock climbing—like Julian's cave—would come to stand for a kind of initiation, and rugged landscapes and detailed geography would function both literally, as for example when she precisely described the historical terrain of her Greek characters, and metaphorically, as she used rock faces and caverns, rural drives and walks through the hills to reflect and reveal her characters' inner experiences. More than a pathetic fallacy of landscape, Renault's treatment of the natural world, often opposed to the world of the city or of institutions, allowed her to explore forbidden spaces, the psychic territory her characters feared or were ignorant of, and their sexuality, which was often forbidden on several counts as socially unacceptable, violating taboos against heterosexual activity between unmarried partners (as in *Purposes of Love*) or between partners one of whom is married (as in *Kind Are Her Answers* and *North Face*), or against relationships in which the woman is the older, more experienced initiator (*Return to Night*), or against lesbian sexuality and bisexuality (as in *Purposes of Love* and *The Friendly Young Ladies*) or male homosexual activity and identity (as in *Purposes of Love, The Charioteer,* and many of her Greek novels).

Rock climbing specifically forms a central motif and geography functions in just this intimate way in *North Face,* in which Renault draws most explicitly on her experiences with Caesar. During the course of the book Neil Langton's new understanding of himself and his relationships is a result of his love for Ellen Shorland, whose very geographical name suggests a coming home, a reanchoring, a reaffirmation. Neil is not in any way transparently Caesar. In his struggle to become a writer he functions in fact as a persona for Renault herself, but he has Caesar's technical knowledge, as to a lesser degree does Ellen. Neil had initially intended solitary expeditions, not exactly a safe practice but suggestive of his own psychological and sexual isolation and self-destructive impulses. On one of the first climbs of his holiday, however, he spies Ellen bathing naked in the sea below. Projecting onto her his own suicidal tendencies, he first fears for her life, then recognizes the social awkwardness of his situation, then reflects "on the loss of his private wilderness" (*NF,* 106). From resentment, Neil soon moves to an awareness of Ellen's body as female and erotic. Renault focuses the rest of her novel on Neil's efforts to deny and then to express his sexuality and on Ellen's own sexual awakening. The metaphor throughout is rock climbing—as the reader might well have surmised from Renault's chapter headings, an unusual feature in her work and here a rather obvious structural and even heavy-handed symbolic device as "Approach from the North" (chapter 1) gives way to "Guideless Ascent" (chapter 4) and later to "Bivouac" (chapter 9), "Slip by the Leader" (chapter 15), and "Summit Ridge" (chapter 17). With their sexual innuendo, Renault's headings are even so broad and explicit as to be humorous in a rather camp way: "Difficult Crack" (chapter 11) is followed by "Fixed Anchor" (chapter 13), "Exposed Traverse" (chapter 14), and "Straight Pull Out" (chapter 16). Indeed, such headings seem intentionally "queer," unstable in their ambiguity, sexually unclear (who is doing what to whom literally or symbolically?) at the same time that they are definitely sexual.

The novel also contains rich passages of geographic description, often from Neil's point of view, that reveal his fascination with and fear of the female body. The novel in fact opens with just this sort of feminized and eroticized landscape:

> The land was deep—an outpost of Devon, which was within walking distance if one took walking seriously—and for a couple of hundred yards it ran straight between banks filled with fern, higher than one's head. Towards the end, meeting trees made it a tunnel, from whose nether end one could see at the other a round hole of twisted light. Until one emerged, the tower was wholly concealed; to a redundancy of dramatic effect was super-added the element of surprise. New visitors, if alone, would refocus their eyes in suspended belief. . . . They were off the beaten track, discriminating individualists: their contempt for the promenade at Bridgehead, and even for the nearer cosiness of Barlock, knew no bounds.
>
> The tower reared, sensationally, above the trees. . . .
>
> Feasting on these visions, visitors would press forward with the excitement of conquistadores. This coming sharp bend in the lane must bring them in sight of the house itself.
>
> It did.

Here the tower is a curious protrusion in the cuneal space whose erotics are initially presented as self-contained and dependent on the depth and verdure of the lane. The new visitor, "if alone," would be surprised to find the concealed tower here. (What is this phallus doing in this female space?) However, if one reads the unanticipated tower not as phallic but in fact clitoral, then this passage becomes a daring depiction of female sexuality whose erotics are primarily masturbatory or cunnilingual and only secondarily a matter of heterosexual intercourse. Renault stresses in fact the purely pleasurable function of the tower, which is no mistake or deformity: "Very naïve explorers took it for part of a ruined castle; the more sophisticated knew it at once for a Folly of the most extravagantly Gothick kind" (*NF,* 7–8).

Neil must come in the course of the novel to accept his own sexuality and attraction to Ellen, while Ellen must overcome her frigidity through her developing relationship with him. *North Face* is not finally a very successful novel, but however pat its happy heterosexual ending (ironically, the one element contemporary reviews generally praised), it reveals throughout Renault's technical knowledge (of rock climbing, of the body, of sexuality) and her use of precise and scientifically observed detail to portray subjects (nature, love) conventionally romanticized. Renault would never for many reasons publish her early sentimental fiction of knights and troubadours; by the late twenties and early thirties, perhaps in part through the experience of rock climbing and her friendship with Caesar, she had come to recognize the importance of physical reality.

This "gray period" also taught her a great deal about the experience of poverty. A child of solidly middle-class parents, Renault's experiences had in many ways been circumscribed by a mother who wanted and managed to keep things "nice" and a father whose secure livelihood had insulated her from the rough realities of economic deprivation. Growing up in East Ham, Renault had certainly been aware of her father's largely working-class patients, the shopkeepers and local residents in the immediate neighborhood, but she had never herself experienced a life of physical or financial need. She was in fact dependent on her family to pay her bills and provide both food and lodging, but until she struck out on her own in the late twenties, she had little conscious awareness of that dependence which she seems to have accepted unreflectively, taken for granted rather than understood. Her return to her parents' home in 1928 as an unmarried woman without a promising profession made her situation abundantly clear, and she recoiled from the dependence that came to horrify her.

Throughout her work and as a dominant theme in *Purposes of Love,* Renault would emphasize this problem of dependence. Her characters struggle from childhood to become independent of their parents and to retain their independence in their friendships and romantic relationships. Vivian and Mic in this first published novel cannot develop their relationship until both are liberated from a sexual, even mystical, symbiotic dependence on Vivian's brother Jan and from the institutional infantilism both experience in the hospital world. Even when the dynamics of the love between Vivian and Mic are most confused (a function of their own inexperience as young lovers and of Renault's inexperience as a young writer), the central issue in the characters' difficulties is Vivian's increasingly conscious but barely expressed fear of dependence, of losing her developing identity in a sexual relationship, of becoming a subsidiary of another person (sister, girlfriend, lover, wife). This matter of imperative independence and consequent physical, emotional, and moral self-reliance, often gained and maintained at great personal and even political cost, remains a feature of Renault's contemporary novels and of all of her mature historical fiction. Her trilogy about Alexander the Great (*Fire from Heaven* [1969], *The Persian Boy* [1972] and *Funeral Games* [1981]) is unified in part by this theme: Alexander struggles from earliest childhood to develop his own gifted nature without becoming a derivative product either of his demanding parents or of his teachers, while of his friends and cohorts only Ptolemy is able after his death to maintain the independence necessary to political as well as personal and moral success.

This need for independence, beginning consciously for Renault in the summer of 1928, would also become a dominant force in her own life. It was countered in these years of national economic depression by a sense of her own insufficiency: She was an amateur actor playing parts; she was an inexperienced writer who had as yet published nothing professionally; she was a young woman on her own without an adequate income. Julie recounted an incident that reflects the sharp awareness of poverty and deprivation that Renault developed during this "gray period." Years later, when the South African Progressive Party leader Colin Eglin came unannounced to see Mary at her home in Cape Town, he expected a large financial donation. Renault was characteristically offended by his supposition and by the impingement on her work time, while in an effort to elicit her support, Eglin recounted his childhood on a South African farm. When he pompously concluded, "Those of us who have known poverty . . . ," Mary, according to Julie, "just went over the top":

> "You don't know poverty. I was brought up in the East End of London and I saw poverty, and I saw poverty and degradation during the war. . . . You don't know what you're talking about. You don't know what it is to see people looking in dustbins for food and people who have no one to turn to—the man or the woman who has been providing has gone; they've got three children and one of them is sick, and they are just sitting in rags in a room, and this is England. I have seen it and it happens, and I've seen people coming into hospital. . . ."[10]

The examples here, taken from Mary's London childhood and her work in hospitals during both the Depression and the war, suggest her vivid awareness of poverty in the lives of others. It was, however, her own experience of poverty after 1928 that made deprivation real for her, provoking the sharpness of her response to Eglin despite the characteristic impersonality of her evidence. Most of her income during these years went to rent, first for lodgings in a Bristol council house, then for a basement flat in Charlotte Street. In an effort to economize, she cut down on food, and a rare early photograph taken on a hike with a group of friends from Citizen House shows her as a very slender young woman indeed—obviously happy but certainly slimmer than she would appear in any later surviving pictures. Despite the lively and comfortable leisure of Citizen House, Renault was undernourished and barely managed to support herself while writing at night and working during the day at depressing "dead-end jobs."[11] By 1932 she became too ill to continue living on her own.

Dr. and Mrs. Challans had moved to Barleston near Stoke-on-Trent, where the rather restless Dr. Challans had taken up a new post in the middle of this year. It was to their home in this Staffordshire village that Renault was forced to return when she contracted rheumatic fever, a serious disease particularly dangerous to the heart in the days before antibiotics. The standard prescription was enforced rest, flat on one's back, with as little movement as possible—the patient was not permitted even to sit up and on no account to get out of bed even to use the toilet. The low-grade fever, aching joints, and persistent headache, usually lasting several months, were debilitating if not in themselves incapacitating. The rest-cure under her parents' care would be for Renault far more enervating than the symptoms of the disease, and her

10. Mullard, interview by Sweetman, tape 15, side B.

11. Renault, interview by Sue MacGregor, *The Woman's Hour,* SABC radio program, 1969[?]. I am grateful to Julie Mullard for sharing with me the typescript of this interview.

Mary hiking with friends from Citizen House in the late 1920s. Photo courtesy of Julie Mullard.

debility and inevitable dependence on others would haunt her throughout her life. She remembered the experience in vivid detail. A heart murmur complicated her situation, "and the only treatment was to take three aspirins four-hourly, and lie three months in bed being fed with a spoon. I did just get leave to hold a book up, and for three months I did nothing at all but read."[12] Dependent financially even when physically recovered, Renault would remain in her parents' home for nearly a year.

During this frustrating period of domestic dependence she continued to struggle with her writing. Julie recalled that Mary was still working on her medieval fantasy: "She wrote some of it under the sheets when she was having complete rest."[13] Perhaps not surprisingly, she made little satisfying headway. Her experience was wider now and deeper than it had been at St. Hugh's; she now had had a direct experience of poverty, however brief, and she had certainly come to know the world of amateur acting and actors. She had for probably the first time as well begun to know her own body—its physical limits, for instance, and its ability to represent her on stage or in a heterosexual

12. Renault to Williams, December 23, 1969.
13. Mullard, interview by Sweetman, tape 3, side B.

relationship, which it seems likely was also physically sexual if technically unconsummated. However, setting her narrative a thousand years earlier in a fanciful past was a gross displacement of her own experiences, and it failed to create the impression of reality she also desired, while the metaphors she needed to explore the important issues at the core of her fiction were as yet inaccessible to her.

Renault would later describe the decision she made in 1933 as simple, clear and rational. It is difficult to imagine that it was any of those things at the time, but certainly during those lonely months in Barleston, Mary reflected on her vocation and on her dependent situation and reached a startling conclusion that shaped the rest of her life. She confessed, "I decided I wanted to nurse because this was a thing where you weren't wasting your time, you were doing something for somebody . . . and getting to know something about human beings. . . . Having written this deplorable novel and now knowing it was deplorable, I thought the time had come to get down to a little reality, and I have always been very glad that I did it." She amplified her defense of this unusual decision for a middle-class woman of twenty-seven with an Oxford degree in English: Nursing, she declared, made her "a much more realistic person"; it also, she pointed out, gave her "a sense of responsibility, and I think responsibility is just as important for a writer as it is for a nurse. I mean, one must tell the truth for instance, that's the thing you learn very definitely in hospital." By implication, during the five years since she had left St. Hugh's, she was suddenly aware that she had been unrealistic, even irresponsible, and less than truthful, both in her life and in her art. Julie would stress Mary's sense of her own ignorance at this time: "She said she knew nothing about life except this handful of people that she'd met from being at school and university. And she couldn't afford to travel and she needed a job, and she thought, 'Well, I'll be a nurse, and that way I'll find out about people.' "[14] Towards the end of her life, when David Sweetman asked her if she had ever wanted to be a doctor, Renault reiterated all of these points about her situation and her own psychology in 1933:

> There wasn't enough money for me to study medicine, and if you have studied medicine, you must have a life-long commitment to be a doctor, and I had a life-long commitment to be a writer. But meantime, I had to earn a living, and I wanted to do something where I would meet people

14. Renault, *Woman's Hour* interview; Mullard, interview by Sweetman, tape 3, side B.

and be doing something useful and not just making money for somebody else, and I have never regretted it, because it is a life which teaches you a great deal in hospital. For one thing, you meet every kind of person from every kind of walk of life, from the aristocracy down to tramps and right through the whole spectrum. And for another thing, and I think this is important for a writer, it does teach you a sense of responsibility.[15]

15. Renault, *Omnibus* interview.

three

The Body
1933–1938

On August 26, 1933, a few days before her twenty-eighth birthday, Mary returned to Oxford to begin her training at the Radcliffe Infirmary. For the first seven weeks she lived and studied with other students at the Preliminary Training School in the Manor House in suburban Headington. There Mary learned basic skills and initially experienced the long hours and domestic drudgery of the communal life that would characterize her career as a hospital nurse for the next thirteen years.

Her training must have recalled for her both Clifton High School and St. Hugh's. She was a pupil again, with information to master and exams to pass; she was not living in her parents' home nor on her own but in a lively community of other women in which she was assigned a small space in a large building. To supplement her meager income as a student nurse, she would once more need to rely on an allowance from her family. Nursing was more demanding, however, than any of Mary's previous educational experiences. At the Radcliffe there was no literary library to which she could retreat for unsupervised leisurely hours. Fifty years later, when the Infirmary archivist asked her for memorabilia, she sent a photograph of herself with her Headington classmates. Mary could still identify by surname seven of the eleven student nurses in the picture, but she commented, "Joyce and I were nearly ten years older than anyone else and Maggie Jones [their supervisor] was a bit scared of us. We used to get up on the roof with a ladder we found leading up through the boxroom, but she never discovered this. It was a delightful place to spend a fine autumn afternoon with a book; I wonder if anyone found it afterwards."[1]

1. Renault to "Anne," August 19, 1983. I am grateful to Elizabeth Boardman, who shared this letter with me.

Even when Mary could find the necessary solitude, reading now was only possible in the brief intervals between long stretches of physical labor and much-needed sleep. Her classroom lessons and instruction on the ward were no longer matters of Old English verb forms or French romances, and she could not afford to be bored or undisciplined or even imaginatively transported. It seems likely, however, that Mary knew before she began her training what her decision meant for her literary aspirations, even if she could not have anticipated the exhausting physical life nor the specific and highly skilled medical work that would fill her days and nights. Discussing years later the importance of earning one's own living, she confessed, "I've never had any money I've not earned, once my education was over; but I have never regretted for a moment the jobs I did for my daily bread, before I made enough to live by writing. I never wrote at all during my three-year hospital training, and never expected to do so—nursing is responsible and one can't exploit it as a means to serve some other end." She also contrasted nursing with academic life, pointing out that "I learned a lot about people which I never could at the University, I made good friends, I kept on reading and living; what I learned made me realise that in any case, before, I had not been *ready* to write anything but derivative stuff."[2]

It was also probably impossible for Mary to have foreseen the extent to which her choice would transform her. Publicly, she suddenly became to others not an individual but a representative—of the nursing profession, of the Radcliffe Infirmary with its particularly high standards, and of cloistered womanhood, with its restrictions on appearance, behavior, speech, and friendships. Personally, in taxing her physical and emotional endurance, nursing required a new depth of reflection and self-examination. She would need to confront what her writing meant to her and what individual and creative use she would make of her medical training. Learning to care for sick and injured people, she would need to come to terms with her own body, with her own sexuality.

The best source for information about Mary's experience as a nurse in the 1930s is her own first novel, *Purposes of Love.* Again in no way transparently autobiographical, this book nevertheless reveals in vivid and specific detail the daily life Mary led at the Radcliffe and her own perspective on what it meant. Histories of nursing and personal accounts confirm the hospital world Renault depicts in her fiction, but her experience of that world was unusual in many respects.

2. Renault to Bryher, June 10, 1967.

Up until the Second World War, hospitals seemed for many people mysterious and dangerous places, often associated with pain, disgusting mess, and death. Nursing in the nineteenth century had frequently meant unskilled domestic labor done by working-class women. By the time of the Great War, nursing had become a profession, but one still generally regarded as unsuitable for a woman privileged by background or education. In her interviews with women who worked outside the home during World War II, Mavis Nicholson records the frustration of many who might have made fine nurses. She recounts the aspirations of Jean Wynne who, "like lots of girls of her time, wanted to be a nurse. Her mum had been one. But her father . . . said no." Similarly, Peggy Terry confessed, "When war started I was eighteen and working in a transport office. I'd always wanted to be a nurse but my father didn't want me to do that. . . . He'd had a long illness when he was young, and people often got these bees in their bonnets about hospitals and nurses, and the hard life and the low pay." Since nursing did not pay well, pursuing such a career was doubly difficult for a young woman who often required from her family not only frequently begrudged permission but financial support. Pat Parker is typical: "What I wanted to be was a nurse, but my mother talked me out of that because she said they couldn't afford to keep me while I trained."[3] Thus nursing became a career predominantly for upwardly mobile working-class and lower-middle-class women, for whom the little power they gained within the patriarchal hospital hierarchy mattered a great deal and was often asserted with a vengeance over younger and less experienced staff. Renault was certainly atypical as an older student entering her training with both an Oxford degree and parental support. As a doctor, Frank Challans would have had a clear sense of what his daughter would encounter; his continuing twenty pounds a year seems itself tacit approval, and training as a nurse appears to have been one of the few things that Mary did of which he approved.

Mary was also unusual in bringing to nursing a range of experiences that had given her a comparative sophistication. Not only Oxford and her "dead-end jobs" but her independent reading, her struggle to write, her acting and relationship with Caesar—a decade of literary and first-hand knowledge—separated her from her younger classmates. In contrast, naïveté is a repeated refrain in nearly all of Nicholson's interviews with young women who began

3. Mavis Nicholson, *What Did You Do in the War, Mummy? Women in World War II,* 201, 81, 41.

to work in the 1930s. Peggy Hill, a middle-class woman who joined the navy and married at the age of nineteen within the first year of the war, insisted, "I was very naive. Immature and inexperienced." So was Patricia Pitman, who, after working for three years at the Bradford Post Office, joined the army shortly before her eighteenth birthday in 1943. She admitted, "The medical rather shocked me, with 'Make water in a pot.' I didn't know what was meant by this. I was extremely naive." Well-bred Doris Barry, an aspiring actress who had begun her London career in the 1930s, worked as a "soubrette," an upscale chorus girl, at the Windmill Theatre. She, too, acknowledged an astonishing ignorance: " 'Oh, Windmill girls,' they used to say," yet "I was so naive, I hardly got any of the risqué jokes, but everyone thought we were worldly." While no nurse could have remained ignorant for long about biological facts and the corporeal, material reality of male and female bodies, their lives were generally no more sophisticated than those of Nicholson's subjects. Julie would retrospectively confess to her own naïveté and lack of sexual understanding: She had never made love in any sense of the phrase until she met Mary; despite her additional two years' knowledge of medicine, Julie was much less experienced in the ways of the world, far more "innocent."[4]

The hospital world of *Purposes of Love* is a strange mixture of innocence and experience. It opens powerfully with images of youth and death, childhood and knowledge:

> At a white-tiled table a young girl was sitting, sucking on a bullseye and sewing a shroud. Her hands moved in and out of a pool of red-shaded lamplight, glowing in their passage first crimson and then white. She was nineteen, pretty, undersized and Welsh; hideously dressed in striped cotton, a square-bibbed apron that reached her high collar, black shoes and stockings and a stiff white cap.
>
> Nightfall had simplified the ward, picking out highlights and resolving them into a pattern, drowning detail, subduing movement, fixing for the moment the symmetry for which, all day, everyone fought errant nature as climbers for the snow of an impossible summit.
>
> Over some of the cots that lined the walls lamps were burning, muffled in red. Under one of them, the child who presently would wear the shroud was lying with a pinched, waxy face, breathing jerkily through a half-open mouth. An apparatus of glass and rubber tubing was running salt and

4. Ibid., 131, 169, 196; Mullard, letter to author, November 16, 1995; Mullard, interview by Sweetman, tape 3, side B.

> water into her veins to eke out the exhausted blood. It was all that could now be done.[5]

This red-light district is not an area of sexual knowledge, but a children's ward, and the figure in the glowing lamp is not a prostitute but a white-clad nurse, at nineteen both a child herself and a medically trained woman who sews in preparation for the inevitable death that her technology cannot prevent. The night has created a tenuous symmetry, life's pattern is only momentarily fixed, and the climbing metaphor that juxtaposes the aspiring individual against given nature is, like this hospital scene, drawn straight from the author's own experience.

Still, *Purposes of Love* is neither the young Welsh nurse's story nor the dying child's. It focuses on Vivian Lingard, an older student nurse, and her romantic relationship with Mic Freeborn, a technician in the pathology laboratory. The two meet through Vivian's brother, Jan, a geologist, who had developed an intimate friendship with Mic when both were at Cambridge. Beginning with this first novel, Renault signals her characters' ambiguous sexual roles through their ungendered names. The narrative reveals a symbiotic, trangressively incestuous relationship between Vivian and Jan, who even look alike, and Jan in fact must die before Vivian can commit herself to Mic. Vivian and Jan are not in any trite way each other's female or male half. Rather, both are presented to a degree as bisexual and, at least at the opening of the novel, sexually unawakened. Vivian is neither offended nor surprised and only slightly aroused by her classmate Colonna's lesbian interest in her; Jan's homoerotic relationship with Mic is predicated on Mic's homosexual desire and may or may not have involved any physical expression. The material body is explicitly an issue, an incontrovertible and defining fact in the characters' experiences, in their scientific and technical work and personal relationships, but Renault's task in the novel goes beyond establishing the body's presence as she explores for Vivian and Mic what it signifies and to what end they will devote its undeniable but indeterminately gendered sexuality. Vivian will eventually reject nursing for the jobs of wife and mother; Mic will leave the hospital lab for medical research. Both, however, will define their vocations by devoting themselves to the body and their own relationship will depend on their sexual choices.

5. Mary Renault, *Purposes of Love,* 1. All further references to this novel (hereafter cited as *PL*) will be included parenthetically in the text.

Vivian is at the center of Renault's novel, and Vivian's experience at times is transparently the author's. When Jan asks her why she nurses, she responds, " 'I suppose I like to think I'm satisfying my personal needs in a way that isn't entirely useless to the community' " (25). She later amplifies: " 'It's not being what I thought. . . . I was prepared for the discipline and the routine, of course. But I came here really as a sort of test' " (31). When Jan wonders whether she is testing her capacity to work, Vivian is even more precise about reasons that must also have motivated the author: " 'No, not that. As a matter of fact I rated my practical capacities a good deal higher than I've found them. You've got the usual lay idea about nursing, I see. When people have disabused themselves of the belief that it consists entirely of stroking foreheads, they always conclude that it consists entirely of emptying slops. Actually, it's a highly technical skill, and I've always been clumsy with my hands, you know. That's just one of the things I didn't bargain for. . . .' " Renault suggests the instability of her own identity as well as her character's psychology when Vivian admits, " 'I suppose the real reason for coming here was to find out whether my personality really existed or if I was just making it up' " (32).

Like Mary, Vivian is also acutely conscious of living a divided life in hospital, having "long ago realized that any personal life had to be lived in the hospital's teeth, and continual protest made the effort more tiring" (15). The hospital becomes to a degree society and convention writ large; "personal life" is to a degree sexual life, especially a transgressive or "queer" one. The routinized hospital contrasts as well with sexuality's intellectual counterpart: an independent life of the mind and creativity, the personal life that for Renault meant writing. The author draws on climbing for a number of metaphors—when we first see Vivian, she is sorting wet diapers and looking out at the city's black skyline "as irregular as a Dolomite range" (3)—but Renault even more frequently draws her comparisons here from geology, emphasizing what is underground, buried, within, invisible, hidden. Jan specifically is a geodycist, Vivian explains to Colonna, someone who measures "the specific gravity of minerals under the earth's surface" (15) who has chosen his profession because "it takes him to the back of beyond," to isolated places, to a romantic world apart. When Colonna asks, " 'Is he much like you?' " Vivian answers, " 'He's supposed to be' " (16).

The similarity, even doubling of sister and brother, each of whose sexuality is hidden (partially from themselves yet especially from others, suppressed but also self-acknowledged and consciously concealed), is made wittily clear when in the next scene Vivian knocks on the door of the flat where Jan and Mic are preparing to live: "A voice, not Jan's, said, 'Push it, my dear, it isn't locked'" (16). Obvious in and of itself, "my dear" will become for Renault from this point on in her work a personal hallmark of especially male homosexuality, the coded phrase that reveals to those who know (the reader, the other characters) that the speaker is gay. In contrast to the hospital with its restricted and regulated spaces, the flat "isn't locked"; like geology and medicine with their secrets open to those with special knowledge, the flat is open to the invited, who are welcomed into sexualized territory that must be individually charted.

Mic, of course, is distressed at having mistaken Vivian for Jan, embarrassed at having revealed himself unintentionally to another, but covers his feeling with pleasantries just as he has been painting the floor when Vivian interrupted. Mic, like Renault, is not only obscuring his sexuality when Vivian meets him but has also been hiding his literary interests behind his profession. Vivian notices on his shelves volumes Renault herself would have had in her hospital cell had she been allowed to display more than six "personal items": "Froissart, Baudelaire, Lawrence (both T. E. and D. H.), Morgan and Huxley, the *Chanson de Roland* and *Don Juan*," as well as Plato's *Symposium*. Vivian thinks, "an odd jumble . . . for a scientist" (21).

This motif of the hidden and its counterpart, the intimate revelation, which if made public would mean personal embarrassment and professional danger, pervades the novel. The hidden is both sexuality and literature. Sister Verdun says to the staff nurse about a young probationer, "'Don't like her. Can't make these girls out who cut their hair off to look like boys. I've seen her out. *She'll* never make a nurse. Too many outside interests'" (14). As Sister has "seen," the student is inadequate because her gender isn't traditional, because she has "outside interests," a coded phrase that suggests serious hobbies (such as reading or writing) but also signifies sexual desire. The danger and erotics of revelation create a good deal of the narrative tension. As Vivian's friendship with Mic develops, she repeatedly sneaks in and out of the hospital, exhausting herself with the stress of the subterfuge and the hours spent with Mic, often making love in his bed when, according to hospital regulations, she was supposed to be asleep alone in her own. Acting is another characteristic metaphor—Vivian muses that "In every civilized personality there ought to be a green-room and a looking-glass at which to remove make up and change it for the next act" (27)—and the novel is replete with scenes of dressing and undressing, with much attention given to the characters' clothing. Nurses, of course, wear uniforms, which Renault presents as complex and restrictive.

When Jan wonders if it is " 'the physical horrors' " of nursing that upset Vivian, she responds, " 'No. One faints, or retches, or whatever one does, the first time, and that's that. It's the purely childish things that get under my skin. The social survivals. Like being forced to wear a hat when you go out' " (34). Preparing to visit her brother after a long day of work, Vivian must struggle "to collect the energy for unstrapping and unpinning and unhooking her uniform. (It was the stockings, though, that for some reason were the last straw)" (16). During compulsory chapel, just as at the services that Mary had to attend daily at the Radcliffe, "The nurses sat in tight rows, arranged in strict order of seniority. Their shoulders were dragged back by the straps of their aprons, their heads were kept stiffly upright by the effort of balancing their high starched caps. Sisters, sitting at the back, found chapel-time very convenient for reviewing these caps, and noting aberrations for future criticism" (28). In contrast to these physically constricting outfits, which signify the enforced institutional order that each nurse must herself represent, is Jan's informal attire, the clothing he wears unselfconsciously whether at work or on holiday. He remarks to his sister, " 'I hate clothes that you know are there' " (30).

What clothing represents is traditional values, social convention, fixed gender roles and the erasure of sexuality. Constricted by her nurse's uniform, Vivian reflects that "Its purpose was partly that of a religious habit, a reminder of obedience and renunciation; partly, as such habits generally are, a psychic sterilizer, preventing the inconvenient consciousness of personality. . . . The tight stuff strained to waist and shoulder, made her breasts into a hard, shallow curve like a doll's. Her movement felt faintly indecent: it seemed improper, as well as improbable, that there should be a body underneath of which these clothes did not form a permanent part" (104). The body underneath is not the "physical horrors" of the medicalized body, which, after the initial fainting or retching, is quickly accepted, but the sexual, eroticized body, the "personal life" that goes on "under the skin."

The distinction between the material, medicalized body and the sexualized body of a potential lover is an issue throughout *Purposes of Love.* Rosenbaum, the gentle physician whose sensitivity to others makes him a less reliable surgeon than the cold and selfish Scott-Hallard, will remember Jan, whom because of the seriousness of his injuries he finally cannot save, as having had " 'such a beautiful body. Beautiful, beautiful.' " Mic himself imagines Jan in the operating theater, and the night nurse's officious adherence to hospital regulations cannot prevent his homoerotic vision of his friend. Mic's awareness of the medical setting—"the position of the instrument cabinets and sterilizers, the anaesthetic apparatus . . . , the great Zeiss lamp over the table . . ."—is obliterated by his intimate knowledge: "Jan stripped well. A skin tanned like thick brown silk, over sleek hard curves of muscle; open shoulders, narrow waist; the down of his chest and belly golden with sun" (320).

When Vivian helps a staff nurse with "the last offices" for a young man who has just died as a result of an industrial accident, she is made painfully conscious of these medical and sexual distinctions. Washing his body, she regards it first dispassionately as a reflection of the man himself, noticing his "square, vigorous hands tempered with various skill, the hands of a good engineer." Still distancing herself, Vivian next thinks, "His body was faultless; it would have been accepted by Praxitiles." Finally, her detached aesthetic appreciation is ruptured by the realization that his fiancée, "who looked quiet-living and religious," who has watched beside his bed until he died, "had probably never seen it." Vivian's response is a torrent of tears as she rinses "the blood-soaked blankets" (86). Mary must have been made sharply aware by her hospital experiences of the many ways of reading the body, of the importance of detachment for a nurse, the significance of sexual response for a lover, and the deep misfortune and anguish when physical intimacy is forbidden, erased, or made otherwise impossible.

Renault develops her exploration of this issue most specifically through the relationship at the heart of her novel. After their first, very passionate kiss, Vivian is furious when she realizes that Mic has misread her body, has in fact been aroused not by her as a woman or by herself, her own "personality," but by the masculine in her, by the ways in which she physically resembles her brother. Having later worked out her feelings, in part through her response to the factory worker's death, Vivian prepares to see Mic again at what will be an important meeting: "She put on her everyday clothes with a kind of defiant carelessness, knowing that she was only trying to deceive herself, and forget how long she had spent on her face, her hands, her hair" (88)—in fact, on her body, of which she is now increasingly conscious. After an intense evening in which Vivian and Mic are again physically close, they kiss goodnight and "Her mind fled, comforted, into the warmth and darkness of her body" (102). Renault's language here is no romantic euphemism for explicit lovemaking. Her earlier account of the two young people together is characteristic in its frankness, humor, and eroticism. Sitting on the downs after a long walk, they watch magpies flying at dusk; pointing one out, Mic leans across Vivian: "She sat still, looking up at the branch which the bird had left. Mic was still too, leaning on his arm. His cheek was resting, so lightly that at first she had not felt it, against the curve of her breast. For a second she held her breath; and knew that she had communicated her knowledge. He made a small sound like a hidden sigh, and she saw as if she watched him that he had closed his eyes" (92). Such a tender and precise physical description of sexual expression seems the result of direct experience, of firsthand knowledge of the tentative movements of new lovers—as does Renault's later account of Mic and Vivian, a bit tipsy after cider at a country pub, together in the dark. When Mic takes her in his arms, Vivian notices that she "had slipped somehow from his knees, and he was lying beside her. Her shirt was open to the waist. When had that happened? She couldn't remember . . ." (96).

Mic becomes such a physical, intimate, and private reality for Vivian that she can barely imagine what it would be like "if Mic were ill" and she were "an anxious-faced girl," not a nurse nor Mic's lover but a woman like the worker's fiancée, who "had to sit with him always under the stare of crowds of people; to ask how he was and to be answered, tolerantly, with what was good for her to know" (115). Vivian at this point in the novel has passed through an initiation that makes such ignorance and publicness impossible: As a nurse and as a woman aware of her own and another's sexuality, she knows too much about the ill body to approach it as a mere onlooker; her awareness of the corporeal is such that it cannot be repressed or concealed by propriety (what "the stare of crowds of people" requires) nor mediated by information imparted by others, limited to "what was good for her to know."

When Vivian and Mic finally do go to bed together, Renault contrasts Vivian's medical knowledge with the understanding that comes from such personal intimacy. Just before they enter his bedroom, "The hospital veneer of sophistication cracked away and her ignorance spread in a huge blank before her mind. Their nursing lectures told them nothing. They traced the growth of babies from the first cell, but dismissed their cause with the brevity of diagnosis. She thought of the elementary psychology, outside their course, which in her brief leisure she had imperfectly assimilated. There were so many things, never adequately explained . . ." (127). Renault comments, however, with characteristic wisdom and seasoned confidence, that "they might both have taken things less anxiously; for they found that, in this as in most other matters, they understood one another very well" (128). When they repeat the experience, Vivian candidly confesses to Mic that she no longer minds if they keep the light on: " 'apart from the fact that I love you, it's very restful to see a body that isn't a case and doesn't look as though it could be.' " Mic responds, " 'Did you find so many bodies rather overpowering, coming suddenly at first?' " (133). Vivian then distinguishes between the medicalized body in contrast for her to Mic's individual erotic body: " 'Hardly at all. One's mind somehow insulates them, at least, mine did. I suppose it's the only comfortable way to carry on. But I didn't realize how completely one does it till last night. All the men I'd bathed and dressed were as irrelevant as so many tables' " (133–34).

Both soon relax in their new physical intimacy, however, and humor plays an important role in their comfort with each other in the private space they have carefully negotiated beyond the literal and symbolic confines of the hospital. For instance, when Vivian tells Mic she is going to buy a new frock, she asks, " 'What sort would you like me to have?' " After a brief pause he retorts, " 'One that buttons down the front' " (231). Frequent exhaustion as a result of Vivian's nursing schedule and occasional illness on both their parts also defines their lives and relationship in physical terms. When Vivian returns from a holiday granted in part because she has had a debilitating bout of flu, she is enervated from the emotional tensions of her week away with Mic. The matron greets her with the news that she has been assigned peremptorily to night duty. With an hour and a half before she has to report, Vivian reflects that she ought to have expected the change: "She had been at hospital ten months, and they were eligible for night duty after nine. Her eyes were sticky with sleep, and she felt as if she were carrying her body on a skeleton borrowed from an old woman. Well, she had no excuse for self-pity. If she chose to come to work in this condition, having expended herself elsewhere, she must take the consequences and do her best to see that no one else suffered" (202–3).

Exhaustion, like humor and the tension between personal "interests" and professional obligations, was to play a similar role in Mary's life, especially during her training, and Vivian's experience of three months on night duty vividly suggests the hospital world in which Mary found herself in the 1930s. The "strange life," to which Vivian gradually grows accustomed, was "dyed in different colours from the daytime world, with its own rhythms, its own emotions and qualities of thought." Renault writes that, like most of the other nurses, Vivian suffers as a result, "in health, in power to perceive and even to think, since the mind was perpetually drugged with more or less fatigue", but Vivian also suffers "in the continual pain of longing for Mic which their brief meetings always seemed to sharpen beyond their power to appease. . . ." Renault then describes in detail the routine of night nursing:

> One woke, heavy-eyed, in the last light. . . . Half-way through breakfast the lights would go on; the little handful of them, bunched in one

> corner of the huge dining-room, already spoke under their breath as if unseen sleepers surrounded them. They walked to the wards, wondering what changes the lost and unknown day had made there; lit by the yellow corridor lights and by the rusty glimmer of the west through the high windows. The ward on most nights would be quite silent; . . . the lights, dimmed with their red shades, lit over the patients just operated on or very ill; the humped white covers of the beds, dyed with the faint reflection, leading in a long perspective to the table at the end and the green lamp-shade where the Sister sat, waiting to give the senior nurse the day report.

Shifting to Vivian's experience, Renault continues to convey the generic routine that she herself, like any other nurse on night duty, must have followed:

> Vivian, if none of the patients needed her, would go into the sluice or clinical room to clean the bedpans or testing things. The work, carried on in quiet and alone, seemed different from the daytime scurry even when, on a busy night, the haste was greater. . . .
>
> The nurses had their midnight meal in two shifts, the seniors going first, so that from twelve to half-past she watched the ward alone. Sometimes she was running errands all through the time, and sometimes had to stand beside the bed of a man who was light-headed or about to die. She would look into the face and listen to the broken life-sounds or wandering speech, feeling, with an awareness impossible in the day, a sense of some permanence behind the ungeared mechanism; that while she tended the body which slumped lower into the filth and squalor of disintegration, an impersonal essence, freeing itself slowly as her own in this stillness was half-freed, shared with her a secret silence. . . .
>
> If the work were slack they might get several rests in the two or three hours after the midnight round; during a heavy taking-in week they might be working at racing speed for the whole of the night. They made their own tea on the ward, when and if they had the time. (204–6)

For Vivian, the tasks that occupy her nights are punctuated by her longing for Mic and by her underlying sense that "Mic wanted her" (207). For Mary, too, who would often seek out night duty despite its fatigue for its special rhythms and privacy, nursing would soon be intermingled with the pull of a conflicting personal world that included not only writing but affection for the woman with whom she would eventually spend the rest of her life.

In October 1933, Mary was transferred to the new nurses' quarters, built the previous year, attached to the Radcliffe Infirmary, Oxford's large hospital just down the Woodstock Road from St. Hugh's. Having consciously put her writing aside, she concentrated on learning the technical skills her present profession required. There was not a great deal of free time in any case for a first-year student, and the social life, as Mary would later recall, was limited to the world of the Radcliffe, but it was invariably interesting: The earthy conversations among students during meals may not have been scholarly, but they were never dull. Mary also had the stimulating offerings of Oxford, both the city and the university, at her disposal. Certainly she continued to attend dramatic performances of all sorts, and she now maintained and developed college friendships interrupted by her years in Bristol. Occasional visits back to St. Hugh's were less rewarding than her renewed acquaintance with a former classmate, Phyllis Hartnoll, who during the thirties worked at Blackwell's bookshop only a few blocks from the hospital.[6] Hartnoll would go on to edit the *Oxford Companion to Drama,* and the two women must have nourished their shared fascination with acting, attending together local plays and consolidating a friendship that would last, through correspondence, for nearly fifty years. Mary's own interest in acting would result in her taking responsibility for the hospital's annual Christmas play, a position that brought her into contact with students beyond her own set.

Julie Mullard at the age of twenty-one was already a senior student. She quickly decided Mary must think herself "a very fancy character having a BA, and I bitterly resented this."[7] Such unfounded prejudice, the seven years' age difference between them, and the general discouragement of friendships between students in different years made it unlikely that Mary and Julie would develop any sort of affinity beyond the professional relationship of coworkers occasionally on the same ward. Hospital social life was limited in any event to organized gatherings, such as the annual Christmas celebration, and to less formal and smaller parties in the students' rooms where, as at St. Hugh's, several women would gather to drink cocoa and chat between tiring shifts on the wards and "lights out."

Despite the difference in their ages, however, both women soon felt an unacknowledged interest in each other. Julie was a committed nurse, almost finished with her course, and clearly saw nursing as her calling. Still, training

6. Phyllis Hartnoll to Sweetman, August 30, 1992.
7. Mullard, interview by Sweetman, tape 4, side B.

at the Radcliffe was for her, as for Mary, also an avenue of escape from an oppressive home. Mary's respectable middle-class family, despite its internecine tensions, presented a pleasant social front. Julie, however, was an illegitimate child of an absent father and an unmarried woman who lived in Hampstead. The relationship between mother and daughter was not warm or supportive, and Julie grew up feeling unloved and perhaps even unworthy. She would remain acutely sensitive about her illegitimacy well into adulthood, an understandable response when revelation carried social stigma and would specifically have resulted in her expulsion from the Radcliffe. Julie had not needed the experience of nursing to teach her the importance of keeping secrets, of separating the private and the public.

Mary corralled quite a group for her Christmas play in 1934 and included Julie in one of the central roles. The two knew each other, but only as fellow students whose spheres seldom overlapped. They had great fun together in Mary's Victorian melodrama, a broad spoof in which the author cast herself as a young apothecary whose rival in love was the rich and evil surgeon Sir Jasper Ruthless, a part that Julie took on.[8] Like the festivities recounted in *Return to Night,* the play and accompanying celebration were an occasion for bending the rules. The spirit of the season and the general mood of naughtiness and freedom made the rehearsals and three performances a particular success for both the participants and their audience of hospital staff. Then, with the advent of the New Year, the two women returned to leading their separate lives.

Julie, however, was in love without knowing how to name her feelings much less express her attraction. She confessed, "There was something about Mary that made me feel I wanted to meet her again, and Mary would have told you the same [about me]. But we could not express this to each other or anyone else. . . ." Unspeakable as lesbian desire, unacceptable within the hierarchy and restriction of the hospital, so new as to be strange, disconcerting, and apparently without precedent, what was not even understood could not be voiced: "I couldn't say, Can she come out with me? It wouldn't be right, it wouldn't feel right. And she felt the same, but she was working away at it, too. But we never spoke. . . . I never had this experience before of wanting to meet someone—never, never—nothing like this."[9]

When Julie invited Mary to a conventional Twelfth Night party in her room, she included her in a group of several student nurses who celebrated

8. Sweetman, *Mary Renault,* 49.
9. Mullard, interview by Sweetman, tape 3, side B.

with cider and biscuits. The chemistry between the two women was intense, and Mary stayed on after the others had left. Every bit as young and tentative and passionate as Vivian and Mic in the dark of the downs, they made love that night for the first time. Concerned that David Sweetman might not understand the very sexuality of this important night, Julie would try to make what happened between them as clear as she could while observing the boundaries of privacy and taste: "We were young and healthy and tremendously attracted to each other physically. . . . We behaved as everyone else behaves in the circumstances."[10]

Mary "wasn't innocent of love-making but I was," Julie later admitted, "she had more experience than I"; but neither at the time knew quite what was happening. Struggling to explain their relationship in retrospect, Julie described her own youth as having included a few heterosexual experiences, which went as far as some "light petting," while Mary "had known people before." What these backgrounds amounted to in terms of sexual awareness, especially for Mary, remains vague. Julie insisted that Mary had never before had "a sexual affair," and there is no evidence that before Mary met Julie she had ever felt passionately about a female partner. Julie is clear, however, that "once we met, neither of us ever looked at another woman." Thinking back, Julie suspected that some female friends had previously felt romantically possessive of her, yet she had not returned their feelings, had not even recognized them as possibly sexual. Both women would bring to their relationship differing degrees of heterosexual experience and continuing heterosexual desire. It seems no mere cultural acquiescence that both women, in fact, would see themselves as bisexual, and Julie would insist that "we were both attracted to men and women," a statement that is at once a comment on what they brought to their friendship in 1934 and on what they continued to feel throughout their lives.[11]

At the time, however, any impulse towards conscious labeling was obliterated by an intimacy entirely new to both of them. Julie attempted to describe their relationship: "It was all tremendous romanticism and we thought it would last forever. I mean it was just a moment and I mean every moment counted and we must grab moments, both of us. We found we had so much in common. And neither of us ever wanted to get married—the idea of being

10. Mullard to Sweetman, October 12, 1990.
11. Mullard, letter to author, November 16, 1995; Mullard, interview by Sweetman, tape 4, side A, and tape 3, side B.

tied down in marriage, not because of being with a man, but being married, tied down. . . . We were both mad to be free." They connived to be together whenever their separate schedules and energies would permit. Julie was finally very frank in trying to convey their experience: In addition to the exhilaration of discovering in each other similar interests and values, there was a great deal of physical attraction between them and they had sex "every opportunity we had . . . we didn't make the bed until after duty in the evening. And it was really, it was beyond belief—the experience—it honestly was."[12]

This physical intimacy created for both women an extremely close friendship that pervaded all aspects of their lives. They would ever afterwards celebrate January 6—"the date we found ourselves in bed together"—as a special anniversary, the beginning of their union. Still, life was certainly not simplified by their relationship. Julie notes that "From then on our greatest problem was to arrange a time and place to be together." The vicissitudes of the depression and the war that followed were in part responsible; so was the structure of nurses' training, which Julie finished two years ahead of Mary, and the sorts of nursing positions both women took between 1935 and 1946. Julie noted that "from 1933, when Mary came to the Radcliffe, until 1946, she never slept for more than a few months in the same room."[13] With limited possessions of their own, the two women would move constantly during this period from one sort of accommodation to another (hospitals, schools, rented rooms, tiny flats, summer cottages). They were often in different cities or towns and seldom shared the same bed overnight, although they would strive to do so despite the Home Sister's vigilance, hospital schedules and rules, limited funds for holidays or out-of-hospital lodging, and finite energy.

Their friendship reshaped their lives immediately. The oppressive clothing that Mary found so complicated was less burdensome to Julie who, more dexterous and less self-conscious about her appearance, quickly took over the task of folding and pinning up the traditional crisp white cap that Mary, like all nurses at the Radcliffe, wore perched on the back of her head whenever she went on duty. More generally, Julie would begin the process of taking over the more domestic side of their lives, freeing Mary from mundane obligations so that she began again to think of writing. In February 1935, Mary told Julie about her aspirations: "I've only got another year and nine months [of training] to go; after that, I'm going to be a writer." In the spring, she showed

12. Mullard, interview by Sweetman, tape 3, side B.
13. Ibid., tape 14, side A; Mullard to Sweetman, October 12, 1990, and December 19, 1990.

Julie her early novel, whose fantastic medievalism now seemed to both of them irrelevant if not also dull. Mary decided to destroy the typescript and began to think about a new novel, to be called "First Love," which would in fact develop into the narrative of Vivian and Mic. "First Love" certainly had its roots in her early days with Julie; their love with its physical, emotional, and intellectual dimensions is at the core of the novel, while the Radcliffe provides the immediate setting. Reflecting on the book's autobiographical sources, Julie revealed that Vivian was in some ways like Mary, although unlike Vivian, "Mary wasn't domestic"; in fact, "Mary is more Mic, but it's mixed because Mic is also me because he's a bastard and he has this to drag with him. But he also wants to be a pathologist, and because he hasn't any money to get a degree, he won't be, and that is Mary."[14]

This splitting and doubling further suggests the novel's fascinating sexual and gender confusion and fluidity, which contemporary reviews frequently commented on as an attribute of Renault's "style." Edith Walton stated somewhat paradoxically that "Renault's style has a sure, fluid quality," while another reviewer emphasized the author's "fluid technique" and Roger Galway drew attention to the novel as "fluent and intelligent." To call an author's work "flowing" may have been standard praise for elegant prose in 1939, yet these reviews nevertheless suggest readers' uneasy awareness of the sexual ambiguity and gender instability at the center of *Purposes of Love.* Walton praised the book on "a double count" and went on to note "a fusion between background and personal drama, between inner and outer reality," stressing the novel's "important dualism," which she nevertheless attributed only to the fact that the central characters are presented "at work as well as in love" and "are governed, in short, as most of us are, by financial stress and the kind of job they hold." Other reviewers were more obviously confused by Renault's first book. Galway saw it as an indictment of the nursing profession, yet concluded with more discomfort than such social criticism alone might elicit: "one does not look forward to its successor without alarm." Conversely, Norah Hoult found the hospital scenes "something of a relief from the strains and stresses occurring in this notable story of modern love." Forrest Reid attributed his uneasiness to Renault's lack of "reticence" and "insistence on the physical side," and stated that he would have preferred more emphasis on what he called "the spiritual relation." His discomfort with Renault's treatment

14. Mullard, interview by Sweetman, tape 4, side B, and tape 3, side B; Mullard, letter to author, November 16, 1995; Mullard, interview by Sweetman, tape 5, side A.

of bodies in the text, with her interest in gender and sexuality, led him to conclude defensively that "after all" the spiritual "is the only relation that is interesting." An anonymous reviewer for the *Times Literary Supplement* explicitly attributed what he saw as the novel's vague weaknesses to gender, but located the "problem" not in the characters but in the author: "This story the author has told with . . . a peculiarly feminine sensitiveness, which should earn her a large public, particularly of women." He decided that Renault "will do even better when she has stripped her style . . . and filed it down into a harder and more austere vein"—in other words, when she becomes more conventionally masculine.[15]

Such contemporary responses suggest the challenges Renault faced as she struggled both to voice and mask the issues raised for her by the relationship with Julie and by her consequent confrontation of her own bisexuality. Using terms drawn in part from the work of Jacques Derrida, Diana Fuss focuses on just the sort of negotiations Renault encountered at this time, on just the sorts of dualities and contractions she confronted in that realm where "the visible, the speakable, the culturally intelligible" vie with their opposites. Fuss posits that "most of us are both inside and outside at the same time." As Mary and Julie, like Vivian and Mic, moved in and out of their hospital world, in and out of the public and private zones they inhabited, in and out of their at least double roles and identities, Renault struggled not only with her literary subject (her plot and characters) but with her point of view. As Fuss indicates, "We really only have the leisure to idealize the subversive potential of the power of the marginal when our place of enunciation is quite central." Indeed, "To endorse a position of perpetual or even strategic outsiderhood (a position of powerlessness, speechlessness, homelessness . . .) hardly seems like a viable political program, especially when, for so many gay and lesbian subjects, it is less a question of political tactics than everyday lived experience."[16] For Renault it was not so much a question of lesbian object choice (being a "lesbian subject") as of bisexual identity; it was not so much a question of "political tactics" as of "everyday life": the practical as well as emotional complications of her love for a woman in addition to the problems of living within the hospital

15. Edith Walton, *New York Times,* March 12, 1939, 24; Rose Feld, *Books,* March 12, 1939, 3; Roger Galway, *New Statesman and Nation,* February 25, 1939, 290; Norah Hoult, *Saturday Review of Literature,* March 18, 1939, 7; Forrest Reid, *Spectator,* February 4, 1939, 320; *Times Literary Supplement,* February 25, 1939, 119.

16. Diana Fuss, introduction to *Inside/Out: Lesbian Theories, Gay Theories,* 4, 5 (ellipses in original).

hierarchy while—now that she had discovered her characters—wanting to write. Thus Renault found herself struggling with boundaries, definitions, and behavior, with personal feelings and actions as well as with the appearance and performance of gender and sex roles in both public (social, professional) and private (intimate, physical, and literary) space. Yet throughout 1935 and most of the following year, the pressing responsibilities of nursing filled her days and, despite early efforts on the new novel, Mary would not have time to devote to writing until after she left the Radcliffe in late 1936.

During their training together, Julie and Mary forged a special and distinctive partnership. Pressed for funds, as most students were, they freely pooled their finances. Mary's twenty pounds a year from her father made, Julie pointed out, "all the difference. It meant that she could buy books occasionally. But she spent money; she was a great spender, but that was part of the way we lived. . . . Tomorrow may never come. . . . There was a great sort of feeling of people being fatalistic at that time before the war. Anything could happen, and things were very bad—depression, talk of war and Fascists coming, Black Shirts in Oxford." Comparing the two women, whom she came to know when they worked together on the neurosurgery ward of the Radcliffe Infirmary during the war, A. D. Day remembered them both as good nurses, although she called Julie "fine," well-disciplined and organized, very "practical," while Mary was caring, intelligent, clearly not so dedicated to the profession, and above all "less practical." Mary's carelessness with money encouraged her reliance on the more pragmatic Julie, who kept better track of their resources while making little distinction between what belonged to one of them and what to the other.[17]

Julie recounts an incident that reveals not only their personalities and their intimacy but the degree to which, as a lesbian couple, they were invisible, unreadable to their contemporaries. Discussing Mary's being "hopeless with money," Julie reflected on their poverty as nurses when, because she was senior, she had a bit more than Mary: "I was scrubbing up at the sink, and under our aprons we had huge pockets." When Mary, as was the routine for juniors, came to tell Julie that she was going off duty, "Mary said, 'I haven't got any money.' So all I did was I lifted my arm and Mary put her hand under my apron and into my pocket and took out my purse—and went off with it.

17. Mullard, interview by Sweetman, tape 4, side A; A. D. Day, interview with author, Bicester, Oxfordshire, November 25, 1992.

And one of the other nurses . . . said, 'You let Challans take your purse like that?' And I said, 'Yes, she did take it, didn't she?' . . . It was interesting to me that they were not aware of how close we were. Yet they were aware of it. And yet over money they wouldn't be."[18]

The desire to spend time together as well as to share the same bed without the danger of the Home Sister's detection forced Mary and Julie away from the hospital, and they developed a pattern of occasional overnight escapes to a rented room near the Radcliffe and brief holidays in the nearby countryside. Their relationship was triply forbidden: It was unprofessional, as a friendship between students in different years, violating the strict hospital hierarchy. It was against the rules as sexual—women, especially nurses, were to be and appear chaste. It was taboo certainly as lesbian both within the hospital and in the larger society. As a lesbian relationship, however, it was ironically capable of erasure (of being unreadable, unread) and thus it was invisible and allowed, as heterosexual relationships would not have been in a traditional institution where gossip about (female) nurses and (male) doctors was rife and marriage engagements had to be reported, resulting in the nurse's immediate discharge.

Together the two women made jaunts to London, when they could afford it, to attend the ballet and to see Gielgud perform. They went on escapades into the Oxford night, and like school girls reveled in their momentary freedom from bedpans and the pressing demands not only of patients but of the matron and her cohorts. Once, in their costumes for a hospital concert that evening, they paraded to a local coffee stall—Julie wearing a white tutu and a shiny red jacket, Mary in drag, sporting white tie, tails, and a top hat. Such outrageous behavior was perhaps only possible in a student community tolerant of a wide range of eccentricity. Much as they would enjoy their more frequent and affordable country rambles, they both were well aware that they could never have lived for long away from a town. Their training was preparing them for work in highly sophisticated urban hospitals; neither knew much about country life, and both recognized they could never achieve in an English village the privacy their life together required.[19]

Yet their finances and their limited time off generally made possible only rural excursions, and they relished them. They became accustomed to taking long hikes into the Oxfordshire countryside. A shared interest in literature

18. Mullard, interview by Sweetman, tape 1, side A.
19. Ibid., tape 7, side A, and tape 3, side A.

was a strong bond between them, and they used to walk along reciting poetry, especially Shakespeare, Donne, Keats, Shelley, and a great deal of Byron. Julie remembered talking about "Keats and Shelley and what their relationship must have been like and how difficult Shelley must have been and poor Mrs. Shelley and what it must have been like living with Shelley. . . . We took sandwiches with us and we'd just go on walking, and when we felt like turning back we'd turn back. We'd spend the whole day just doing that."[20]

After Julie finished her course and passed her State Finals in the spring of 1935, she was certified as a State Registered Nurse (SRN) and took a post at the Osler Pavilion, a tuberculosis sanitarium in Headington. For the next year she lodged in the Manor House, where Mary had lived in 1933. Except for occasional nights together in an Oxford boarding house, the two women often met only for the odd meal or evening together in town when they could coordinate their schedules. By April of 1936, when Mary still had eight months of training ahead of her, they agreed that Julie should take up a post at the Royal Northern Hospital in London while Mary finished her course. Julie would be advancing her own career, to which she was committed, and would simultaneously gain more status and freedom within the hospital system as she moved into positions of increased independence and authority. She would also be earning more money. For her part, Mary would remain in Oxford, where Julie would come to visit on her days off as Mary would, when she could, come down to London. Before the new job began, though, they took a holiday in Bourton-on-the-Hill, west of Oxford.

For the first time, for an entire week, Mary and Julie lived together. Staying at a guest house providing half-board, they spent their nights in the same feather bed and their days tramping over the surrounding Cotswold hills, stopping for tea at country pubs and one day walking as far as Cheltenham.[21] Freed from the dangers of intrusion or discovery, they enjoyed a romantic idyll while outwardly appearing as merely two nurses on a well-deserved holiday—as indeed they also were. Their time was especially precious in its contrast to the hospital labor and tensions that preceded it and that they anticipated would follow accompanied by the additional stress of greater physical separation. The new arrangement was going to be more difficult than they expected. Until the end of the year, the two would manage to see each other only about once a month.

20. Ibid., tape 3, side B.
21. Ibid., tape 3, side A.

Over the next decade, Mary and Julie would negotiate a lesbian partnership, a sort of marriage that, because of its transgressive nature and the independence and bisexuality of both women, could rely on no established precedent, no traditional model, no conventional rules or assumptions. By the 1960s, when they had established themselves professionally and settled together far from England, they would appear to South African friends and neighbors, to their English and American correspondents thousands of miles away, and to anyone who cared to look (through their letters, through Renault's work) as the perfect couple. But the friendship, in being initially undefined and certainly in the 1930s undefinable, to themselves and to others, was often at risk. By its lesbian nature, it called into question not only itself but Julie and Mary's complicated sexual identities and their futures together, their possible alternative and separate lives. Julie would be explicit: "So many people think Mary and Julie ascended into heaven and lived happily ever after, but it wasn't that easy." They were both attracted to "other people," that is, to men, and "we could have been broken up." They came to realize that they would need to work at their relationship in personal terms.[22]

Soon after beginning her job at the Royal Northern in Holloway, during Easter of 1936, Julie met Lazarus Aaronson, a lecturer at the London School of Economics. A private patient recovering from an appendectomy, he was quite a sophisticated man and focused his attentions on Julie. Two weeks later, fully recovered and released from the hospital, he sought her out, took her to restaurants in taxis, flirted outrageously, talked about sex. Julie was flattered, interested, and attracted. Having become conscious of her own sexuality only when she first slept with Mary, she had not defined her desire as lesbian nor did she see her sexuality as exclusively directed towards women, nor even towards only one woman, towards Mary herself. Aaronson was an urbane Jew, a committed and wealthy socialist, an educated man in midcareer—different from Mary, different from anyone Julie had previously encountered. He was also very much in London, and he was first man with whom Julie could talk frankly about sex, the first person to whom she could speak openly about Mary.

Julie felt that he "filled in" for Mary, but he also, as boys tend to function for adolescent girls, as men tend to do for women, became the subject of the women's conversations with each other, the object of their discourse, substituting for but also displacing and logically threatening their own sexual relationship. For women, traditionally, talking—or in this case writing nearly

22. Ibid., tape 4, side A.

daily letters—about sex, about heterosexual relationships, often functions itself as a kind of sexual bond with its own erotics playing themselves out between the female speakers. "Girl talk" is conventionally talk about "boys." But such customary behavior is predicated on the assumption of an uncomplicated heterosexuality: Girls and boys are attracted to each other; girls discuss boys, giggle and are aroused together, but are not themselves in love with each other; boys are what girls talk about in part because society assumes that women are not transgressive, assumes that they do not accept, permit, or admit being sexually attracted to each other.

Julie and Lazarus Aaronson soon went to bed together, a novel and satisfying initiation about which she wrote to Mary in their regular correspondence. Mary was understandably upset and jealous, but Julie felt her affair with Aaronson did not make a difference in their love and attraction for each other. Rather, this new relationship had a special and exciting status for, as she noted later, up until she slept with him, "I retained my virginity so far as that [heterosexual intercourse] was concerned." The affair lasted into the autumn, continuing throughout Mary's last months at the Radcliffe. While fascinated, Julie was not apparently romantically committed to Aaronson, and his interest in her was not exclusive either, diminishing the intensity of an affair that might ultimately have destroyed the friendship between the two women. Mutual sexual attraction sustained the heterosexual romance until the end of the year, when Julie left London, but in fact, she admitted, it continued on and off until "after the war."[23]

Geography would be at the heart of both the problem and the solution of Mary and Julie's friendship for the next ten years. Mary finished her training at the end of November 1936. She spent a few weeks in Oxford gathering her things together, then set off for her parents' home in Barleston for the Christmas holidays, where Julie soon joined her for a few days. Julie's responsibilities at the Royal Northern required her return to London, but early in the New Year she became ill with pneumonia and left again to be with Mary at Barleston while she recovered. During December and January, Mary began to plot out "First Love." Having received her SRN but hoping finally to leave hospital nursing with its consuming routine, Mary had secured a position as a school nurse, which would allow her time for writing, and in February of 1937, she took up a temporary post for the winter term in the sick bay at Marlborough, the boys' school in Wiltshire. Having decided to leave the Royal Northern,

23. Ibid., tape 4, side B.

Julie took a similar job at Stowe in Buckinghamshire. Now Renault started at last to write the narrative that would become her first published novel.

Over the Easter holiday, they met in Oxford, where for two weeks they rented a small flat much like Mic's in the novel. Skipping breakfast in order to save money, Renault would write all morning, then break for a huge lunch with Julie. In the afternoons they would go out together on the river, and later they would have fish and chips for supper. Up until this time, Mary had kept the details and shape of her work to herself. Now, making exciting progress each day, she would at intervals read pages aloud, then cut and destroy sections, develop ideas for others, and enthusiastically go on to them. From Julie's memories and from the intense and episodic character of *Purposes of Love* itself, it seems clear that the novel has, in fact, a kind of organic growth, a potential hugeness. Renault did not, despite her months of thinking, plan it all out beforehand, but took it as it came. For her part, Julie was a responsive audience: "I thought it was wonderful, and it was."[24] Julie's affirmation bolstered Mary's wavering confidence, and her domestic support as they structured their vacation days around Mary's literary work defined their roles and deepened their partnership as it began to assume its life's pattern.

At the end of the Easter vacation, in April 1937, Mary took up a nursing position at a girls' school in Colwyn Bay in North Wales, where she remained for over a year. This was a permanent job that, as she had hoped, allowed her time for writing. In her turn, Julie accepted a permanent post at Christ's Hospital, the famous public school in Horsham in West Sussex. The two women were geographically quite far apart again but could now count on meeting during the school holidays. During the summer of 1937, they took a tiny cottage, primitive but cozy, not far from Julie's school, in Horsted Keynes in Sussex. Julie remembers: "There we lived [together for six weeks] for the first time, with me doing the cooking and Mary working." There was no running water, but the cottage had a living room, a bedroom, and a lean-to kitchen; there were two bicycles; and Mary had a typewriter. As at Oxford three months earlier, Julie again assumed the domestic duties: "I did the local shopping, meals on a paraffin stove. Mary worked. That was our first taste of a normal life." Here, in relative isolation, they briefly established an independent union, a home apart from the labor of nursing and the restrictions of family or institutions. They also had a camera, and as if to assert their claim on

24. Details of the period between November 1936 and March 1940 are taken from ibid., tape 5, sides A and B. This statement occurs on side A.

Mary in Sussex, mid-1930s. Photo courtesy of Julie Mullard.

their private territory, they used to cycle around the countryside where, Julie recalled, "we photographed each other in the nude. . . . We were into a lot of taking our clothes off in the fields—a bit of D. H. Lawrence, I suppose." The image of the two nurses, escaped from their boarding schools and cavorting naked in the Sussex fields, is more suggestive of Mic and Vivian, however, than of Laurentian characters who take themselves a good deal more seriously than Mary and Julie tended to do, either at the time or in retrospect. On their week of holiday "sick leave," Mic and Vivian pretend to be married, stay at an inn named the "Live and Let Live," and strip outdoors to swim in a lake and to make love afterwards—until interrupted by society in the form of Girl Guides with their leader, "a bright adolescent in the late thirties," who ironically affirms the couple in their unorthodox union by telling her troop, " 'in Nature there's beauty *everywhere*. . . . Nature never makes a mistake,' " then flees when she notices Vivian's knickers "caught on a low spray of bramble" (196). Julie's memory of her time with Mary at Horsted Keynes is one of two young people in love having a good deal of fun. With both amusement and affection, she reflected later, "We were very arty, the two of us, in those days."[25]

25. Ibid., tape 5, side A.

Mary on vacation at Horsted Keynes in Sussex, 1937. Photo courtesy of Julie Mullard.

Having left hospital work for school nursing, Mary was struggling to shape her career on her own terms, to move from professional nursing to professional writing, to earn enough to enable her to leave nursing altogether and to devote herself to literature. More than a "year and nine months" had passed since she had announced her intentions to Julie early in 1935. Her first novel was taking longer to produce than would any subsequent book; the money it would earn would indeed allow her to leave nursing, but ironically circumstances beyond her control would require her to return to hospital work just as she had achieved an income that would have allowed her to leave nursing permanently.

Her medical training, enriched later by her hospital nursing during the war, would provide knowledge and metaphors, experiences and attitudes, an atmosphere and settings that would influence all of her writing. All six of her contemporary novels concern hospitals, nurses, doctors, or medicine in some way; Renault's intimate knowledge of the material body as a trained and experienced professional would inform every one of her books. On the one hand, she would never shy from physical truths, and her writing has throughout a characteristic frankness and attention to explicit realities. On the other hand, her awareness of the material body would make her wary of natural details that to her recalled the medical rather than the erotic body, the ward rather than the bedroom, human commonalities rather than individualities. Her response to Colin Spencer's *Tyranny of Love* in 1967 was typical. Generally positive in her comments, she praised the novel's natural dialogue and its excellent visual descriptions, especially of landscapes and interiors, but she was careful to add, "To be honest, I could have done with fewer cocks and cunts. After ten years' nursing one takes the human anatomy more or less in passing, what arrests about the human being is his basic human condition, physical and mental; one has a general impression of various organs up which one passed catheters, or put on fomentations, or whatever, but with the process of time it escapes one's memory which of them belonged to which person."[26]

Renault never shied from natural or scientific facts, however, never treated reality delicately, was always careful to render the world of her fiction correctly and precisely. For her historical novels, this commitment meant extensive scholarly research; for all of her books, it meant sound science and a responsible and accurate portrayal of the material body. For example, she was finally made uneasy not by the sexual energy and transgressive behavior of Spencer's characters, but by their dangerous physical practices. She was amused but also horrified by reading in the autobiographical *Tyranny of Love* of "Eddy's gimmick with the cointreau," and while explaining her moral view of this character, cautioned the author about the medical consequences: "If you know anybody who actually has this kink, do give them a timely warning. . . . Nature hasn't constructed for these eccentricities; there is a direct opening into the peritoneum, and one woman is known to have died of embolism just from being *blown* into." Renault reflected, "I think it is my nursing days that have put me against Eddy. I've met men with his background by the hundred, both soldiers and civilians, and many of them not at all short of vitality mental and sexual. . . . It's not their obscenity, a lot of men are obscene when disinhibited by drugs etc.; it's their gross, thick bloody selfishness and determination to get what they want no matter who else is kept waiting." She concluded, "If you'd ever nursed Eddy with a really ill patient in the next room, you'd feel the same." Julie explained specifically the sense of moral responsibility and attitudes towards the body that Mary developed during her years at the Radcliffe: "A nurse is a nurse, which meant there was nothing she couldn't do. And a patient was a patient, which meant that there was

26. Renault to Spencer, June 7, 1967.

nothing that should not be done for him by the nurse." Mary and Julie had been trained "to do everything," to feel that "no function of the body was such that a nurse cannot or should not act on that totally. . . . She must never tell a junior nurse to do anything that she had not done or would not do herself."[27] Mary's medical experience would anchor her writing in the body; her relationship with Julie would commit her personally to the exploration of the sexually transgressive; but it was her experiences during the war to come that would develop her interests in the explicitly cultural issues of martial violence, masculinity, and social responsibility.

27. Renault to Spencer, July 10, 1967; Mullard, interview by Sweetman, tape 2, side B.

four

War
1938–1945

In September 1937, Mary returned to Colwyn Bay, where she spent the Michaelmas term working on the novel. Her plans for uninterrupted time away with Julie over the Christmas holiday were upset by an outbreak of mumps at Christ's Hospital, which kept all medical staff on duty, so Mary joined her in late December in Horsted Keynes. It was not until the very end of the year, when the two women visited Mary's parents in their new home in Essex, that they had the freedom to speculate on their future together. The novel would be finished in a matter of weeks, and Mary was eager to send it off and to establish herself as a published writer. For her part, Julie was in a real quandary, which they now discussed at length. During the autumn, Julie had developed a friendship with a married teacher. She was wary of an extramarital affair and had kept an emotional distance despite the chemistry between them. When Roland's wife died soon after giving birth to twins, Julie's feelings were in turmoil. She was certainly attracted to him, and the tiny babies elicited all her maternal affection. A desire to nurture combined with her trained commitment to care for those in physical need created a conflict for her more serious than any problem posed by her affair with Aaronson the previous year. When the teacher asked her to marry him, she was caught between her feelings for Mary and a possible conventional future that promised a number of personal rewards. It must have been a very difficult New Year.

In January, both women went back to their separate schools. In Colwyn Bay, Mary completed the novel and sent it off to Chapman and Hall for consideration. Julie resumed her romantic relationship, having resolved nothing and intensely aware of her divided loyalties. When Chapman and Hall rejected the novel as too loose and too long, Mary's understandable disappointment was somewhat mitigated by the editor's encouragement: He felt the novel was promising in spite of the need for revision and suggested that Mary begin the process of looking for a literary agent by sending the typescript to Curtis Brown.

After a year of school nursing in north Wales, Mary accepted a new post, to start at the beginning of the summer term of 1938, at Cheltenham Ladies' College. In the familiar Cotswold countryside, she would be nearer to Oxford and to Julie. She was on the brink of her career as an author; meanwhile, Roland, pressing Julie to reach a decision, had invited her to spend the holiday with him on a car trip to Wales. Years later, Mary described her "curious feeling of sudden vacuum." In part because she knew that Julie's romantic relationship might end in marriage, might lead her to an important, separate future, Mary felt that she should encourage her to "go off for a bit with him and see." Heterosexuality, with marriage as its traditional consequence, was an issue; so was the individual lover. It was a tremendous relief to both women when, after less than a week away, Julie left Roland to join Mary in Bourton-on-the-Hill, where they had been so happy two years earlier. Mary felt that Julie had made her decision not because of any sexual dissatisfaction ("the bed part had gone all right"), but because she finally realized that she simply did not like the man sufficiently to devote herself to a marriage with him.[1] Certainly her return to Mary was a reaffirmation of their partnership, although it did not resolve for either of them the issues of monogamy or sexual identity.

In the spring of 1938, Naomi Burton at Curtis Brown agreed to serve as Mary's agent and sent a draft of the novel to Longman's, which promised its author a contract and an advance of fifty pounds, nearly as much as a school nurse's annual salary, once the book was cut in length and its narrative tightened. Despite the months of revision still ahead of her, Mary was naturally elated.

In July 1938, Julie resigned from Christ's Hospital and accepted a position to begin at Mary's school in the autumn. For six weeks of their summer holiday, Mary and Julie took a room in a small hotel on the French coast at Equihen, just south of Boulogne, at a physical distance from England that both must also have seen as symbolic of their distance from the routine of school nursing and from Julie's involvement with Roland. Having finally finished

1. Renault to anonymous recipient, undated, quoted in Sweetman, *Mary Renault,* 68. Other details from this period are drawn from Mullard, interview by Sweetman, tape 5, side A.

Purposes of Love, Mary began serious work on a second novel and reveled in the foreignness of a country she had never before visited but whose language and literature she loved. Her French, unlike Julie's, was good, and together they swam in the sea, cycled in the countryside, went shopping in Boulogne. They both read *The Well of Loneliness,* still banned across the Channel as obscene. Neither woman could identify with the lesbian characters, and their general reaction was to discount the experiences Radclyffe Hall recorded as in no way like their own, even ridiculous. Mary remembered that "Every morning, before getting up and starting out for the beach, we used to read it with the coffee and croissants, accompanied by what now strikes me as rather heartless laughter. It is a fact however that we both found it irresistibly funny . . . ; it does, I still think, carry an impermissible allowance of self-pity, and its earnest humourlessness invites irreverence."[2] The two women on their own in a foreign land affirmed their friendship but rejected naming it as lesbian. Julie commented, "Thank God we were not like others," suggesting the real gap the two women felt between themselves and the lesbians in the novel, between their friendship and any model union they might have found, could they even have imagined a real lesbian community. As it was, they were delighted to be on their own, away from their respective institutions, away from England and its legislated sexual morality.[3]

With the announcement of the Munich agreement in August, world events loomed as yet another factor beyond their control that would determine their lives. They left France and spent a week in London, then returned together to Cheltenham Ladies' College. Renault signed her contact with Longman's that September, receiving her promised advance, and $250 soon followed from Morrow, which would bring the book out in America. When *Purposes of Love* appeared in February 1939, it met with very positive reviews and sales were excellent. Mary now began to think seriously about reshaping her life, about leaving medicine, about establishing a permanent household with Julie.

Mary was now especially pleased to have Julie with her, in part because she herself was uncomfortable there; neither the town of Cheltenham nor the school was particularly appealing for her, and she longed increasingly for an independence and freedom to write that nursing never permitted. She was hard at work on *Kind Are Her Answers,* and both she and her flat needed the domestic attention she had become accustomed to receiving from Julie. She

2. Renault, afterword to the Virago edition of *The Friendly Young Ladies,* 281.
3. Mullard, interview by Sweetman, tape 5, side B.

Mary in 1938, publisher's publicity shot. Photo by Ramsay and Musprat, courtesy of Julie Mullard.

probably also missed her friend as a literary critic, the personal and supportive audience for her creative work.

Their schedules, however, as at the Radcliffe, seldom allowed them time off simultaneously, and both soon grew frustrated. Splurging, Mary used her American advance to buy a sporty red MG, which, despite their dual failure to pass the driving test, they often drove into the Cotswolds on free afternoons, exploring the countryside that they had always found so liberating. When Mary wrecked the car in June, she precipitated decisions that were perhaps unavoidable in any case. Julie was hospitalized with facial injuries, while Mary, despite painful bruises, returned to her work at the college for the few remaining weeks of the summer term. At the end of July, both women resigned their posts, taking a flat in Oxford for a fortnight before moving to a small cottage in Cornwall in the middle of August 1939.

Mary and Julie settled quickly into life in the countryside. They were well situated between Cubert and Crantock and within walking distance of

Newquay on the north coast, a position of peaceful solitude that still allowed them some contact with civilization, just the sort of freedom they had been struggling for since 1935. Financially secure for the first time, they lived off the income from *Purposes of Love* and on the advance that Longman's had already paid on the second novel. Julie again saw to domestic tasks while Mary wrote, and during the summer afternoons they would set out on local excursions. But their rural isolation was a brief respite whose duration was inevitably tied to the increasing political tensions throughout Europe.

Mary had nearly finished *Kind Are Her Answers* when war was declared in September. As the Emergency Medical Service required of all trained personnel, they sent off their credentials, and in fact were eager to participate in the war effort, eager to contribute to a communal cause that demanded their skills. Without word from the authorities about where they should go or what they should do, however, they stayed put and were still in Cornwall at the end of 1939. They enjoyed a "wonderful" Christmas together; the weather was like "spring" and they walked down to the sea. Julie recalled:

> . . . we had a little cat, a kitten, which we felt bad about really because we had to give it away when we left. When we went for a walk, Mary used to put it into her jacket. It was frightened of the sea; when it heard the sea, it used to cry. However, we had this place with all manner of beds, and we thought we'd fill them with children, evacuees. Of course, they never turned up. . . . Still, we knew what was going to happen. Meanwhile, we did lots of things we'd never done before—like riding. Mary was very fond of riding, and I loved running the cottage, doing the washing and all those sorts of cottage things. Mary was very upset about this; I had to try and do it in secret. . . . But now we had run out of money. . . . We couldn't go on staying there.[4]

Julie's details vividly convey the tenor of their life at the end of 1939. It was a time of innovation (they rode horses, as they had never done before; they lived together for months as a couple); it was a time of conventions (national feeling; and Julie's joy in traditional female tasks, which Mary apparently saw in part as evidence of her self-effacing and even compulsive willingness to assume menial chores). Julie's memory also suggests the degree to which Cornwall became home for the two women: Their time there established

4. Ibid.

their partnership in the cottage as a household with domestic elements, a marriage with even the possibility of children, for whom the kitten in Mary's coat symbolically substitutes. Julie's images here contrast Mary's figurative pregnancy (the second novel nearly completed at this time, the kitten they must leave behind, the evacuees who never materialize) and war, life and death, spring and winter, confirming their state as transitory and halcyon, threatened from without despite the relative peace within, inevitably to be determined by war.

The next six years would demand from Mary both physical and emotional stamina as she was once again defined not by her literary achievement but by her medical training. Looking back on this period, Renault wrote to Kathleen Abbott: "I suppose the National Service Act broke up your pastoral seclusion and swept you back into teaching again. . . . For myself, I went back to nursing all through the war."[5]

Writing to Bryher, who had sent her a copy of her *Days of Mars: A Memoir, 1940–1946,* Renault offered a vivid overview of her own experience. She was concerned to explain to her wealthy lesbian correspondent her decision to put aside her writing for nursing. Bryher had not had to work at any time in her life, and primarily for patriotic and philanthropic reasons had left her home in Switzerland in 1939 in order to take up residence for the duration in her London flat, which she shared with her companion, the American modernist writer H. D. (Hilda Doolittle), whom in her memoir she duplicitously calls her "cousin." Renault's war experiences were very different, and she wrote Bryher somewhat apologetically, "You do seem to have had a very interesting war. I can't say mine contributed much to culture." Mary apparently felt she needed to defend the choices she had made: "We were told there was a war on the day after it was declared, my birthday [September 4], by a man on a footpath wheeling a bike. We enrolled of course and awaited call up." Indeed, during the "phoney war," the Emergency Medical Service put off the civilian conscription of medical personnel until it was clear that additional staff were needed. Renault saw her second book through proof, and, she reported to Bryher, "It came out felicitously in the week of Dunkirk and sold about 2000 copies, which I find astounding as it wasn't even good."[6]

By May 1940, however, Mary and Julie had been placed in an EMS hospital in the hills outside Bristol, where they took care of "bone cases" and gunshot

5. Renault to Abbott, undated, probably written late in 1947.
6. Ibid.

wounds. Reluctant to reveal personal details or difficulties, Mary stressed the humor and social camaraderie of her situation. The hospital had been quickly constructed and expanded "in the middle of nowhere, without any staff accommodation, and they had to convert a ward. The sisters were in the same hut as the nurses, an arrangement loathsome to both parties," but the soldiers "were nice to be with. Our special friends were Bombardier Black and Bombardier Keen, with whom we played darts at the pub. . . ." Bryher thought of herself as a boy in a girl's body, preferred the friendship of homosexual to heterosexual men, and was actively hostile to heterosexuality; Renault seems to be aware of Bryher's mixed feelings towards men and offers her correspondent just the sort of account that would appeal to her. Thus, she writes of "one really awkward lout, name of Smith, a sort of great shambling ape, an ex-docker or something, practically a moron—poor devil, he had all the stigmata of hereditary syphilis—who would sleep through anything, ack-ack, shrapnel on the roof, bombs in neighbouring fields, the lot. If we had to get them under their beds he would just sleep like a log on the bare floor until we shook him. In the morning he had to be extracted from his slumbers by force. He was quite well, a convalescent arm wound. . . ."[7]

Most of the war, however, Renault spent "doing neuro-surgery (which means mostly brains)," she explained to Bryher, "under the late Hugh Cairns, a surgeon of the very finest kind." Continuing in her jocular mode, Renault was nevertheless careful to point out the significance of her work and her own understanding of the institutional hierarchy: "Nursing, by the way, gives you a somewhat ambivalent attitude to the Establishment. On the one hand, one had stupid old trouts of Home Sisters who thought they were running Miss Prism's Academy for Young Ladies; on the other, one had people like Sir Hugh, who were the *real* Establishment; who were what it was all about; who made the fundamental rules. If you horsed around with those, someone would die, and it wouldn't be you; you would only wish it had been. Hospital leaves one with little time for anarchists." But, Renault told Bryher, as soon as it was possible—that is, after VE Day—"I managed to get put on part-time nursing, which meant I only worked an eight-hour day. In hospital it was about nine and a half on day duty, eleven or twelve on nights."[8]

In fact, the physical work on the ward and the nursing of wounded young men threw Mary's life into sharp relief. Responding to her editor John Guest's

7. Ibid.
8. Renault to Bryher, December 30, 1971.

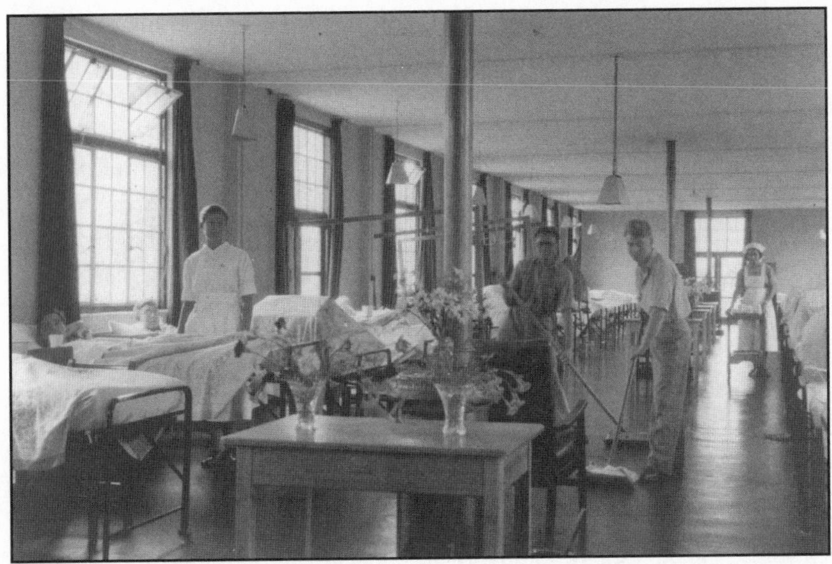

Nurses and orderlies (Conscientious Objectors) at Winford Emergency Hospital, Bristol, during World War II. Photo courtesy of Tim Evens.

account of his war experiences in *Broken Images,* Renault reflected seriously and sympathetically that "it is the sudden glimpse in the midst of some chore or other which takes one for a few minutes out of doors, the dawn seen through the window of a hospital corridor during a busy time on night duty, that one vividly remembers. . . . I used often to wonder while the war was on, nursing soldiers as I did part of the time, whatever it was like for a civilised and sensitive man to be pitchforked into the daily primitiveness and workhouse squalor of Army life."[9]

Such experiences would specifically influence Renault's depiction of war and individual characters in *The Charioteer* (1953), the last novel in which she would draw directly on her own life. This book, the transitional text between her five contemporary novels and the eight historical fictions that followed, has the pace and focus, the art and insight of a mature writer who has found her voice. Renault's experiences during the war would allow her to winnow and sift her material, to develop the perspective that would enable her to

9. Renault to Guest, March 8, 1960.

combine subjects and themes already defining themselves in her early work with concrete illustration of a particular time and place. However, as she wrote to Bryher, her daily life during the war was not one of contributing directly to "culture" but of pressing practicalities, the first effect of which was to break up the "pastoral seclusion" that she and Julie had been enjoying in Cornwall.

In order to qualify for service in Queen Alexandra's Royal Army Nursing Corps, Julie decided to apply for a midwifery course, and in March 1940, they moved to a flat in Bristol and set up yet another household. The plan was for Julie to prepare for overseas nursing, while Mary would continue to write as long as possible. Before Julie could finish her course, however, both women were assigned first to the Bristol Royal Infirmary, then, in the early summer, to the Winford Emergency Hospital, where they worked for several months with wounded soldiers evacuated from Dunkirk. By the end of the year, they would move back to the Radcliffe in Oxford.

This brief period introduced Mary to the hospitals, soldiers, and Conscientious Objectors she would fictionalize in *The Charioteer.* Winford was one of the first hospitals to employ the young men who refused to fight in the armed services. Denis Hayes described their role:

> C.O.'s were only accepted because the authorities were crying out for staff, not so much in the skilled technical grades as for plain portering, orderly work, or stoking. The hospital worker, though there were exceptions, was essentially a labourer, taking cases from the ambulances to the casualty department, taking the post and the meals round the wards, helping the undertakers to put the corpses in coffins, mopping down the corridors, emptying the bins of soiled dressings and keeping the furnace going. . . . A few hospitals, such as the Radcliffe Infirmary, Oxford, and the Winford Emergency Hospital, near Bristol, employed numbers of C.O.'s who were thus able to maintain a real corporate spirit.

The camaraderie Hayes notes was indeed rare, but the group at Winford maintained an enduring coherence and identity. In 1946, Tim Evens and Stuart Walters chronicled their experiences in *The Winford Team,* which—with Evens's own personal recollections and those of other staff—provides a specific and perceptive account of the hospital and men Renault later depicted in her novel. By the end of August 1940 the first group of eighteen C.O.'s had arrived at Winford to take over, among their other duties, the domestic tasks of the maids who had just walked out for more lucrative work in munitions factories. Ward jobs included scrubbing and polishing floors and endless washing up as well as minor nursing work—shaving patients and giving them their baths. Some C.O.'s were trained to help with surgery, transporting patients to and from the operating theaters and assisting with anaesthesia and sterilization. By October there were twenty C.O.'s at Winford; by November, twenty-two.[10]

The physical circumstances at Winford fostered an unusual degree of community as staff cooperated to organize the new rural facility. Clifford Worrall, another member of the "team," noted in his memoirs the hospital's relative isolation "on high ground, surrounded by meadows, up a country lane, overlooking the very pleasant, small village of Winford." Meriel Eyre-Brooke, who arrived with the first patients as resident Medical Officer, recalled the situation in which Mary and Julie found themselves: "Before the war Winford Orthopaedic Hospital was a small country hospital for orthopaedic children and children with rheumatic heart disease, with only one visiting surgeon . . . and one physician. There was a large amount of land available in 1939. Seven large hut-type wards were erected by the Ministry of Health for the Emergency Medical Service. Four were actually used as wards (30 beds each) and three for nurses [and later C.O.] accommodation." Julie remembered that when she and Mary arrived at Winford with twelve other nurses, the wards were "stark and silent and forbidding"; the site was "an empty camp made up of a small, evacuated children's hospital, around which . . . temporary Nissen huts had been built. When we looked through the windows we could see that these sheds were stacked with unmade beds." Characteristically, Mary and Julie volunteered for "night duty all the time once the patients arrived," effectively forming their own separate community.[11]

The hospital rapidly became full and busy, and the new staff quickly defined their roles in the emergency enterprise. Eyre-Brook remembered "the arrival of sixteen or fifteen soldiers from the Dunkirk evacuation. They had had a wonderful reception on arrival [in England] and the more serious cases were off-loaded near the Southeast coast. Ours were actually pretty fit and rather bored at having to live for a while at a quiet country hospital (one mile from an R.A.F. aerodrome and five miles from Bristol)." Pauline Clark, the operating theater staff nurse at Winford, recalled the atmosphere early in the war: "It

10. Denis Hayes, *Challenge of Conscience: The Story of the Conscientious Objectors of 1939–1945*, 218, 14–15, 47–48.

11. Meriel Eyre-Brook, letter to author, June 12, 1993; Mullard, letter to author, September 2, 1993, and a description based on Mullard's memory of Winford from Sweetman, *Mary Renault*, 90; Mullard, letter to author, October 4, 1993.

was an extremely fraught time, with frequent air raids on Bristol and transfer of civilian casualties to us, plus service personnel with orthopedic injuries"—like those depicted in *The Charioteer.* Having read the novel, Clark "could easily recognise Winford, particularly the mention of the covered way and air raids. . . . Patients who were fit enough were permitted passes (day and late) to go into Bristol by our bus." She felt that "the nurses' attitude to the C.O.'s was indifference." There were no long discussions of their perspective on the war; the nurses "were glad to have them as members of the Team, and as friendly, mostly well-educated individuals. . . . In those days I suppose one was very ignorant. Homosexuality [as depicted in Renault's novel] just didn't enter our thoughts. We were far more interested in the C.O.'s as possible boyfriends, so it is a surprising idea to me to equate C.O.'s with possible sexual deviation. They seemed to be a sincere bunch of men, who in some cases had had to face quite a lot of criticism and even imprisonment."[12]

For Renault in *The Charioteer,* however, Conscientious Objectors formed a community whose social transgression suggested also the possibility of sexual transgression. Through her fictional re-creation of the actual setting and situation at Winford in her last hospital novel, Renault revealed her capacity both to use history and to transmute experience (her own, that of others). Misreading fiction as fact, Sweetman suggests an unlikely reality: "listening to their stories and trying to understand their motives," Renault felt that "the most fascinating thing was that some of the conchies were homosexual. . . . These were young men interested only in each other." Sweetman stresses "the special form of courage" that it must have required to be both "a conscientious objector during a world war and avowedly homosexual." It would have been unusual indeed for a night nurse to have had the opportunity for the personal discussions Sweetman suggests; it would have been even more surprising to find an "avowedly homosexual" C.O. in England at this time—as Johnathan Dollimore points out, from 1939 to 1953, prosecutions for "homosexual offenses" increased fivefold. The only "safe" position for a homosexual was a covert life masked by apparent heterosexuality, a public erasure.[13]

In fact, Renault would draw on her early experiences in South Africa for her depiction of male homosexuality in *The Charioteer;* at Winford she only came to know the C.O.'s from a distance. Renault's presence at the hospital

12. Eyre-Brook, letter to author, June 12, 1993; Pauline Clark, letters to author, June 11 and July 7, 1993.

13. Sweetman, *Mary Renault,* 92; Jonathan Dollimore, "The Challenge of Sexuality," 61.

was vitally important to her as a writer in providing a social situation—comprising medical personnel, soldiers, and Conscientious Objectors—that she could later use both historically and symbolically to comment on sexuality in wartime England, but during the few months she and Julie worked at Winford, they developed no friendships, became in fact invisible to others. Evens and his fellow workers during that time remember neither woman, and none of the former staff recalls the two young nurses who chose to work under the cover of darkness during the late summer and autumn of 1940.[14]

Renault would not be ready to write *The Charioteer* for thirteen years. Instead, as bombs began to fall on Bristol, she started work on *The Friendly Young Ladies,* a novel that constant nursing would prevent her from finishing until 1944. Not yet prepared to focus on war, on the larger political and social issues that shape culture, Renault would again set her work in a late thirties prewar period, in a town and countryside unmarred by war but over which war hangs as an inevitable determining factor beyond the characters' control. The coming conflict will have its greatest impact on Leo and Joe, the two writers in this novel whose self-chosen diminutives, differing in only one letter, suggest their intimate relationship: They are reflections of each other, mirrored opposites, doubles, halves of one whole, a split of their author into two parts.

More literally, this book has at its center two women (Helen, a nurse-artist, and Leo, a hack writer of westerns) living in a lesbian relationship; it also features two forceful men (Peter, a physician interested in psychology, and Joe, a realist-modernist writer of the highest order). Men, in fact, beginning with Lazarus Erinson, would become the most serious threat to Mary's and Julie's lesbian relationship. Their unstable position, which resulted from their bisexuality, made it especially difficult to negotiate a permanent union in an environment (hospitals, cities, war) that brought them into constant contact with individual men. In *The Friendly Young Ladies,* Renault confronted head-on the difficulties of bisexual women struggling to define a lesbian relationship in a heterosexual world.

14. I am grateful to Dr. Meriel Eyre-Brook, who went to a good deal of effort to locate someone from Winford's early days who would have known Mullard and Renault. On June 12, 1993, she wrote to me, "I have been trying very hard to chase up any possible contacts who might remember Mary Challans or Julie Mullard (and have much enjoyed talking to old friends of fifty years ago or so!). Very sadly it has been without success so far. I have talked to three nurses and two physiotherapists who were all at Winford at that time—but, like myself, cannot remember Mary and Julie." Arthur Eyre-Brook, Meriel's husband and a visiting orthopedic surgeon at Winford, did not remember either woman, nor did Margaret Tiley, assistant to the hospital secretary.

Renault's novel begins and ends with sequences that explore the problem of how to read reality, particularly when that reality is sexual and especially when it is lesbian. In the opening section, Leonora Lane's naive younger sister, Elsie, tries to understand her sister's situation. She reflects on Leo's escape years earlier from their unhappy family in Cornwall, imagining a conventional melodrama based on her limited knowledge of adult love and on her reading of sentimental novels. Elsie later follows Leo to suburban London, where she discovers that her sister lives with Helen on a houseboat, a home whose unusual nature suggests the women's transgressive union—both house and boat, yet neither one completely, forming something else altogether, a *houseboat.* Renault cleverly juxtaposes the fantastic world of romantic fiction with the realistic realm of the river and its characters, including the expatriate American Joe Flint who lives on a nearby island. She thus evokes allusively Mark Twain's classic novels—Tom's literary fantasies in *The Adventures of Tom Sawyer* are amusing episodes that demonstrate his wit and creativity, but in *Adventures of Huckleberry Finn* the realistic Huck is no longer the butt of Tom's jokes but the true adventurer, forging ahead into new moral territory on the richly symbolic river that is not America but outside it, in being neither shore but a forbidden escape route both for Huck, fleeing his abusive father, and for Joe, the runaway slave. Renault's parallels stress Elsie as the bookish Tom who, in the adult river world, cannot understand or cope, who misreads and must finally return home, having lost his charm (for Huck, Joe, the reader) but not his innocence and delusions. Leo in turn becomes the boyish Huck, society's reject who can briefly dress up in a calculated effort to fit in, but who finally finds his identity on the river, aligning himself with Joe against society for moral and personal reasons.

Renault's literary gloss complicates her novel as social commentary while developing its transgressive center as she depicts the partnership that Elsie cannot read. Arthur Lane's conventional attitudes are communicated to his youngest daughter when he complains to his wife that Leo is "outside the pale of decent society," living in "the *demi-monde*" (*FYL*, 8). He is here condemning Leo for leaving her family, for not behaving like a dependent woman, for probably living with a man—he cannot envision a lesbian relationship, and Leo has given him no information about her actual situation. Elsie can barely conceive of heterosexual misbehavior, deciding that "There was only one thing too bad to talk about. . . . Her sister was living in sin" (12). Her biblical euphemism hints at both the traditional immorality of Leo's actions and their forbidden attractiveness, implying paradoxically a broader range of human sexuality than Elsie is capable of imagining, but she soon meets Dr. Peter Bracknell, whose surname, recalling Oscar Wilde's Lady Bracknell, suggests another literary context for Renault's novel. Peter tries to calm Elsie's distress by explaining a situation he projects and does not himself understand: " 'Everything has a name, my dear. And some things have several. Don't you think, knowing your parents as you do, that perhaps the reason they don't talk about her is that they haven't got a word for love?' " (35). The Lanes' silence may well have its source in their incapacity for love; however, Peter ironically foreshadows here his own as well as Elsie's inability to recognize that "love which has no name" when both are later introduced to Leo and Helen.

When Elsie first boards the houseboat, she marvels " 'It's just like a house' " (*FYL*, 64), but cannot believe that Leo is not expecting a male "visitor," that she is not living with a man, that what seems so "normal" could be anything other than heterosexual. Elsie fails to understand when Leo tries to clarify the situation—" 'No one belongs here except Helen and me' " (68)—and misses the point when Helen reveals that she and Leo share the same bedroom (71). Renault plays wittily with Elsie's persistent ignorance throughout the book. When Peter, who understands that Leo's relationship with Helen is sexual, notices Leo's close friendship with Joe, he remarks jealously to Elsie, " 'Your sister's interests seem remarkably versatile' "; Elsie responds, " 'Yes, Leo's interested in all sorts of queer things' " (203). While the experienced Peter is far more broad-minded and knowledgeable about sexuality than Elsie, he is still unabashedly heterosexual, patriarchal and selfish. He patronizes Helen when he insists that he accepts her lesbian relationship: " 'There's too much loneliness in the world not to be glad of any human happiness one sees, however unorthodox—and precarious, perhaps' " (221). Despite their differences, Peter, like Elsie, is finally unable to "read" lesbian experience. He decides that Leo is "fundamentally lonely," that "what she needed was a really constructive relationship." He concludes: "Eccentricity in women always boiled down to the same thing. She wanted a man" (222).

Renault is outraged by these misreadings of lesbian experience, but chooses to present the resulting situations so broadly, with such irony and humor, as to render them camp. The satiric scenes punctuate a novel with a far more complex and serious center, even diverting attention uncomfortably from the novel's and Renault's own unresolved conflicts. The book concludes with Peter's misinformed and misguided musings on Leo's imagined heterosexual future, first, with him, and after, with "a friend of his who liked women of her type and whose psychological layout, as observed by Peter, ought to link on to hers very nicely" (*FYL*, 280). Such an ending undermines Leo's painful decision to leave Helen for Joe, to relinquish a lesbian life for what may become a heterosexual marriage, to reject an identity developed at great personal and moral cost for a much more conventional union that would essentially erase that other self.

Years later, in the afterword to the Virago reissue of *The Friendly Young Ladies,* Renault confessed that "On re-reading this forty-year-old novel for the first time in about twenty years, what struck me most was the silliness of the ending" (*FYL*, 281). Ironically, it was not her final emphasis on Peter's misunderstanding that Renault was rejecting, but the idea that Leo and Joe would have a satisfying future life together: "Sexual harmony apart, one cannot contemplate without a shudder their domestic life, hitherto so well arranged. Of course, more doomed and irresponsible unions happen in real life every day; but it is naïve to present them as happy endings" (281).

Indeed, as Erin Carlston has persuasively argued, the novel does not actually present such a happy ending, and in her afterword Renault seems to be bristling at implied lesbian feminist criticism, calling in fact for a "queerer" reading of her text, a reading that would see it not as an insufficiently politically correct lesbian novel (a lesbian "cop-out") but as a bisexual text contrasting the virtues of a lesbian relationship over heterosexual alternatives. The novel's presentation of bisexuality, difficult for readers at the end of the twentieth century, was particularly challenging to contemporary readers. Kate O'Brien, for instance, was ultimately baffled and stated, "I could not quite make out what was up with Leonora." Henry Reed was equally confused. He liked the character of Elsie and enjoyed her point of view, but declared that as soon as Elsie arrives on the houseboat, "Miss Renault's troubles begin." He felt that "whenever things are seen from Elsie's angle, the book is lovely and real," but "a fog descends whenever Miss Renault tries to get inside her grown ups." He attempted to define what had gone wrong, attributing his own inability to read Helen's and Leo's bisexuality and lesbian relationship to Renault's ignorance of "the preliminary necessities of organization" and to her "real lack of invention." He concluded by complaining that the novel's love scenes "do not bring the characters any more clearly before us" and, with an obtuseness evocative of Peter's in the novel, that "One cannot even tell precisely *how* friendly the young ladies have been to each other."[15]

15. Kate O'Brien, *Spectator,* September 1, 1944, 204; Henry Reed, *New Statesman and Nation,* October 14, 1944, 256.

Elsie and Peter are finally humorous figures who diffuse the novel's focus on Leo and her two sexual relationships, while Leo's difficulties are, indeed, not entirely clear. Like Vivian in *Purposes of Love,* she is desperate for an independence on which her very identity depends. That this identity is at once human and female is problematic, because it calls into question (as does lesbian or bisexual identity itself) what it means to be a woman. Renault struggles with these issues throughout the novel, and it is their facile apparent resolution of them she later stresses as "naïve." In *The Friendly Young Ladies,* as it seems likely was true for Renault and to a lesser degree for Julie in the early 1940s, the physical act of going to bed with a man had for Leo and to a lesser degree for Helen a defining importance. Heterosexual love may finally have been for Mary and Julie of another order than the deep affection and sexual expression that bonded them as women to each other; it was nevertheless, especially during this period, fascinating.

When in London, during the intermission at the ballet, Leo by chance sees Joe with a woman, she feels jealous, hurt, thwarted, insecure. She is embarrassed to discover that she wants what the other woman has—the "prideless assurance" (*FYL,* 211); "maturity, sexual poise and confidence" (212). Leo also realizes that she desires Joe, and longs suddenly and with very mixed emotions for an intimacy that she feels can only come from sleeping with him. Renault explores Leo's predicament through her response to the afternoon's performances. Leo had enjoyed the first ballet, Frederick Ashton's *Façade,* a series of folk and theatrical sequences without a linking plot, which was "an especial pet of hers." She was particularly entertained by "Tango," in which an oily gigolo attempts to seduce a dim-witted debutante; "the Dago" had "epitomized what seemed to her the more comic aspects of the heterosexual scene." Her mood changes utterly after the interval: Having "forgotten what the last ballet was to be" (210), she buys a program, is pleased to discover Ashton's *Horoscope* on the bill, sees Joe and "the woman in the seat beside him" (211), wishes for invisibility, then has difficulty responding to the opening sequences of the second ballet. Initially amused by a heterosexuality perceived as alien to herself, belonging to the comic "Dago" and his foolish partner, she now recognizes her own heterosexual desire—she had indeed "forgotten what the last ballet was to be," having in fact neglected to register what was on the program, failed to recognize the complexity of her own sexual makeup, the possibility of her erotic feelings for a man. She is simultaneously awakened to a previously suppressed side of her self and numbed by both the shock of the acknowledgment and her own inexperience with heterosexuality.

Renault poignantly presents Leo's psychological distress as *Horoscope* begins: "The lights went down, the curtain parted, a blue drapecloth displayed the signs of the Zodiac. The orchestra began. She sat alone, not penetrated by the music; the warring measures of the planets, disputing moral destinies, had nothing to say to her, nor the young lovers caught in their beams. With a passing irony she recalled that she had been born in August, between the signs of the Lion and the Virgin. . . . The lion, she remembered, was fabled to humble himself before the virgin. But this legendary reconciliation had, it seemed, somehow failed to take place . . ." (*FYL*, 213). Leo feels herself unable to sympathize with the young heterosexual lovers, ruled by the opposing signs of Leo and Virgo, whose shared moon in Gemini eventually brings them together; larger issues (war in the universe, moral destinies) have "nothing to say to her"; she is "not penetrated by the music." Like Renault, as yet unready to write more largely about war and morality, Leo is detached from the grand themes around her because of her personal struggle: Her identity is too simply split into unreconciled male and female parts; she is "alone, not penetrated." Having called herself "Leo," having fashioned a boyish male identity (as a modern-day Huck; as the androgynous but suggestively masculine "Tex O'Hara," the author of popular westerns; as Helen's champion, Joe's sidekick), she has remained "naïve," a (hetero)sexual virgin—and now feels that it is vitally important to be "penetrated," initiated, reconciled.

Leo's—and Renault's—newly awakened heterosexuality is no simple matter. Renault will always contend for bisexuality as a sexual identity, but for Leo—as seemed possible for Renault in 1944—the discovery presents a painful and, in terms of the novel, an exclusive choice between a lesbian and a heterosexual life. Renault presents two quite different women in Helen and Leo; for Helen (as perhaps for Julie by 1944), heterosexuality was less pressing because it was more explored, less new, because she had by then slept with several men. Helen reveals the relative stability of her own sexual identity when she realizes near the novel's end that Leo has slept with Joe. She confronts the possibility that Leo is likely to leave her and reflects, "I got all this over before we met each other; if not, I might have been the one. It's luck, it's a shape that makes perfect sense, it's perfectly fair" (*FYL*, 269).

Earlier, she recounted to Peter her own sexual past in an effort to explain herself to him. Peter is a clever foil for Renault in this case: As a conventional heterosexual man, he has great difficulty comprehending the bisexual identity Helen describes. Trying to seduce her, he cannot accept that while she apparently enjoys his kisses, she is not particularly attracted to him: "She was sweet and yielding, but . . . he felt the smooth surface of her self-possession as undisturbed as a pool in the rock" (*FYL*, 216). Presuming that she is less responsive than he wants because she has had unhappy heterosexual experiences in the past, he tries to persuade her to "trust" him: " 'All men . . . aren't alike, my dear. Does it seem odd that I'm not content simply to kiss you, satisfactory as that is; that I want you to trust me too?' " Helen responds pragmatically, " 'One doesn't simply trust people. One trusts different people for different things.' " When Peter asks if she trusts Leo completely, Helen describes their unorthodox relationship: "I don't trust her to count the change in shops, or to remember to bring things back when she goes to town. . . . I know what to expect of her.' " When Peter wonders if Leo knows what to expect of Helen, she retorts, " 'She'd be pretty stupid if she didn't, after five years.' " Peter concludes " 'Yours must be a very—unusual relationship.' " Helen replies insightfully, " 'I expect most relationships are unusual when one knows enough about them. We're pretty well used to ours; it seems quite ordinary to us' " (217).

Peter feels that such a friendship " 'must demand great courage' " from both of them (*FYL*, 217). Helen declares: " 'What a queer thing to say. It takes less effort than any other relationship we've either of us tried. That's why we go on living together, naturally' " (217–18). Here Renault uses word play to criticize conventional notions of sexuality: Peter's traditional ideas are "queer," while Helen and Leo live together as lesbians quite "naturally." When Peter wonders melodramatically if Helen " 'would sacrifice a great deal' " (that is, a possible heterosexual relationship) to protect Leo, Helen is surprised: " 'You do have odd ideas. I don't need to sacrifice things not to hurt her. I keep telling you, we live together because we enjoy it. Anyone would think, to hear you talk, that we were a married couple.' " Peter taunts her with an imputed fear of marriage, declaring that since she is obviously " 'normally sexed,' " she may want to marry someday. Helen explains, " 'if I wanted to, I should.' " Peter wonders if, " 'when it came to the point,' " Helen might be afraid to let Leo know. Helen is shocked and Renault stresses their failure to communicate: "She might have been repeating an incomprehensible phrase in a foreign language" (218). Helen tries once more: " 'I think you must have read a lot of novels, or something. People don't live that way. . . . You have . . . such sensational ideas. . . . I like men. They're perfectly all right in their way. I lived with one once . . . for several months, while I was at the Slade. He was quite pleasant, but a bit of a cad. . . .' " Peter cannot seem to grasp what Helen is saying, and she describes specifically her healthy decision to reject a heterosexual for a lesbian relationship. There was nothing wrong with her male partner as lover; indeed,

> "He did all that very well. He was just a cad to live with. Things like wanting all the space for his own work and not leaving me any room for mine. Or time. I don't think he liked, really, seeing me work at all. I was better at it than he was, that might have been one reason why. Between women, you see, an issue like that is bound to come out straightforwardly, but a man can cover it up for ages. And then, he thought I ought to like his friends but he needn't like mine. If I had a cold or a headache or wasn't feeling bright for the usual sort of reasons, he just used to go out; it never occurred to him to do anything else. Leo isn't any more domesticated than most men, but she isn't above filling you a hot-water bottle and fussing you up a bit. Well, anyway, he kept on assuring me he loved me, and I feel sure he believed it. When he asked me to marry him he was thunderstruck that I didn't fall into his arms with tears of gratitude. . . . Finally he tried to make me have a baby so I'd have to. He said it was for my own good. I was tired of arguing by then so I just packed and went. . . . Shortly after that I took up nursing, and met a great many people, as one does. But instead of asking myself what they'd be like in some romantic situation, I always found myself imagining them shut up with me in a three-room flat. Only two people passed. One was an honorary surgeon who was fifty and happily married. Leo was the other. I've never regretted it." (219–20)

It is tempting to see Helen here as Julie, who finally left Roland not because he was an awkward lover but because she did not like him sufficiently. It is also possible to see Helen as Mary, whose relationship with Caesar taught her a good deal about men as she struggled with her literary art before she "took up nursing." However, Renault's portrayal of Helen is less important for these biographical parallels than for the fact that Helen's "self-possession" depends both on sexual experience and on her acceptance of sexual identity and object choices as personal and individual. Leo, ironically like Peter, is still struggling with the concept of sexual identity as exclusive and with the idea that lesbian desire is conflicted, immature, unwomanly. Renault, born at the beginning of September, a Virgo with strong sympathies for her central character, portrays Leo as caught between the lion (herself) and the virgin (herself again).

Renault introduces Leo as masculine in language, gesture, and dress, especially in contrast with Helen, who is more traditionally feminine and nurturing. Even Leo's physical appearance appears boyish: "Her body was straight, firm and confident," with a "slender, fluent shape . . . small, high breasts, straight shoulders and narrow hips" (*FYL*, 74). She is attracted to Peter despite his egocentricity, and Renault writes that "Both the woman and the boy in her" (170) respond to his enthusiasms. Leo carefully controls her double-gendered personality by conscious masking and occasional revelation. When she dresses up for a party, she looks so femininely alluring in a scarlet dress that Elsie cannot recognize her. Leo reassures her: " 'It's me . . . up to a point' " (123). When she can indulge in boyish behavior with Joe, Leo is comfortable; awakened to him sexually, "There came over her, like a kind of sickness, the consciousness of being a woman, detached for a moment from all accompanying thought. She could feel it, even before she spoke, invading her voice, the way she stood" (237). These heterosexual feelings distress her in that she cannot control them, in that they call into question her conception of herself. Initially, the fraternal companionship she enjoys with Joe seems to her without erotic tension, and Renault writes that "With him, and through him only, she had the company of her kind; freely and simply, without the destructive bias of sexual attraction or rejection, he let her be what her mind had made her and her body refused." Leo's "way of life," her lesbian relationship with Helen, "had always seemed to her natural and uncomplex, an obvious one, since there were too many women, for the more fortunate of the surplus to arrange themselves; to invest it with drama or pathos would have been in her mind a sentimentality and a kind of cowardice" (164). This vision of lesbian life as "natural," "uncomplex" and pragmatic, a choice not to be "fussed" over, is very much Renault's own position—but Leo is not a boy; despite her posing as Huck Finn or Tex O'Hara, she is undeniably a woman, and she needs to come to terms with her female body.

Such a process does not necessarily mean choosing a heterosexual life, but it does seem to imply for Renault a degree of heterosexual experience. Helen's past suggests her choice of a lesbian partner as somewhat arbitrary. That is, since the male surgeon is married and thus unavailable, she chooses Leo. But Leo, still a "virgin," must inevitably in the novel sleep with Joe before she can attain the level of maturity to make the informed decision Helen recounts. When she and Helen discuss men early in the book, Leo reveals her own fear and inexperience. Explaining why she broke off a romantic friendship with Roger, she declares that she could not bring herself to sleep with him: " 'I liked him too much. I couldn't risk it. . . . But it has to be someone you like. You see, there's no answer. It's time I gave up looking for one. . . . After all, what does it matter? My life's good enough as it is. I'd only spoil it. The only thing I really mind is—well, just knowing there's something one hasn't got the guts to face' " (*FYL*, 95).

Renault may have been "naïve" in portraying Leo's heterosexual relationship with Joe as a happy ending in itself, but she did indeed see heterosexual initiation as playing an important part in the development of a bisexual identity. Towards the very end of *The Friendly Young Ladies*, Joe writes to Leo to explain his feelings about her and about their lovemaking: " 'There are two people in you. One of them I have known much longer than the other. I am missing him, already, as much as I ever missed a friend. I should like him back—sometimes. But you know, now, how much he counted for when he came between my woman and me . . ." (*FYL*, 274). Despite the apparent possessiveness of Joe's cowboy language, the reader is sympathetic here with his understanding of Leo's personality. She needs to learn that being a "boy" is finally childish while being a "woman" does not necessarily imply heterosexuality; rather, it signifies honesty, maturity, and an acceptance of the body and the possibility of sexual choices.

Renault's own real and lasting interest in men, her erotic feelings toward them, her recognition of the body and herself as a woman depended on her personal acknowledgment of the broad range of human desire. During the war, she had several intense relationships with men, beginning in Bristol in 1940 with Robert Wilson, a London physician whose interest had been sparked by his reading of *Purposes of Love.* Like Peter Bracknell, Robbie's enthusiasms were often naive and manipulative, but he was also spontaneous and engaging. His interest in Mary as the author of a frank book about medicine and love, about the body and transgression, led to a friendship that lasted, through correspondence, even after she left England in 1948. Probably through her publisher, he discovered her address, began a correspondence, then one evening came down by train to visit unannounced. Whatever letters had passed between them had evidently encouraged him and had not mentioned Julie. Mary may have failed to understand the erotics of his interest, or she may have wondered about a heterosexual relationship apart from her relationship with Julie—in any event, his arrival at the flat was a surprise, according to Julie, to both women. When Mary made clear to him that she and Julie were lovers, he was not in the least judgmental or daunted. In the midst of a divorce, he would go on to remarry during the war, but his friendship with Mary persisted and it seems likely that he always hoped for more emotionally and physically than she was prepared to give him. Julie would recall that Robbie "really loved Mary," although they never had an affair.[16] Mary's reluctance probably had more to do with common sense than reserve—Robbie was extremely attractive and vivacious but unreliable; he was sensitive and exciting, but also wayward and self-centered.

By the end of 1940, Mary and Julie had arranged to leave the provincial hospital at Winford for the Radcliffe, where the celebrated physician Hugh Cairns was assembling sophisticated personnel to staff a special neurosurgical unit. Once more in the familiar surroundings of Oxford, Mary enjoyed a position of increasing autonomy and responsibility. The nursing of patients with complicated head wounds in an atmosphere of exciting innovation and purpose was gratifying, even if it seriously interrupted her literary work. The nearby flat she took with Julie provided both women an occasional escape from the wards, even though Mary now had neither the free hours nor the concentration for the writing that she had hoped might be possible in rooms away from the hospital. Wartime nursing did not allow them much time alone together, either, and the flat became a retreat but not a settled home.[17] Julie remained in Oxford on these terms for a little over a year, but personality conflicts within the hospital hierarchy made life at the Radcliffe difficult for her, and in early 1942, she took up a position at St. Mary's Hospital in Paddington. Within a month, Mary found a post at the London Clinic, and the two women moved into rented rooms in an attic in Cleveland Square.

During the worst of the Blitz, they remained in London, nursing civilians as well as the occasional soldier who passed through their wards. In 1943, Julie transferred to the Redhill Maternity Hospital in Edgware, but their situation was not materially improved: Their shifts seldom coincided; their accommodation was uncomfortable and grim; and the bombing was a constant and unnerving threat. Unable under the circumstances to focus on her writing, Mary grew increasingly frustrated and sometimes depressed. Her father had died in 1941 after a painful bout with cancer, and she now felt cut off from even the unlikely possibility of parental approval for her achievements as an author. She was struggling to define a life with Julie, but the two had little opportunity to see each other, working different shifts at separate hospitals in a besieged city.

16. Mullard, interview by Sweetman, tape 12, side A.
17. Ibid., tape 4, side B.

When Julie decided to return to the Radcliffe in late 1943, Mary found a position at the Acland Nursing Home across the street. They soon reestablished themselves in Oxford. Beyond the range of nightly bombing, life was marginally calmer, although working at different institutions and now once again living within their walls, Julie and Mary had little opportunity to meet. Mary took a room a few blocks away, where she finished *The Friendly Young Ladies* in the spring of 1944, then put aside all hope of writing until the war was over. As D-Day neared, she accepted that the daily round of hospital work demanded nearly all of her professional energy.

From 1942 until the end of the war, Mary and Julie would live and work more separately than at any other time in their relationship. Julie continued to form passing romantic friendships with men, and both women became clearer about their bisexuality. Through the intimacy of her heterosexual affairs, Julie affirmed her own bisexuality while learning, as perhaps one only does through direct experience and pillow talk, about the individual sexual lives of other people. She confessed, for example, that "During the war we had an American surgeon working in our Neuro-surgical department: very male, very 'normal.' It wasn't until we were in bed together that I realised he was bisexual." Neither woman would have a lesbian affair, but the issues of heterosexual virginity and experience that Renault explored in *The Friendly Young Ladies* were pressing realities in her own life. Julie reflected that during the second half of 1944, while nursing at the Acland Home in Oxford, Mary realized that "there was something in her that suddenly seemed to attract men," and from this time until the two women left England, "there was always at least one man who was important in her life." Robbie visited in Oxford as he had earlier in Bristol, and there were, apparently, other interesting men as well—visitors, correspondents, people whom Mary met and went out with both in Oxford and on occasional trips to London.[18]

There are no letters during this period that suggest the nature or extent of these relationships, no direct or indirect accounts from Renault herself that convey the tenor or significance of her personal life. The clearest sense of the intensity of these experiences comes from the early novels themselves, from Renault's treatment of complex fictional relationships, most of them predominantly and all ultimately heterosexual in spite of the varied homosexual and lesbian friendships or affairs that the author makes clear are vital elements in her characters' histories. If *The Friendly Young Ladies* has a lesbian center,

18. Mullard, letter to author, May 14, 1996; Mullard, interview by Sweetman, tape 12, side A.

it nonetheless focuses on the tensions between Leo and Joe; and *Return to Night,* with its rare dedication—"to R. R. W." (Robert Rowand Wilson)—is unabashedly about the fraught erotics of a woman's relationship with a man. Julie herself suggested that Mary's precious free time was spent with other people. She developed friendships beyond the confines of Oxford, and both during and after the war, "There were times when she would go up to London and seemed quite cheerful when she came back." Somewhat more specifically, "There was a man who was attracted to her"—not Robbie, Julie is clear, but "someone else . . . and I think actually it was quite serious in a way. It didn't affect us, as she constantly told me." Despite some understandable jealousy and unease, Julie believed Mary's affirmation of their lesbian partnership in large measure because of her own affairs, which, with the possible exception of Roland, had always been secondary to her relationship with Mary. Mary, too, evidently saw these romantic heterosexual friendships—two of which were intense and at least one of which was a fully physical affair—as other than primary. She appears to have been open about them with Julie; it would seem that they discussed individual men both at the time and after, and these affairs were the subject of the "girl talk" that is traditionally about men and sexual frisson and bonds women to each other.[19]

These heterosexual relationships were extremely important to Mary, in part as the sort of initiation that she describes as so exciting, complicated, and stressful for Leo. She herself shared few of Leo's naive notions, but she was certainly a novice in heterosexual experience; whatever her friendship with Caesar had amounted to, whatever acceptance of the body she had arrived at through nursing, whatever joys she had discovered in her emotional and physical relationship with Julie, she was indeed a heterosexual virgin until at least 1943. When asked about Mary's earlier relations with men, when asked if there had been any affair with a man that could have provided Renault with material for her treatment of Vivian and Mic in 1939, Julie was emphatic: "The answer is no."[20]

By the end of the war, Mary had returned to her writing: She was no longer emotionally or physically involved with a man; the hours required by her nursing had decreased; she was thinking ahead to *Return to Night.*

19. Mullard's statements are taken from her interview with Sweetman, tape 12, side A; the conclusions I draw are based on material in this interview and on a letter to me from Mullard, May 14, 1996.

20. Mullard, letter to author, November 16, 1995.

This creative renewal—in part a matter of energy and attention, in part a result of changing circumstances—was an important counterbalance, perhaps even to a degree an artistic response to the distress she must have felt when the "short and sharp" affair was abruptly broken off. Her established lesbian partnership ironically made heterosexuality transgressive, and it seems unlikely that Mary's experiences with men seriously undermined her devotion to Julie. There was nothing formal about their bond to each other, and Julie declared that "we hadn't planned to remain friends, or whatever we call ourselves." Like Helen with Peter, both women would have scoffed at the idea that their partnership was a "marriage," although what it was remained unnamed, even unnameable. Years later, however, they agreed that they never would have left each other: it "just seemed that we liked each other best."[21]

21. Mullard, letter to author, May 14, 1996; Mullard, interview by Sweetman, tape 12, side A.

five

Leave-Taking 1946–1953

In October 1945, Mary finally left nursing. She had continued to work at the Acland Home, despite the end of the war in Europe in May, until six months later, when released from compulsory service in the EMS. From this time on, she would define herself and earn her living as a writer. Oxford would be home for three more years, as it had come to be, despite interruptions, since she first went up to St. Hugh's in 1925.

Settled in a small flat on Banbury Road, she briefly considered returning to historical fiction. In late 1946, she wrote to the artist Rowland Hilder of having abandoned a novel about Byron; aware of scholars at work on newly discovered letters, she indicated that she had "scrapped" this project and "begun another, contemporary."[1] She would complete *Return to Night* in July 1947, followed by *North Face* early in 1948, but the postwar period was not so clearly focused as these two novels written within less than two years might suggest. Rather, Renault continued to be attracted to the idea of historical fiction for a variety of significant reasons, while war itself as a subject persisted in the background of her work at the same time that she avoided exploring it directly. Socially, life was far from comfortable: Throughout Britain, extended rationing restricted food, fuel, and clothing just as it had done during the Blitz, and Mary's accommodation in Oxford was especially uncomfortable: the three attic rooms included no bathroom, while the lavatory, with a cold-water tap, was on the landing below. Julie further remembers the "horrible" owners

1. Renault to Rowland Hilder, undated (the approximate date of composition of this and other correspondence with Hilder is clear from internal evidence). Hilder illustrated the cover of *Return to Night.*

as complaining that she visited "too often." Julie was technically required to sleep in at the Radcliffe, and Mary now felt particularly isolated; she had little daily contact with other people and knew no other writers. Both women at first accepted this pattern, for Julie noted that Mary "hadn't imagined a life outside it. As far as she knew, she'd be living in Oxford for the rest of her life; I'd be working at the Radcliffe, and life would go on like that." They initially resigned themselves to their situation because in being less than they could have hoped for, it was not unique; in disillusioned postwar Britain, "Everyone knew nothing was ever going to turn out the way it was supposed to be."[2]

Soon, however, Mary and Julie began to think that it might be possible for them to be happier elsewhere, in another flat, another city, even another country altogether. During the summer of 1946 Mary and Julie left England for a holiday in Ireland. They visited Dublin and toured the countryside, which was foreign to them in its simplicity and peacefulness. With the war over, they were eager to explore the world beyond Oxford and the neighboring Cotswolds. Early in 1947, they left England again briefly for France, where they had been on the eve of the war nine years earlier. This time they spent a week in Paris, a new and thrilling city for both of them, replete with aesthetic and cultural surprises. They wandered at will and saw Cocteau's film *La Belle et la Bête*. Writing to Hilder on her return, Mary told him exuberantly, "I hardly did any of the things that one is supposed to, I spent so much of the time just walking about and looking. . . . I did get twice to the Louvre; but it's more painful than pleasurable, really, to try and do it in so few hours. You keep rushing away from things before you have had time to half take them in, for fear of missing something else. Five Leonardos at one go is enough to knock you silly by itself, before you start on the Rembrandts, let alone the Greeks." A frequent visitor to London's National Gallery, Mary was a sensitive critic of the art she saw, and responded with characteristic humor and sensitivity: "I couldn't make anything of the Venus of Milo, though. I thought the original might be different (Mona Lisa is; an absolute explosion, I found) but she wasn't. She doesn't seem to have any personality somehow—I should never be surprised if she suddenly said in a refined voice "Ladies! YOU too can possess a Perfect Bust!" I thought the Aphrodite of Cnidos—you know the one, just a torso and legs down to the knee—was far more beautiful. . . ."[3]

2. Mullard, letter to author, October 1, 1995; Mullard, interview by Sweetman, tape 6, side A.

3. Renault to Abbott, dated only "Sunday," but on the basis of internal evidence clearly written in late 1947; Renault to Hilder, undated.

Although both women were advancing and increasingly secure in their careers, limited funds and the logistics of their separate lives continued to pose problems. Early in 1947, Julie began to think of leaving the hospital to train as a "health visitor," a nursing position that would free her from institutional restrictions and night shifts. This change would not materially affect their financial situation, but it would allow them to begin at last to think of a "permanent home."[4] Then, in the autumn, Mary was notified that, as a result of efforts by her American agent, she had won an award from MGM for *Return to Night.* Hollywood was recognizing her work as a novel of outstanding literary merit, and although the book would never be made into the film that theoretically would follow the prize, Mary was awarded a sum of twenty-five thousand dollars. While a portion would go to her publishers and agents, most of it would come to her. The two women were ignorant of the hefty British tax levied on such income during the war and postwar period (as high as 19 shillings and 6 pence to the twenty-shilling pound) and were simply amazed at Mary's apparent and undreamed-of wealth. Their first expenditure would be £500 for a surplus gunboat they discovered in Devon. Their plan was to moor the boat near London or Oxford, then fix it up as a houseboat, to create for themselves the free and independent life that Renault had depicted in *The Friendly Young Ladies.* Unfortunately, the boat was too large to pass through the necessary locks, and after several months they had to abandon their idea and reckon the investment as a loss. Undeterred, they next decided to buy a large house near the Radcliffe, divide it into flats, and rent one to create a steady income while living in the other. When they received council permission to renovate, they were all set to go ahead, but the plan to buy the house fell through because the owners abruptly changed their minds, having cagily decided to renovate themselves. Frustrated, Mary and Julie began to consider imaginative alternatives to Oxford, to London, and even to England itself.

Because of publicity generated by the MGM award, Renault was now invited to lecture both in the United States and in Canada. Julie, in turn, having made clear her interest in alternatives to hospital nursing, found herself asked to join an ambulance team in Athens. Having simultaneously put her name in for a medical exchange, she was also offered a place in a pediatric nursing course in Sweden. These exciting prospects were certainly tempting, but they rejected them all. Julie notes, "The only options in making a change in our life-style seemed to be possible if we were willing to part. We were not willing,

4. Mullard, letter to author, October 4, 1993.

even for six months or so." However, by early 1948, they began to consider leaving England together. Mary later wrote about their decision to Kathleen Abbott: "We emigrated in a burst of released claustrophobia in 1948 after that dreadful winter when it froze for three months and there was no heating and we had a flat with a frightful landlord and notice and couldn't find anywhere to live." In contrast, South Africa, about which the two women knew very little, offered warmth, palm trees, exotic foods—everything apparently that England did not. The king and queen with Princesses Elizabeth and Margaret had made a four-month trip to South Africa in 1947, a much publicized visit that celebrated the Commonwealth. Mary and Julie certainly heard radio broadcasts and saw the frequent newsreels of the royal tour, but they had no notion of local realities or of the political turmoil that would escalate in South Africa with the formalizing of racial laws in the 1950s. Before their departure in April 1948, they hadn't imagined anything such as the apartheid to come, and nothing they read would have informed them. Julie remembered, "We only had two books. One was called *South Africa and Madagascar.* So we thought Madagascar would be like the Isle of Wight."[5]

The two women began their journey in London, traveling by boat train to Paris and then on by train to Marseilles, where they boarded the SS *Cairo,* a small and crowded Italian ship that took them through the Mediterranean and, via Port Said and the Suez Canal, down the east coast of Africa, stopping at Aden and Mombasa. Mary and Julie disembarked at Beira in Mozambique, then traveled overland in order to visit briefly with a cousin of Mary's in Sinoia, Rhodesia, before going on by plane to Johannesburg and then by train once more to Durban, where they would live for the next decade.

Although the legislated apartheid that came in after the election of the Nationalist Party in 1948 brought escalating racial oppression to South Africa, Durban in the late 1940s and early 1950s was a mecca for white immigrants looking for a new life and particularly for economic opportunity not available in postwar Britain. Renault described this promising city as "sub-tropical, built on sand-dunes, lazy and green with a thick warm sea full of sharks, and topsoil washed down by tropical rains from the hills above . . . [a city with] lovely flowering trees and a relaxed charm."[6] She also found in Durban a South African "wild west" populated by ex-soldiers in search of financial and

5. Mullard, letter to author, September 14, 1993; Renault to Abbott, undated, probably written in December 1958; Mullard, interview by Sweetman, tape 1, side B.

6. Renault to Abbott, probably written in December 1958.

personal stability. Heavy drinking and drug abuse were common problems among the expatriate population, and the boom-and-bust mentality did little to curb the excess.

Here the two women would be able to live more independently than they could previously have imagined. Mary was eager to settle down to writing and Julie was interested in finding a nursing post, but both women were also open to ideas about how they might invest Mary's money. On the *Cairo,* they had met two homosexual men, Peter Albrecht and Jack Corke. The instant friendship resulted in their moving into a shared house in June 1948. At Jack's and Peter's suggestion, the four of them formed a construction company, an ill-fated and misconceived project of land investment and speculative building that was mismanaged from the start by the inexperienced women and by the duplicitous young men, who had no reservations about using Renault's prize. Initially bound together by a free-spirited camaraderie, the two couples were soon embroiled in domestic and financial discord. It would take Mary and Julie until late 1949 to disengage themselves and their interests from the joint business. Jack, whose drinking became a serious problem during the year they lived together, made painful scenes, while Peter, an aspiring actor with a more charming personality, introduced Renault to acquaintances in the South African Broadcasting Company. The often wild and outrageous homosexual community that formed their circle during this first year in Durban would provide the basis for the vivid underground depicted in *The Charioteer.* Julie commented: "Had Mary not met Jack and Peter and got to know them on very close terms, she would never have been able to write *The Charioteer,*" whose homosexual underground was based primarily on "the people we met and the parties we went to in Durban where so many ex-servicemen turned up just out of a probably sentimental memory of the good times they had there on the way out to the east as soldiers or airmen."[7]

These men whom Mary came to know in Durban had once been active participants in world events, but now were doubly marginalized by their sexuality and by their status as "ex-servicemen," still defined by a war that no longer provided them with a clear professional position. Renault's treatment of male homosexuality in her novel reflects her understanding of this complex reality that was for her both the specific experience of particular gay men and an analogue to her own predicament as a bisexual woman in a lesbian partnership and an English writer far from home. *The Charioteer,* Renault's

7. Mullard, letter to author, October 22, 1995.

last contemporary novel, anticipates the mature achievement of her historical novels while it also serves as a kind of leave-taking, an *ave atque vale* to England, to the war, to her own childhood and youth, to a rich literary apprenticeship.

Drawing directly on autobiographical experience for the last time, Renault insists that the novel's protagonist, Laurie Odell, must come to terms with himself within the contexts of twentieth-century England and Englishness, but, as in all of her later fiction, Renault is here also concerned with both historical specificity and universal themes. The Second World War, the one Renault herself experienced as a nurse in England, provides a historical and social framework for the novel finally written in Durban thirteen years later. The author also emphasizes in her title a more obviously displaced framework for understanding her material: the struggle of the charioteer from Plato's *Phaedrus,* the book sixteen-year-old Laurie is given by Ralph Lanyon, the head prefect, who at nineteen is about to be expelled from school for a homosexual incident with a younger student. The narrative thus becomes at once the story of Laurie Odell and Renault's own story of war and recovery, of transgressive sexuality and the struggle for companionship, of the body and expression negotiated at personal and moral cost.

Renault situates Laurie by his ambiguously gendered name in a long line of characters whose sexual and gender identity are at the core of her work, but he is the first for whom homosexuality is not life's undercurrent but its main current. Laurie is introduced as a child of five in 1922. Awake in the dark, he is alone in a mythic and symbolic Africa, an unknown and forbidden zone: "Seven o'clock was familiar and domesticated. . . . Eight was unusual, and associated with trouble: having been punished, or being sick. Nine was the wild outpost of an unknown continent. Ten was the mountains of the moon, the burial-place of the elephants: white on the map" (*TC,* 1). In this psychic landscape of waking dream, Laurie confronts the universality of death and recognizes his own identity. He realizes "that sooner or later everyone died; not only old people like Grannie, but Laurie, Laurie Odell, I. He sat bolt upright in bed, a point of protesting, passionate identity in echoing space" (2). For the first time he recognizes "the burden, prison, mystery of his own uniqueness" (8). This understanding arises not only because of his awareness of his limitations but because of his location of himself within the world of adult sexuality and gender difference.

Getting out of bed and entering a room where his father is packing, Laurie witnesses the end of his parents' marriage, as Michael Odell prepares to leave his wife and child. Trespassing on the "private and personal" world of his father, of adulthood and maleness, Laurie feels "the absolute impotence of childhood." When Lucy Odell enters and his parents confront each other, Laurie is "seized with a panic sense of insecurity and loss." His mother's physical comfort, the apparently "absolute reassurance of her soft breast," is transitory, however, and he can only listen with half his attention to her retelling of his formerly favorite story about St. George and the Dragon, the quintessentially English narrative (*TC,* 5–7). The tension between his parents alienates Laurie and divides his loyalties: separated now from his father, with whom as the male child he identifies, as well as from his mother, despite the continuing oedipal bond, Laurie can no longer fully accept the traditional national identity suggested by the nursery tale. Instead, unfamiliar experience, this venturing into unmapped territory, confirms his own identity and difference: "It had come to him that no one would ever look from those eyes but he: that among all the lives, numerous beyond imagination, in which he might have lived, he was this one, pinned to this single point of infinity; the rest always to be alien, he to be I" (8).

The Charioteer has received more scholarly attention than any of Renault's other novels, but it has often been willfully misread by critics eager to see it as a case study in abnormal psychology. Claude Summers has written that "Clearly, Renault offers the oedipal entanglement of Laurie and his mother as an explanation for the young man's homosexuality . . . providing the details of a clinical case history to explain her character's gayness as symptomatic of disease." He concludes: "Renault's portrayal of Laurie's family situation in the stock psychiatric clichés of the 1950s is so obvious as to render trite and predictable what might have been an insightful study of the dynamics of mother-son bonding."[8] Renault does not focus on "mother-son bonding" because she is interested instead in locating Laurie within a specific social context and in exploring how he, like herself, will live with his difference in a heterosexist society. Most gay people, as Renault well knew from her own wide experience, were not the products of divorce or of the stock weak or absent father and domineering mother. The novel does not attempt to "explain" male homosexuality or the particular erotic dynamics of Laurie's "gayness"; instead, it explores Laurie's character, especially in ethical terms. Further, Laurie does not appear unhappy or psychologically maladjusted; in fact, the opposite

8. Claude J. Summers, " 'The Plain of Truth': Mary Renault's *The Charioteer,*" 162.

seems to be true: He is a unique product of his environment and has "normal" needs for companionship, security, sexual affirmation, and expression.

While Renault is clearly invoking Freud in the opening section as a way of accounting for Laurie's psychological development, as Joseph Cotter notes, "Renault's characters are not approached as if they were merely case studies; they are always free to choose." A contemporary reviewer similarly stressed that Renault "offers no hashed-over sociological explanations." Responding to Peter Wolfe's psychoanalytic treatment of her work, the author herself emphasized that she found Freud "often absurdly dogmatic and inadequate to the totality of human experience" and indicated that Laurie is "naturally homosexual" rather than sexually compromised as a consequence of a broken home.[9] The novel's opening section, in fact, reveals the child's traumatic witnessing of the *reverse* of the primal scene: Ironically, he does not intrude upon his parents in sexual union; he discovers them at the moment of disruption and parting, echoing the situation and feelings Renault emphasized when she described her own childhood to Colin Spencer.

Laurie does not ultimately identify any more than Renault herself did with either parent in their power struggle, and both parents are understandably hurt and self-absorbed. Lucy Odell seeks to substitutes Laurie for the inadequate father, and while never stating her feelings explicitly, to the child "she seemed to have declared in the clearest language that he was her only solace and the last refuge of her violated trust." For his part, Michael Odell is an alcoholic who dies within a year of leaving the marriage. As a husband and father, he is irresponsible and duplicitous. Laurie is aware that "his father had done something wicked while he was away from home" (*TC,* 3–4)—perhaps he has taken one or several lovers, although whether the "wickedness" consists of conventional adultery with other women or of sexual acts with men is not made specific. Laurie experiences what Bernard Dick, referring to Alexander's youth as depicted in *Fire from Heaven,* describes as a "typical Renault boyhood" in which "a son is forced to choose between a bisexual father whose ambition he admired and a possessive mother whose affection he craved."[10] Dick's generalization provides further evidence that we are to read Laurie as a psychically healthy if unusual male child within a common family constellation. Additionally, such a "typical Renault boyhood" supports

9. Joseph Cotter, "Mary Renault," 133; Siegfried Mandel, *New York Times,* May 10, 1959, 6; Renault to Peter Wolfe, February 27, 1970, and December 7, 1971.

10. Bernard F. Dick, *The Hellenism of Mary Renault,* 101.

Renault's vague implication here of Michael Odell's bisexuality. Whatever Michael Odell's "wicked" acts, he is portrayed as needing to hide them; the author remarks humorously that "He was often away, covering things (it was not so very long since Laurie had first understood that his father was a newspaperman and not a kind of upholsterer)" (4). Michael Odell, like Laurie, participates in forbidden acts (the father's drinking and "wickedness," and the son's staying awake, leaving his bed at night). Renault suggests that for both characters sexuality is vital and transgressive.

Her portrait of Laurie's sexuality within the context of an Edwardian household is particularly vivid. Alone in bed, where he is at once obedient and disobedient, Laurie is acutely aware of this night as "strange, and different." Isolated, the boy sees on his cupboard his "especial things":

> the blue and gold cap from a broken fountain-pen of his father's, a knob of pink quartz which had been the head of one of his mother's hatpins once. . . . He wasn't allowed them in bed since the quartz had slipped down while he slept and made a sore place on his leg. He remembered this; but everything was different tonight, lawless and wild; if he were dying, he must have at least one of them with him. The pen-cap was the newest and most dear; his father had given it to him only the week before. With the desperate courage of an invested garrison making a sortie, he jumped out, snatched it up, and curled back again, still alive. (*TC*, 3)

This episode is richly symbolic as Laurie, a nascent soldier in a sexual struggle here configured as war, claims the phallic pen cap rather than the clitoral knob of pink quartz, which is simultaneously and ironically also both scrotal and penile, also his, the genital "knob" of British schoolboy slang. Laurie's maleness here and throughout the novel is never in question, but significantly it is sexuality itself that is forbidden rather than a gendered version of it or a particular mode of expression or object choice. All of Laurie's "especial things" are "forbidden," and Renault stresses his violation of the rules in claiming a sexuality he needs and wants.

While the novel's first section emphasizes sexual identity and Laurie's difference, the second is less a deeply psychological episode and more clearly a moral confrontation. Ten years have passed. During the spring of his fifth-form year at boarding school, Laurie is informed of Ralph's impending expulsion. Outraged by what he sees as an unfair accusation, Laurie confronts Ralph, declaring that he will rally support for his prefect and go to the master, Mr. Jepson ("Jeepers"), alone or with others, to refute the charge. Laurie's impetuous chivalry is admirable but foolish. Urging Laurie for both their sakes not to protest against the social order, Ralph tries to direct the younger boy's attention from naive idealism to the " 'quite material facts' " (*TC,* 28).

Laurie's world, like Renault's during her own adolescence, is one of literature and inexperience, "a kind of exalted dream, part loyalty, part hero-worship, all romance. Half-remembered images moved in it, the tents of Troy, the columns of Athens, David waiting in an olive grove for the sound of Jonathan's bow" (*TC,* 28). However morally admirable, Laurie's perspective on life, while clearly homosexual, is theoretical and abstract. Renault further stresses that he has chosen to draw attention to his difference, of whose nature he is only vaguely aware, without understanding the consequences. For example, Laurie had for a while affected an Irish identity: "His brogue, however, was of literary origin, consisting of stock phrases carefully acquired. . . . [H]e had even gone through a phase, till stopped, of writing his name O'Dell, and had opted out of the O.T.C. [Officers' Training Corps], which was theoretically allowed but almost never done except by boys with rheumatic hearts" (14–15). Laurie struggles to take on a role that will be his own, although as yet that identity is an acted part, derivative and in fact alien to him. It also, significantly, places him in a special situation of difference: that of the conventionally despised Irishman among his English peers, the Irishman who, in 1940, would be neutral in a war in which England suffered. He changes his name in an attempt to name himself, in an effort to give a name to what has no name, to name something he as yet has no name for, to voice an identity that (had he been more experienced) he would have known was that which dared not be named. But his renaming is "stopped," one presumes, by those in power, whose institutional records depend on consistency, regularity, obedience. Laurie's decision to opt out of the O.T.C. will later have specific consequences in wartime England; here it places him in a pacifist position—a nonposition of neutrality or conscientious objection, a theoretical position, as it were. Yet the only actual or common reason for opting out was illness or impairment, from neither of which Laurie suffers. Ironically, the only really positive result of this adolescent phase is that Laurie acquires the nickname "Spud," a name given to him affectionately by other boys, a name that later helps him to negotiate the difficult boundaries of class ("Spud" situates him comfortably amid working class and military contemporaries), a name that, with its variant "Spuddy," becomes a term of endearment and even intimacy.

Ralph, in contrast, is a realist who knows, like the adult Renault, that desire involves the body. Still, Ralph is not entirely sympathetic. Renault describes him as "marked already with the bleak courage of the self-disciplined neurotic" (*TC,* 22), and we are not to trust him completely when he gives Laurie his copy of *The Phaedrus of Plato* and declares that it is " 'an antidote to Jeepers. It doesn't exist anywhere in real life, so don't let it give you illusions. It's just a nice idea' " (29).

Renault presents the metaphor of Plato's charioteer as the framework for Laurie's understanding of his moral choices. Discussing desire, Socrates compares the tripartite soul to a charioteer who must master two mismatched but yoked horses, one dark, the other light; one base, the other exalted; one lustful, the other temperate. For Plato, the lesson is to strive for purity, a sort of sublimation of erotic desire to some theoretically more moral and ideal affection characterized by moderation and restraint. That is, corporeal sexuality is to be generally repressed and replaced by intellectual and verbal exchange; physical homosexual union is to be refigured as intimate but "pure" companionship.

For Renault, physical love was always important; it seems impossible that she is advocating chastity in *The Charioteer.* While misreading Renault as basically homophobic and arguing that she, like Ralph, adheres to a medical model of homosexuality as a form of illness, Summers makes this very point: Plato's myth is not "a recommendation for asceticism" but for "a balance of the sensual and the spiritual." Further, it would be uncharacteristic for Renault to recommend repression, suppression, even rechanneling of homosexual desire for Laurie. The issue is not finally sexual expression (to do it or not to do it), but expression on what terms. Dick has noted that "The tragedy of Plato is ultimately linked with his whole system of philosophy, which was never intended to leave the realm of the abstract." Dick continues with particular relevance to the use of the trope of the charioteer in Renault's novel: "One should read Plato's *Dialogues* as one reads poetry, marvelling at their subtlety and language but never expecting them to yield a *modus vivendi.*"[11] Plato's metaphor is thus best understood as ultimately a moral one. The dark horse is shameless and wants only lustful indulgence; the more admirable steed is noble and temperate, sensible of shame and capable of restraint. Laurie is challenged to find a way of living as a homosexual man in a homophobic society that will offer him few options, few ways of being. He must fulfill his erotic desires while behaving admirably with worthy companions; he

11. Summers, " 'Plain of Truth,' " 160; Dick, *Hellenism of Mary Renault,* 98, 99.

must express his sexuality within a relationship that is ennobling rather than diminishing.

When Ralph mocks *The Phaedrus* as offering " 'just a nice idea,' " he is, Renault suggests, capitulating to moral relativism in the face of a homophobic society. This point is later stressed when Ralph reveals to Laurie the facts behind his expulsion from school. Ralph was accused by Hazell of deriving sexual pleasure from beating him. The homophobic Jeepers confronted Ralph, who admitted his guilt. In fact, he was not guilty of sadistic pleasure. Actually, Hazell had panicked in response to his own homosexual and masochistic desires. Initially, Ralph had befriended the awkward younger boy, but when the prefect found Hazell's constant presence cloying, he rejected him, first threatening discipline, then administering a traditional beating. When Ralph realized that Hazell was physically aroused by his punishment, he became disgusted. In fear of revelation, Hazell went to Jeepers. Brought in front of the master, Ralph felt he could not extricate himself from the situation without revealing his own homosexuality and capitulated as the easiest course in what he anticipated as inevitable condemnation and exile. Telling this story to Laurie years later, Ralph prevaricates, " 'Of course one sees if he [Hazell] was like that he couldn't help himself. . . . I didn't see very much future in arguing. . . . I realized afterwards, some time afterwards, a perfectly normal person wouldn't have been so angry. He was sick, after all. That was what I had against him. I'd been trying to work up what I was into a kind of religion. I thought I could make out that way. He made me see it as just a part of what *he* was' " (*TC*, 194).

Renault presents Ralph throughout the novel as more admirable than many of the work's homosexual characters, but he is by no means her voice or Laurie's, whose principles come closer to the author's own, but who is defined by his youth and inexperience. Ralph may speak with the voice of experience, but he also speaks as one who has given in, given up, capitulated to a heterosexist and homophobic society. The medical model of homosexuality he offers to Laurie—in which Hazell and he himself are "sick" in contrast to "normal" people—is not one to which Laurie or Renault ascribe. Thus Ralph is surprised at Laurie's psychological health, commenting, " ' . . . you're remarkably well balanced for the offspring of divorce. Quite often being queer is the least of it.' " Laurie responds, " 'Well, my mother's pretty well balanced' " (*TC*, 196).

Alec, another homosexual character, articulates a position closer to Renault's own. Laurie recognizes the medical student as "a speaker of his own language; another solitary still making his own maps" (*TC*, 124). Discussing contemporary laws against sodomy and solicitation and specifically "a recent blackmail case," Laurie remarks that "the present state of the law seemed to encourage that sort of thing; it was unenforceable, and merely created racketeers." Alec agrees: " 'You could add that it gives the relatively balanced type, who makes some effort to become an integrated personality, a quite false sense of solidarity with advanced psychopaths whom, if they weren't all driven underground together, he wouldn't ever meet' " (215). Stressing her own view of homosexuality as other than a sickness, Renault commented that while writing *The Charioteer* she felt strongly that "if people are going to be homosexual—which they are, if they are—they and society will both be far better off if they are exposed to a proper set of standards, as was the case in Greece, rather than driven underground where the best are thrown together with the worst."[12]

Alec's lover, Sandy, however, argues against "coming out," the alternative to living "underground": " 'What about his job, what about his dependents, what if his mother's got a weak heart and the news will kill her?' " Alec counters:

> "It's a matter of what your self-respect's worth to you, that's all. . . . In the first place, I didn't choose to be what I am, it was determined when I wasn't in a position to exercise any choice and without my knowing what was happening. . . . I don't admit I'm a social menace. I think that probably we're all part of nature's remedy for a state of gross overpopulation, and I don't see how we're a worse remedy than modern war, which from what I hear in certain quarters has hardly begun. Anyway, here we are, heaven knows how many thousand of us, since there's never been a census. I am not prepared to accept a standard which puts the whole of my emotional life on the plane of immorality. I've never involved a normal person or a minor or anyone who wasn't in a position to exercise a free choice. . . . I am not a criminal."

Ralph is shocked by Alec's radical position: " 'Anyone would think, to hear . . . Alec talk, that being normal was immaterial, like whether you like your eggs scrambled or fried" (*TC*, 215–216). Renault is not sympathetic with sexuality itself as a matter of mere "preference," an identity trivialized by the notion of "choice"; rather, she shares Alec's view that sexuality is so deeply a part of "the whole of [one's] emotional life" that it cannot be denied.

12. Renault to Wolfe, January 10, 1970.

Additionally, Alec contends that homosexuality poses no "social menace" but may even serve a social purpose as a form of birth control, a position that echoes the author's own feelings. Writing to Jay Williams, Renault confessed: "I half suspect that you are one of those thoroughly nice people who don't know a homosexual when you see one unless it is some screeching queen, or a stomping old butch in a hard collar and brogues. You want to get out a bit and meet some nice normal ones; actually I expect you know about half a dozen of various sexes already, who have never mentioned it to you lest you should be embarrassed." Then she went on to make her serious point: "Unless the world is decimated by some holocaust, there will have to be more and more of them with each succeeding generation, to cope with the population explosion. Why none of the learned writers on this subject have mentioned this solution I don't know, but I suspect they haven't the nerve."[13] Despite her obvious humor here and her more subtle irony—she never made Williams aware of her own homosexuality—Renault presents in this letter and in *The Charioteer* her own view of war as a means of coping with overpopulation. She also stresses that, through technology, war's horrible carnage is becoming increasingly vast and devastating, as Alec is aware after the debacle of Dunkirk in 1940 and as Renault well knew, in 1953, looking back on the destruction of Hiroshima and Nagasaki. Further, she juxtaposes war and homosexuality, suggesting that human homosexuality is the opposite of technological war; homosexuality is potentially a matter of love and peace in contrast to war's hatred and violence.

Alec's use of the word *normal* should not detract from Renault's radical argument here. He seems to be using it *not* in contrast to *sick* (as Ralph does), but in a more conventional and scientific way, suggesting the norm, what is standard; that is, heterosexuality. That such standards are arbitrary is made clear first by Sandy—who points out that if heterosexual " 'sex were ever made illegal, you'd get decent married couples meeting each other in brothels and dives and getting tarred with the same brush' "—and then by Laurie, who brings up Athenian society with its different standards of sexual behavior.[14] This argument is ironically underscored by Ralph, who concedes " 'They were

13. Renault to Williams, May 28, 1961.

14. Interestingly, Renault's language here—Sandy's "tarred with the same brush" and Ralph's rejoinder to Laurie's introduction of ancient Greece as an alternative culture that " 'You'll get yourself lynched if you don't look out' " (*TC*, 217)—recalls racial tensions in the American South and implies a parallel between contemporary English society's treatment of homosexuals and South Africa's treatment of its black population. Strict apartheid laws began to be passed,

tolerant in Greece' " as he emphasizes the admirable homosexual figures in the ancient world. Ralph, however, has missed Renault's point: Alec is arguing not for "tolerance" of something "sick" or "weird" but for affirmation of the emotional wholeness of huge numbers of people. Ralph further reveals his misunderstanding of Alec's view of homosexuality when he adds that "civilized people had better hang on to a few biological instincts. . . . They've learned to leave us in peace unless we make public exhibitions of ourselves. . . . [C]an't we even face the simple fact that if our fathers had been like us, we wouldn't have been born?" (*TC*, 216–17).

Alec (and Renault) are arguing for more than being left in a peace that requires remaining hidden, closeted; however, Ralph introduces another idea significant for Renault when he brings up the sexual orientation of fathers, the sexuality of those who engage in heterosexual intercourse. Ralph assumes (wrongly, Renault implies) that fatherhood is certification of heterosexuality and implies himself that heterosexuality and homosexuality are exclusive. But Renault has already suggested that Laurie's own father may have been bisexual and emphasizes this range of sexual orientation and behavior in her portrayal of Dave. This older man serves as a father figure to Laurie's friend Andrew and, Renault makes clear, is prompted in this role by affection for Andrew's dead father, with whom Dave was in love and who returned his feelings even if, naively, he did not recognize his response as homosexual.

Renault also explores in the novel's second section Laurie's inexperience and enthusiasm, much like her own when she was at school. He is not yet ready to understand literature or to write, and he has only a nascent awareness of political and sexual realities. The section opens with the young Laurie, drowsy in the warm sunlight, composing an essay on Shakespeare's *Julius Caesar* in which he is to compare Brutus's dilemma with Hamlet's. Renault writes that "the ink, flowing incontinently from his warmed pen, made blots on the page." As yet, Laurie's sexuality manifests itself merely as masturbation. His response to the assigned topic is adolescent: He thinks "poorly enough" of both protagonists (*TC*, 10). Just as his essay on Shakespeare is naive, so is his sexuality as yet inexperienced and without a clear object. He can in his essay dispose "of Portia quickly" as "the ideal Roman wife" (11), but he has no awareness of the social realities that will problematize his own sexual nature

formalizing a system of discrimination previously enforced primarily by prejudicial attitudes, in 1948. Renault was acutely aware of the links between racial and sexual oppression.

and writes that while " 'Shakespeare understood politics,' " he " 'saw them chiefly as a field for the study of human . . .' " Laurie pauses to look up the spelling of *psychology* in his dictionary. Renault thus implies how little he really understands what is meant by the term, how ignorant he is as yet of his own complex psyche. In fact, he goes on to write adolescently of Cassius as " 'a familiar type, whose temperament modern science links with gastric ulcers' " (9), as if personality—and by implication his own homosexuality—could be explained in simple biological terms. Here, Renault also takes another opportunity to make clear that Laurie's psychology is not the simple product of some classic and unresolved oedipal conflict. While he fails to understand Brutus's struggle, an ironic analogue of his own, between friendship with Caesar and political morality, Laurie concludes that "In Hamlet's place he wouldn't have hesitated for a moment" (10).

The school world of this section is still a childish universe in which the sounds of boys playing cricket are a "lullaby" and even the urbane Ralph is only relatively sexually experienced. Thus when he declares his resolution to go to sea, he assures Laurie he will be all right: " 'I can get a ship quite quickly. I know a man who'll fix me up.' " Ralph's familiarity with a sailor implies a homosexual relationship, the young toff and his working-class lover. Defensively, in case Laurie might suspect more than Ralph would like, the older boy continues: " 'We ran into each other. He's not so bad. I don't know him very well' " (*TC*, 30). Perhaps, in fact, this man Ralph knows does not exist at all and is a product of mere boyish bravado. Renault emphasizes that Ralph's understandable adolescent inexperience is not so far, in fact, from Laurie's own masturbatory level. At the beginning of Laurie's encounter with the head prefect, Ralph is nervously "doing something with a pen-knife to a propelling pencil" (21). Later, he puts the knife away, only to keep his hold on the pencil, gesturing with it, placing it briefly in his pocket, then getting it "out again" and "screwing the lead up and down" (26). The level of Ralph's sexuality is as yet primarily onanistic, a physical innocence to a degree enforced by and in stark contrast to his sophisticated understanding of homophobia.

By the end of this section, Laurie is less naive. Ralph has explained to him the social consequences of his morally admirable but childish protest on behalf of his friend, the "politics" of his intended rebellion. Laurie's classmate Carter is much more savvy. Kidding about Laurie's kind treatment of a much younger boy, Carter says " 'Now, now. . . . You want to sublimate, you know. Collect antique doorknobs, or something.' " Laurie's playful response is more ironic than he knows: " 'It's too strong for me. . . . I can't get him out of my head.

Those long eyelashes. Would he look at me do you think?' " (*TC,* 13–14). Laurie intends to speak ironically, mocking the imputation of homosexual desire by broadly assuming it, but the double irony is that his own feelings for the youngster are in fact erotic, although he has not yet consciously realized it.

The more sophisticated Carter finds "Laurie's conversation disconcertedly uninhibited" (*TC,* 14) and later tries to point out the personal danger in Laurie's intended protest. Urging him to calm down, Carter explains, " 'Lanyon likes you, and other people have noticed it if you haven't' " (18). When Laurie goes to Ralph and declares his willingness to defend him by rallying the whole house to confess to "immorality" (the housemaster's word for masturbation and homosexual—even, perhaps, to a degree, all sexual—behavior), Laurie exclaims, " 'It makes me sick, the way people will let anything by, even something like this, sooner than come into the open about—anything you're not supposed to.' " Like Carter, but more explicitly, Ralph tries to make Laurie see his naïveté: "And tell me, what makes you so cheerful about coming out into the open yourself?' " Well aware of the dangers of "coming out," which Sandy lists later in the book, Ralph tries to make Laurie see the issue in practical rather than moral terms. Significantly, although without a full understanding of what he is saying, Laurie maintains his moral ground and responds, " 'Well, somebody's got to' " (25).

Renault introduces in this section two issues central to the novel and to her own development: the political realities of transgressive sexuality and the physical aspects of erotic desire, the fact of the body. In this second section, Laurie confronts the first issue in his response to Hazell's accusation; he confronts the second as he and Ralph part. Here Renault is more oblique, placing physical sex in a gap in the text. When Laurie and Ralph have finished the conventional business of leave-taking, language (the intellectual, abstraction) fails them: "Suddenly they had come to the end of all there was to say." Ralph turns to the younger boy: " 'That's all, goodbye. What is it, then? Come here a moment . . . Now you see what I mean, Spud. It would never have done, would it? Well, goodbye' " (*TC,* 30–31). This important kiss, which it seems obvious has occurred in Renault's own ellipsis, is especially significant for several reasons. First, Laurie's immediate response to the kiss is to want more. He asks, " 'But when can we—' " (31), implying, in another textual gap, "see each other again?" the common euphemism for "do it again." Laurie's homosexual desire is, at sixteen, even this early in his life and in this novel, fully developed. His sexual identity ("Is he or isn't he?" asked either by himself or by the reader) is not in question. Second, the kiss here also suggests more than a kiss (for when is a literary kiss—any more than a cinematic or biblical kiss—ever only a kiss?) It stands at least for carnal expression of erotic desire. This physical fulfillment, Renault makes clear, is something Laurie wants even before he knows he wants it. The body is inescapable, as much a fact of life as desire itself. Renault thus insists that sexuality is no merely academic matter. The material body is a final reality, and it should not surprise us that the physical pleasure of the kiss that concludes the work's second section should in the novel's third and main part be initially replaced by the physical details of Laurie at twenty-three, wounded at Dunkirk.

The central section of *The Charioteer* is set in the autumn of 1940 in a coastal city, denominated as Bridstow but in actuality Bristol, and in the neighboring Somerset countryside overlooking the Severn. Recovering in an English hospital, which has replaced the institutions of the family and the English school as the social microcosm in which he will have to work out his sexual orientation, Laurie is preparing himself and being prepared by nurses for another in a series of painful operations. Lying in a traditional ward, in which "two lines of beds converged in a neat perspective on the desk at the end," he is a patient among other injured young men, a casualty of war, a medicalized body. Discussing his case, the ward sister tells the charge nurse, " 'Don't forget that Major Ferguson is doing the sequestrectomy *after* the arthrodesis. . . . And do see there's no muddle about the injections this time' " (*TC*, 31). This medical language and specialized hierarchy alienate even as they specify and make possible Laurie's physical recovery.

As a patient, Laurie struggles to maintain and assert some individual control over himself, and especially over his body, as he becomes to the medical establishment merely another soldier awaiting surgery, recovering with other evacuees whose camaraderie further defines him socially as one of the "boys." The sister continues, " 'I want Wilson moved out of the side ward for today, and Corporal Odell put in there when he comes back from the theatre. He was very noisy coming round last time' " (*TC*, 31–32). Laurie, in semiconsciousness, when he is not in control of language, may be not only be upset himself but upsetting to others, a social problem.

Laurie's friend in the next bed, Reg Barker, a working-class soldier who met Laurie at Dunkirk and remained next to him on the boat back to England, jokes with Laurie, as he apparently has done before previous operations. In the way of soldiers, Reg imputes to his friend a high level of heterosexual desire. "Solitary confinement" serves Laurie right, Reg feels, and laughs at Laurie's retort that he will at least get some sleep: " 'Sleep! *We* know. Mind now, I'll be listening. Minute I hear a woman scream, I'll be there. You watch out, Spud, she might be more oncoming when she gets you alone'" (*TC*, 32). Laurie must hide his real self behind conventional good-natured repartee. At the same time, he is reminded of his homosexuality, his difference, which may so easily surface when he is coming out of the anaesthesia and cannot assert the social control on which his public identity depends. Renault continues to stress this issue of self-control—and control over the social, the physical, the sexual—with characteristic frankness. Thus the charge nurse deflects the conversation from what she sees as the "dirty" jokes to Laurie's body: "'Odell, have you used the bottle yet?'" Such a question, like many matter-of-fact medical queries, infantilizes any patient, accustomed in the adult world to being in control of bodily functions and to keeping quiet about them. Laurie responds, "'I can go through, Nurse; I'll look after the leg,'" claiming an authority (he will not under anesthesia pee on himself) that the nurse refuses: "'Don't you dare. If you think we've got time to prep you again at the last minute. Ask for one when you have your injection'" (32).

Laurie has, in fact, an unstable status: He is an experienced participant, an educated man who has had several operations before and knows the routine, but he is prevented from full knowledge by the military and medical hierarchy. He is also a slowly recovering patient, no longer in daily physical danger, able to do many tasks for himself, but unable as yet to get about on his own (he walks throughout the rest of the book with difficulty, at various stages hobbling, limping, with crutches or a stick, with special braces and an orthopedic shoe). He is a soldier ("Corporal Odell"), but he can no longer participate in military life at the front, an impotence underscored by the increasingly frequent bombing raids over the city. Finally, he is a gay man in fear of and close to public revelation, but his social status among the other soldiers in the ward depends on a duplicitous assertion of heterosexuality, an uncomfortable claim made superficially easy by others' presumptions about his sexual orientation. Laurie's existence neither here nor there, his dual status in several spheres where he never quite has a fully realized identity, reflect his efforts to establish in a homophobic society an authentic homosexual life in which he is free to discover and to be himself.

In this muddle of wartime conditions, Laurie's body is no longer clearly his own, and his authority is called into question (by others, by himself) in an increasingly unstable world. Laurie may recover geographical mobility (he is able to get about more and more, to move physically in the city and countryside beyond the confines of his hospital bed) and a degree of physical mobility in his leg, but the war has made Laurie not only physically but also emotionally and morally unstable. Laurie's mangled limb is not symbolic of a "twisted" or "bent" homosexual state (in fact, this is exactly what Laurie's leg will not do—twist and bend). Rather, his sexual orientation, an integral part of his identity before Dunkirk, before he was thrust unavoidably into the communities created by the war—the military, the hospital—must now be understood (by him, by the reader) within a destabilizing social and historical context. Renault emphasizes that it is war that has wounded Laurie, medicine working with nature that has preserved and strengthened his leg, and the understaffed Emergency Medical Service that has initially bungled his treatment (creating a "muddle about injections" and fashioning a surgical boot of the wrong proportions) only to release him into the confusion of nearly five more years of war.

Laurie could realize his own unique identity, celebrate his difference, even within the trauma of his "broken" home. He could at school, however naively, develop and come to the verge of acknowledging and expressing his sexuality. At Oxford, where he had a homosexual affair with Charles Fortescue, Laurie found his position more difficult, for he was brought to see homosexuality for the first time as an affected role. His introduction to a homosexual subculture was not affirming but repellant, in so much as community, for Renault, denies uniqueness and individuality and levels sexuality to emotionally and morally constricting activities and attitudes. For Laurie, the experience of the hospital and the war crystallized the problem of sexual identity, as it would for Renault herself.

Renault's interest in nontraditional gender roles, in the instability of gender and gendered activity, in the range of possibilities within gender and sexual identity, also manifests itself in *The Charioteer* in her depiction of Conscientious Objectors, such as the Quakers like those she and Julie first met at Winford. These young men were fit for military service but were brought in as at Winford to replace the overworked maids who had walked out *en masse.* The C.O.'s are both part of the medical establishment—those healthy people who represent routine and regulations and who care for the soldiers during long shifts on the ward—and the soldiers' counterparts. Like both the staff and the servicemen, the C.O.'s wear special uniforms and are assigned to the hospital by the circumstances of war, but they, like the patients, are in positions of relative impotence, at the bottom of the hospital hierarchy. Their activities in the novel include the basic tasks Renault saw allocated to the C.O.'s at Winford: serving and washing up after the soldiers' meals,

Conscientious Objectors during a meal in their "hut" at Winford, early 1940s. Photo courtesy of Tim Evens.

sweeping floors, cleaning toilets, holding vomit bowls, and changing soiled linen. Like Laurie and his wounded comrades, the C.O.'s have a particular and elemental relation to the body. If the servicemen are infantilized, the feminized C.O.'s are similarly deprived of their peacetime status as independent men.

Renault's depiction of C.O.'s in her novel derives from a broad conception of them as a group marginalized by the war, paralleled to the soldier-patients as products of the military system but separated from them in that the ground of their identity is not physical but moral. Their "problem" is, further, a social one, stemming from convictions at odds with prevailing attitudes of a precise time and place. The hospitalized soldiers, although by chance physical victims of the war, suffer bodily in a way that transcends specific period or locale. It is homosexuals as a group who finally parallel the C.O.'s in the novel, for both communities are socially liminal, problematized by wartime England with its particular attitudes and policies. In the novel, Laurie must finally choose between two possible lovers: Ralph, who has defined himself within the context of a homosexual subculture, and Andrew, an unsophisticated and sexually inexperienced Conscientious Objector.

The homosexual subculture depicted in *The Charioteer* is a hidden and forbidden world of specialized language and high camp. Laurie's own experience, revealed to him and misread by Reg, suggests this sexual underground. The two soldiers had formed a special bond, "a kind of blood-brotherhood," while awaiting evacuation at Dunkirk. Reg, raving with a splintered arm and a concussion, his eyelids "swelled and stuck together," recovered his self-control when Laurie reached over and forced his eyes open. This symbolic act of opening Reg's eyes to reality is also, ironically, what cannot be spoken about later, what must be hidden, for it reveals dependence, vulnerability, fear, intimacy, and the repressed. Renault writes that among the soldiers on the ward "no one discussed what he had really felt"; the men "took it out on other things" (*TC,* 33). In this setting, Laurie's own experience must also remain unexpressed. Reg's version develops poignant ironies, for the man who has had his eyes literally opened for him by Laurie does not "see" the significance of the tale he tells.

Collected from the beach, Laurie and Reg were placed on a crowded ship. During the crossing, other wounded men wondered if Laurie was still alive and summoned the captain to determine his condition. Laurie remembers only that "he had looked up to find a bearded face peering into his. It hung there persistently saying something and asking questions he felt too ill to deal with. Dimly he reflected that he was filthy and unshaved, and that his leg felt like some extraneous decaying mess. The attention was very flattering and suddenly, weakly, funny. His inhibitions must have been at their lowest; for he remembered giving a wry kind of smile and saying, "'Sorry, dearie. Some other time'" (*TC,* 35). The moment of homosexual revelation is signified here in part by Renault's emphasis on the coded endearment. Certainly the captain, coincidentally Laurie's schoolmate Ralph Lanyon, later tells Laurie that he interpreted the response as "'Sending me up sky-high in front of a petty officer and a couple of ratings.'" Lanyon even has difficulty believing that Laurie did not intend to unmask him and confesses his own panic: "'Much to my relief, a Stuka came over a few seconds later and machine-gunned us. I was a great deal more frightened of you'" (129). Homosexual revelation is more threatening than war; social humiliation and rejection are more painful and damaging than the threat of physical harm suggested by the bomber overhead whose machine-gunning mutilates Ralph's hand, a wound that, like Laurie's, will prevent further service in the front lines. Reg has his own reading of the incident: "'Old Spud was a one coming over. The captain took a look at him to see he was alive, like; and old Spud was that far gone, he took him for some tart and give him the brushoff. Chap with a mucking great beard and all. Laugh!"' (35). Reg's heterosexual misreading of the experience both protects Laurie and further differentiates him from others as his homosexual identity is forced into invisibility and silence.

As Renault herself knew from her own experience, to reveal and proclaim homosexual attraction are dangerous acts with serious personal and social repercussions. In *The Charioteer,* she vividly depicts an underground community in which homosexuality can be both recognized and expressed, a broadly camp world that rigidly defines sexuality for its members and is, in its own ways, as limiting and destructive as the heterosexual culture whose oppression it merely displaces. Entrance to this marginalized community depends on coded communication of sexual status. Initiated through his Oxford friendship with Charles, Laurie uses conventional signs to probe the extent of his friend Andrew's self-awareness while simultaneously attempting to disclose his own orientation. For example, in an effort to sound Andrew out, Laurie declares that he misses his gramophone and, propping himself against a wall because his crutch feels "shaky," he continues, " 'I've got quite a bit of Tchaikovsky, ballet music mostly. It's all right when you feel like it, or don't you think so? I read somewhere once, Tchaikovsky was queer.' " Physically and emotionally "shaky" at this moment of possible revelation, Laurie substitutes Tchaikovsky's ballet music for homosexual activity, "it," which becomes "all right when you feel like it," which is in common parlance "queer." Andrew fails to understand: " 'Was he? I hadn't heard. He was never actually shut up, surely?' " Andrew is unfamiliar with the code; he "hasn't heard" and misconstrues even the word *queer* to mean "insane." At first, Laurie thinks Andrew has at least understood the blatant "queer" and is referring to the illegality of homosexuality, but Laurie "saw his mistake, and with a painful jolt caught himself up just in time: "'Not mad, you know. Just queer."' Andrew is still in the dark: "'You mean a bit . . . Oh, yes, I see. . . . I find all Russians slightly mysterious, don't you? Perhaps if one met more of them."' Renault concludes this amusing but painful scene with Laurie's concession, "yes, that was the trouble, probably" (55). The trouble here is exactly inexperience, the fact that Andrew has not met other gay men and does not know the code.

A similar exchange occurs when Sandy meets Laurie in Bridstow after his first physiotherapy session, except that on this occasion both men are in on the game: "Hanging unspoken between them, and clearly understood, were the words, 'Your move' " (*TC,* 117). Laurie had first seen the young medical student on the ward and had bridled at his affected, feminine manner while

Reg had quickly labeled Sandy a " 'Proper sissy' " (41). Laurie senses what he is in for when Sandy asks him for a drink at a nearby pub, recognizing "one who had escaped from solitude, whose private shifts had given place to a traditional defense-system. Somewhere behind him was the comforting solidarity of a group." Renault continues: "This was not the first time he had touched the fringe he was touching now. He knew the techniques of mild evasion and casual escape. Though the Charles episode had been disillusioning, he hadn't given up hope of finding himself clubbable after all. This time, he briefly thought the right moment had come. But, after all, no: and, after all, it was no one's business but his own" (117–18). Laurie longs for the safety to express himself as well as for a partner and sexual comfort, yet he shuns the "solidarity of a group," the club that will, like the hospital and the war, define for him an identity that is "after all" finally "his own." Thus Laurie enters into conversation with Sandy knowing the rules but pretending an obtuseness reminiscent of Andrew's naïveté. The exchange that follows is at once a complex game and a covert battle in which the men are "wary," "circumspect," "equivocal and elusive" (118) and struggle "to resurvey the terrain" and for "self-preservation" as the conversation moves to a "stalemate" (119). When Sandy finally takes a risk and asks Laurie to a party at his flat, Laurie discovers that Ralph will be there and accepts the invitation that introduces him to the local gay community.

The party is a vivid pastiche of homosexual social life. The guests include a wide variety of young men, among them many like those Laurie first met with Charles—" 'awful people you'd never have believed,' " Laurie mutters as he emerges from anesthetic after his final operation (*TC*, 37). Some of them are indeed melodramatic, petty, self-absorbed, and pretentious: "Bim" is high on amphetamines, while "Bunny," Ralph's current lover, is manipulative and catty, encouraging his partner's tendency to drink, only apparently condoning his renewed friendship with Laurie. Before the evening is over, Sandy, in a pique of jealousy, attempts suicide with a razor to his wrists after having swallowed a bottle of pills. Renault's conversations sizzle with realistic repartee. These are men who come "frisking in" (123), spouting gossip and revealing confidences. Sandy treats Alec, whose birthday the group is celebrating, "rather ostentatiously, like a loveable dreamer to be bossed and protected" (122); impatient with the attention Alec devotes to Ralph's present, Sandy gives Lanyon "a shove which turned him half around from the door," and declares "in a voice carelessly audible through the room, 'And now come over here and see what *we've* got for *you*' " (128).

The party reunites Ralph and Laurie, but has other, more complicated purposes. It allows Renault to examine homosexual subculture both critically and sympathetically while developing significant parallels between the social repression of homosexuality and the psychological effects of war. For example, Bim, one of the more offensive guests, is also a flight-lieutenant and one of the few men still alive from his original squadron. His "tough, steely kind of grace" is undercut by the "high girlish voice with which he greeted his friends. . . . You felt, and were meant to feel, that he was playing at it. He was like a little fighting-cock, brave, shining, and cruel" (*TC*, 143). Bim's behavior is attributable to an act that has its source as much in his war duties as in his homosexuality as a despised identity. Alec reports to Laurie that Bim was rather charming " 'a few months ago; well, even a few weeks. He was light relief, you know, pure Restoration comedy. I don't know how long it is since he averaged more than two or three hours' sleep out of the twenty-four. . . . He can't go on much longer' " (147). Soon after, Bim dies " 'Over Calais somewhere. He was seen to hit the ground; he hadn't bailed out' " (213). Bim as a worthy human being becomes a casualty of both social attitudes and the war itself. Renault is more interested, however, in individual responses to experience than portrayal of a group or explicit social criticism, and places Laurie's relationships with Andrew and Ralph at the center of her novel.

Like Mary and Julie, Laurie and Andrew quickly develop a friendship that involves talking alone at night over tea in the ward kitchen and spending autumn afternoons together in the countryside near the hospital. Both are clandestine activities that, as Laurie recognizes his affection for Andrew, become increasingly special, secretive, and potentially dangerous. Laurie escapes early in the novel to his own " 'private Eden' " (*TC*, 74), an orchard where Andrew discovers him reading beside a stream. The land belongs to a Mrs. Chivers, whom Laurie calls " 'the serpent' " (75), a dotty old woman who hands out religious tracts and confuses the present war with the Great War. She initially welcomes Laurie and invites him to eat the ripe apples but later expels the men from her garden because Andrew is not " 'in khaki' " (81). Mrs. Chivers suggests not so much God as society: Her name is that of a jam manufacturer; her distribution of tracts implies a traditional but unreflective religiosity; her blanket condemnation of Andrew's pacifism conveys her hypocrisy and lack of tolerance. Both men later refer to their new retreat on the other side of the stream as " 'Limbo,' " the place reserved, Laurie reminds Andrew, for " 'good pagans' " (84) marginalized by a Christianity never available to them. These biblical parallels serve as witty and ironic correlations that hint at the forbidden nature of the friendship that neither man quite voices.

Laurie feels he must hide his sexual feelings from Andrew as well as from society at large. For his part, Andrew feels that his pacifism, which his conscientious objection makes a matter of even visible difference, may threaten Laurie, endanger his status as a soldier, to which his uniform and even to a degree his wound commit him. From the first appearance of the C.O.'s on the ward, this oxymoron (the threat of pacifism) is an issue at least to others. Reg expresses his concern about Laurie's friendship with Andrew: " 'Spud, you want to watch it. No offense. . . . I mean the law. . . . [I]f you can talk some sense into him, good enough. But if he tries to start in on you, that's where you want to watch it. Because that's an offense. Seducing His Majesty's troops from their allegiance.' " Laurie, suspecting initially that Reg is referring to homosexuality rather than pacifism, takes "a long steadying draw on his cigarette" and replies ironically, " 'Don't worry. I guarantee that if any seducing goes on it'll be done by me' " (*TC*, 91).

Similarly, Laurie's and Andrew's conversation in the orchard is rife with double-talk and ironic actions. Having been told by Laurie about Mrs. Chivers's evangelism, Andrew admits its awkwardness, then adds, " 'I should like to take my shirt off; would it upset her?' " It is of course Laurie who is upset as he pretends to read the tract but is actually reading Andrew's body, which is "slim, but more solid and compact than one would have thought, and very brown, with the tan deepest across the backs of the arms and shoulders, as it is with laborers who bend to their work. His hands, which were structurally long and fine, were cracked and calloused, and etched with dirt which had gone in too deep to wash away" (*TC*, 75).

When Andrew asks Laurie, " 'Do you believe in hell?' " Renault suggests that he may have grasped the sexual nature of Laurie's glance and is raising the issue of the morality of homosexual desire. When Laurie jokes, the more religious Andrew admits, " 'I'm taking advantage of you' " (*TC*, 75), unaware that it is in fact Laurie who is in a way taking self-indulgent advantage of Andrew's innocence. Ignorant of the actualities of battle, Andrew embarks on a series of questions that might as well be about homosexuality as about the nature of Laurie's war experiences. Andrew reflects, " ' . . . you could tell me so much I ought to know; but I don't know if you want to think about it any more,' " then asks, " ' . . . when it started, did you have any doubt about what you'd do?' " He continues, " 'Has it been like you thought?' " Andrew concludes, " 'You've got a sense of proportion out of it, though you didn't say that' " (76), and he finally responds to what he thinks is the tension between them, " 'We can't go on like this, can we?' " (77).

Laurie, for his part, answers Andrew's questions with specific references to the war, but Laurie and certainly the reader must understand these responses as a carefully encoded confession of transgressive identity, desire and acts. Laurie begins, " 'I thought the whole thing was a bloody muckup and ought to have been prevented. But then it just seemed something that had happened to one, like getting caught in the rain.' " Renault comments, "Now for the first time he realized how important it had been not to admit any alternative to the hard, decent, orthodox choice which need not be regarded as a choice at all; how important not to be different" (*TC,* 76). "The whole thing" (that is, war, or homosexuality or socially imposed heterosexuality) seems to Laurie like an accident, veiled in publishable language as a "muckup," which hides behind it the more explicit and sexual "fuckup." Soldiering (that is, heterosexuality, the choice that is not regarded as a choice) signifies the conventional, while pacifism, resistance, individuality, and homosexuality are difference.

Laurie continues, " 'I didn't think too much in case it got awkward. I can't remember now. Of course, one had other sorts of doubt. What would become of one . . . what one would turn into, how one would make out.' " Laurie explains that at first there was a period of boredom, " 'followed by a sort of nightmare version of one of those ghastly picnics where all the arrangements break down. One thing, it shakes you out of that sort of basic snobbery which makes you proud of not being a snob. On the other hand it doesn't alter your own tastes, I mean things like music, and however you look at it the people round you don't share them, and when you feel less superior it seems you feel more lonely. Except in action, of course, which is what one's there for but for me it didn't last very long' " (*TC,* 76). Homosexuality, like the experience of war, is at some level profoundly upsetting in that the ordinary rules and models for heterosexual behavior and relationships do not apply: Something is wrong with the "picnic" and all the arrangements have broken down. One remains the same person with the same "tastes," but self-confrontation and acceptance of one's homosexuality make one lonely, "except in action," except while engaged in sexual activity, which, in Laurie's case, has been so far merely passing physical sensation rather than any sort of expression of enduring love with another man.

While throughout her work Renault wanted to write explicitly about sexuality, about relationships and desire, about social attitudes and physical experience, by the time she came to write her sixth novel, Renault was also capable of using sustained metaphor to encode the discourse. Laurie is occasionally aware of masking his meaning, but he is also frequently unaware of the extent or resonant complexity of this linguistic process. Renault shows us Laurie playing verbally, often subversively, but it is finally she, as the author, who is using these literary devices sometimes to play, more often in dead seriousness, as she offers sharp insight into the covert world of transgressive sexuality and explores the nature of what must be hidden in a homophobic and sexually repressive society.

The result is writing that can be misread by homophobic readers, readings in which homosexuality is misconstrued or even erased. Just as Renault in the orchard scene explores the creation of a discourse that encodes homosexuality with Laurie as author, she also simultaneously examines the (mis)reading of such a discourse with Andrew as reader. Conversely, Andrew is the unconscious creator of a double discourse (" 'We can't go on like this, can we?' ") and Laurie, as the reader, struggles to interpret what Andrew intends and what he both fears and might like in fact to hear. To Laurie's disappointment and relief, Andrew is not here acknowledging the intensity of shared sexual desire. Renault stresses the difficulty Laurie finds in interpreting Andrew's question: "His heart gave a racing start that almost choked him. The sky, the water, the fine leaves through which the late sun was shining, had the supernatural brightness which precedes a miracle." Laurie can only query, " 'Meaning?' " Andrew finally deflates Laurie's expectations and ratifies the self-protective reticence that enables the parrying of one question with another: What Andrew "means" is that he suspects Laurie feels conscientious objection may signify fear and cowardice. Before Laurie goes on to deny Andrew's imputation in a discussion of pacifism that is literally a discussion of pacifism for both men and only to us, Renault's readers, in fact still a discussion of something else, the author writes, "Laurie couldn't speak for a few seconds. The lift and drop had been too much. Then he remembered how silence might be taken." Silence, too, is communicative and may both reveal and hide complex meanings; Renault, like Laurie, knows meaning resides at once in what she does and does not say. The conversation continues, but it is only for the sensitive reader that Andrew's discussion of conscientious objection is also a discussion of sexual identity. Thus, for instance, when Andrew declares, " 'What I finally stuck at was surrendering my moral choice to men I'd never met, about whose moral standards I knew nothing whatever' " (*TC*, 77), Renault suggests that the moral choice is, in terms of the novel, acceptance of one's sexuality and refusal to conspire with either the dominant heterosexual or the underground "queer" society to deform or judge it as other than a viable and individual identity.

Choice, and especially moral choice, is at the center of *The Charioteer,* and it is even possible to see choice as the overarching issue for Renault throughout her life and work. In this pivotal novel, the choice in terms of plot is insistently sexual. Specifically, the story becomes a love triangle as Laurie realizes that he must choose between Andrew and Ralph and the possibilities both men represent. Laurie's relationship with Ralph develops from the gay party scene, an analogue to the war, to the picnic gone wrong. Both men have helped to care for Sandy in his messy suicide attempt, Ralph fetching from the hospital the medical materials Alec needs to stitch him up, and Laurie staying behind in a coordinated effort to wipe up the blood and vomit from the communal bathroom. Afterwards, Ralph reflects that meeting at the party " 'was like meeting during an action. You come out knowing each other a lot too well to begin at the beginning. . . . And yet, not well enough' " (*TC,* 161). Ralph continues, as at school, to insist on his greater experience and thus his greater understanding, while Laurie reveals his narrower sexual experience but ironically deeper understanding of himself, sexual relationships, love, and homophobic society. Thus, for example, when Ralph finally drives Laurie back to the hospital after the party, the two men discuss the evening. Ralph talks about the melodrama of the homosexual underground as they have witnessed it at Sandy's and Alec's flat and concludes, " 'I never go there now without wondering whether they'll start turning up in drag.' " Laurie can only ask curiously, " 'In what?' " Although he is not the morally admirable and equal partner that Laurie deserves and seeks, the more experienced Ralph must serve as Laurie's teacher. When Ralph finally asks with affection that is also condescension, " 'Spuddy. . . . What *do* you know?' " Laurie answers truthfully and admirably, " 'I know about myself' " (163). Laurie's task in the novel is to find a way to live as a homosexual man in the England of 1940, but while he may be initially ignorant of accommodations made by homosexuals in this society, he does know himself, a knowledge Renault presents as uncontaminated and admirable if not finally sufficient to the social challenges he will confront.

In contrast to the inequality of power in his relationship with Ralph, Laurie finds self-affirmation and potential peace in his friendship with Andrew. Wrestling with these issues in the dark of the ward late at night, Laurie is distressed by the pain in his leg and "a terrible consciousness of the world's ever-renewed, ever-varied, never-dying pain." He whispers Andrew's name, having "forgotten there was anything to hide. To return to the innocence of their love was like returning home." Renault writes that "He reached for Andrew's hand as it might be for the hundredth time, as if everything had been accepted and spoken of between them" (*TC,* 174). Renault portrays this friendship as authentic and worthy, innocent of sexual expression but more importantly innocent by virtue of being separate from the world's pain, whose sources are social cruelty and war.

Laurie struggles to choose between Ralph, who woos him, and Andrew, who affirms all that is best in both of them but whose sexual innocence Laurie hesitates to destroy. Ralph confesses to having lost a similar friendship: He was passionately in love with a heterosexual sublieutenant, killed early in the war, to whom he never revealed his homosexual feelings. Laurie reflects, however, that in Ralph's situation there had been "no moral choice," but "only impossibility and a desire excluded by the facts of life" (*TC,* 178). Laurie's friendship with Andrew is potentially sexual and threatened finally by Ralph's manipulations and the inevitable impingement of the homosexual underground, about which Ralph declares, " 'of course we all have to use the network sometime. Don't let it use you, that's all' " (192).

When Laurie and Ralph make love for the first time, the experience is sexually fulfilling for both men, but means something quite different for each. Ralph sleeps peacefully while Laurie lies awake in the dark, as at the opening of the novel, and thinks, "It can be good to be given what you want; it can be better, in the end, never to have it proved to you that this was what you wanted.' " He enjoys physical gratification and the affirmation of his sexuality and desirability that accompany it, but he is deeply wary of Ralph's possessiveness and his encouragement of dependence in others. Laurie realizes that "Andrew was the only one who hadn't believed that one could be rescued from all one's troubles by being taken out of oneself. He had a certain natural instinct for the hard logic of love." Drawn to Ralph but desperate to assert a difference that is at once homosexuality and moral autonomy, Laurie grieves "that life was so divided and irreconcilable, and the good [Ralph and what he offers Laurie] so implacably the enemy of the best" (*TC,* 319)—Andrew and all he promises.

When a series of coincidences and the worst elements in "the network" combine to reveal Laurie's homosexuality to Andrew, the young Quaker panics. He is shocked both by the repellant qualities he confronts in Bunny, who here represents the homosexual underground, and by his own recognition of his feelings for Laurie as homosexual. When Laurie courageously goes to

London in search of his friend, in the hope of working out with Andrew an honest and loving relationship, he is put off by Dave, who persuades Laurie that it would be wrong to rekindle the homosexual relationship: " 'It's not that I think it would be wicked for you to meet. But you'd both suffer more than now, and no good would come out of it.' " Dave is speaking of homosexual desire not as a sin but as so socially unacceptable as to produce only misery. Dave then confesses his own homosexuality and his love for "Bertie," Andrew's father, but he advocates a cruel and hypocritical accommodation: " ' . . . don't think of yourself because of all this as necessarily typed and labelled. Some men could make shift, for a time at least, with any woman out of about ninety per cent they meet. Don't fly to extremes the moment you discover your own needs are more specialized.' " Dave himself has taken this course of sublimation and duplicity, and urges Laurie to leave quickly and unseen by going " 'out at the back' " (*TC*, 361–62). The secrecy of this retreat is particularly painful, as Laurie realizes his own capitulation to a heterosexual system that caters to homosexuality only by typing and labeling it, by forcing it underground, by condemning it as "specialized," different, "queer."

Self-betrayed, Laurie continues to be admirable as he succumbs to external forces he cannot control. He relinquishes his friendship with Andrew through an act of self-sacrifice and from a misguided impulse to do his friend good. Similarly, he sacrifices himself in rekindling his relationship with Ralph, to whom he falsely confesses the romantic devotion Lanyon desires.

With the move to South Africa and the completion of *The Charioteer,* Renault finally achieved the necessary physical and emotional distance to write about the force of social context on the sexually transgressive individual. At last she had the control and vision to present, through chronologically sequential episodes, the span of a character's life. Beginning with this, her sixth novel, her form would be the *Bildungsroman* (in *The Last of the Wine,* in her two books about Theseus, and in her Alexander trilogy) and its more personal variation, the *Kunstlerroman* (in *The Mask of Apollo* and *The Praise Singer*). Her protagonists after 1953 would be predominantly bisexual or homosexual men of increasingly heroic stature, whose success is both a matter of ethical standards in personal relationships and in the larger social and political sphere of the historical periods they inhabit. All of these elements are here in *The Charioteer,* in which Renault reveals a sophisticated understanding of personal politics as well as of the individual's inseparability from social context. With this novel she has also developed the process of encoding, as masking that is performed by her characters consciously as well as unconsciously, and as a literary strategy, whereby she can voice what society silences and speak the unspeakable. Yet while moving beyond the naive ending of *The Friendly Young Ladies,* in *The Charioteer* Renault can offer only the conflicted ending of Laurie's capitulation. Within English society of the 1940s, she suggests, social pressures are such that even the potentially heroic individual cannot triumph socially or personally. In order to explore morality further, she will need to shift historical ground, leaving England behind in her fiction as in 1948 she left it in her own life for South Africa.

six

The Greeks
1953–1962

More than a year before the publication of *The Charioteer* in October 1953, Renault had begun serious research for *The Last of the Wine,* the historical novel that would define and establish her reputation. South Africa had provided both the social experiences and the isolation that she needed to write—the quickening life of the sort that had fed her art since she first consciously sought it out through her nurse's training—as well as the domestic peace that she had struggled to achieve with Julie since 1935. The immediate inspiration for *The Charioteer* was Jack and Peter and their circle. In her fiction Renault had always drawn on her own experiences, especially in matters of setting and situation. In this novel, Winford and the Bristol hospital, to which Mary and Julie had been initially assigned by the Emergency Medical Service, provided the setting. However, for the homosexual underground, Julie emphasized that Mary "had to learn through Jack and Peter. This was her only experience [with gay men and] absolutely hot off the press."[1]

The vivid world to which they were introduced was thoroughly new to them and in stark contrast to what they had known—or more specifically not known—in England. Open homosexuality startled and fascinated, for, as Julie noted, "No one wrote about it; it wasn't in books; no one talked about it unless they were of the fraternity. . . . For instance, we were never in a social gathering of any sort ever in England in which we could talk even slightly about homosexuality, never." England offered both repressive silence and, ironically, "a great deal of freedom" in that the homosexual underground, liberated

1. Mullard, interview by Sweetman, tape 2, side B.

from the larger society's conventions, developed its own rules. Further, the uninitiated, those ignorant of "the fraternity" flourishing beneath the public silence about transgressive sexuality, were "free" to develop their own ideas and identities—although they were always aware of their behavior and very existence as forbidden. For both women, Durban became the first time the subject was out in the open, visible, and discussed socially. There, "we didn't feel pent as we would have done in England."[2]

The liberating world Renault experienced in South Africa was largely a masculine one. The female environments of boarding school, university, and hospital nursing were now replaced by the frontier communities of growing cities surrounded by sparsely settled land. Johannesburg, where the two women stopped briefly on their way from Rhodesia, seemed to them like an American "mining town" of the previous century. Their hotel, which Julie remembered as "very rough indeed," had the atmosphere of a whorehouse: "There were . . . polished brass spittoons, and there really were fat men with tarts on their knees. Mary and I sat with our knees together and our lips closed and thought it was disgusting, which it was." The two women also felt constricted by the attitudes of residents who "didn't think it was right for women to be out on their own."[3]

The threat of rampant male sexuality without style or taste or love was not merely a heterosexual matter, but permeated the homosexual community as well. Among these gay acquaintances, as in *The Charioteer,* behavior was often undisciplined and unprincipled. In Durban, Mary and Julie found themselves having to cope with Jack's alcoholism and the petulant dramatics of unstable relationships gone awry. Julie recalled one awful afternoon when Jack, having taken an overdose of aspirin as part of a calculated suicide attempt, staggered home drunk: "There's Jack lying naked on the bed. He wasn't wearing any clothes. And he kept pushing the [bed]clothes off. I don't know anything more infuriating than when a perfectly well man insists on somehow or other exposing something. It's the only word I can use, because it mattered to us. Somehow it's so infuriating I could have throttled him. He's vomiting—just like *The Charioteer.* Read it all in *The Charioteer;* it's all there."[4]

Durban seemed, however, a more sophisticated city than Johannesburg, being a tropical town in which women could move about more freely. By 1950,

2. Ibid., tape 2, side B, and tape 12, side B.
3. Ibid., tape 1, side A.
4. Ibid., tape 2, side A.

Mary on her first visit to the Cape, South Africa, 1950. Photo courtesy of Julie Mullard.

having disengaged themselves from Jack and Peter and their shared business venture, Mary and Julie settled down to forge a new life for themselves. They became South African citizens, and from this time on had dual nationality, although they would never again use their British passports. Living in one of the houses they had built with Jack and Peter, they let the other two, and in time they would sell off the remaining land investments. Julie was eager to return to her nursing career and found a post as a sister in a tuberculosis ward at King George V Hospital, a position she would hold until 1958. She had always been committed to nursing, and throughout her career she had sought out situations that would help her to advance and specialize. After the war, when she had been offered the post of sister in the children's ward of the Radcliffe, she had been delighted despite her inexperience with children. She explained: "I knew once I had my foot in there, my career would go ahead, which I thought I would need to keep Mary." Their roles in the relationship were to a degree defined by their careers. Julie commented more generally on the separate spheres: "I was expected to go ahead and get a good job. I never doubted that Mary was going to be a writer, but I never dreamed that she was going to make money. . . . And that was what I was quite prepared for. So no one was more surprised than I was to find Mary was bringing in money, and Mary of course was quite stunned by it. And we were no good at money at all."[5] Mary never did become very "good at money," but they now had behind them the disasters of the sports car, the gunboat, and the housing corporation with Jack and Peter, and Julie at least had learned a great deal about managing their finances.

For her part, Mary again focused on writing, completing *The Charioteer* in late 1952 and beginning to gather around her the books, often sent out from Blackwell's, that she would use in all of her future work. Together, the two women established a comfortable home and developed the pattern that, with some variations, would define the next phase of their life together: Mary would work secluded in her study during the mornings and afternoons, while Julie would work outside the home. She would bring in a predictable salary on which, if need be, they could live, but with their local investments in land and houses now generating regular funds and with Mary's increasing literary success, money would never again be a serious problem. Julie would, as she had since 1935, keep track of accounts and look after domestic matters, seeing to meals and groceries, for instance, although from this time on their household would include a daily servant to cook and clean as well as someone to take care of the garden. As soon as they had a home of their own, the two women also acquired a car and two dogs; for the rest of Mary's life, their family would include two dogs and occasionally a cat as well. Exercising these animals became a regular ritual that got Mary out of the house to the countryside or the nearby beach no matter how intensely she was working, but her world was more and more one of the guarded privacy necessary for her writing, balanced by get-togethers with carefully selected friends, frequently gay men from the art world, first in Durban and later in Cape Town. Julie brought her reports of local life encountered at her job, but Mary herself was content for the most part to stay at home, in touch with world events mainly through newspapers and radio, becoming increasingly an independent scholar and writer of distinguished reputation and wide readership who could shape her days exactly as she wished.

5. Ibid., tape 6, side A, and tape 2, side B.

The ancient world and literature generally had fascinated Renault since childhood, and her early novels are replete with mythological references as well as allusions to Shakespeare and a host of other literary sources. When in *Purposes of Love* Vivian sneaks into the hospital through the bathroom window, she comes upon Colonna bathing, seeing her as " 'a lovely boy in Dian's shape,' " a quotation Renault takes from Marlowe's *Edward the Second* (*PL*, 24). *Return to Night* includes numerous passages from Shakespeare that suggest both Julian's theatrical experience and his inner conflicts. In *The Charioteer* Renault scatters references to English canonical authors from Milton to Robert Louis Stevenson to H. G. Wells, while Oscar Wilde's life and work function as a witty gloss throughout: Michael Odell, like Wilde, may be both a parent and a homosexual, while Dave has been in love with Andrew's father, whose name ("Bertie") as well as many of the novel's other gay nicknames ("Bim," "Boo," and "Bunny") recall Wilde's diminutive ("Bosie") for his lover, Lord Alfred Douglas.

As early as *Return to Night,* however, as Bernard Dick has pointed out, Renault begins to develop mythological allusions into literary tropes. She often portrays Hilary, for example, as Demeter, a parallel that becomes allegorical in the cave scenes. In *The Charioteer,* Renault offers in Plato's dialogue a specific trope that informs the entire novel from its title to its conclusion. Thus by the end of the book the reader is to understand that Laurie has saved his friend but sacrificed himself, sacrificed the possible best for an easier good, and Renault's concluding images, drawn from Plato, convey a poignant sadness:

> Quietly, as night shuts down the uncertain prospect of the road ahead, the wheels sink to stillness in the dust of the halting place, and the reins drop from the driver's loosened hands. Staying each his hunger on the pasture the place affords them, neither the white horse nor black reproaches his fellow for drawing their master out of the way. They are far, both of them, from home, and lonely, and lengthened by their strife the way has been hard. Now their heads droop side by side till their long manes mingle; and when the voice of the charioteer falls silent they are reconciled for a night in sleep. (*TC,* 380)

Renault stresses the grief of the final scene: The struggle of the two horses has ceased because of forces beyond their control, because of the night that has shut off the way, making progress "uncertain"; each animal accepts what is available, "what pasture the place affords." Dislocated and lonely, they are "reconciled" by exhaustion and the charioteer's silence.

It is impossible to read this conclusion as triumphant as, for example, Summers does when he decides: "From the beautiful coda, it is clear that in his relationship with Ralph, Laurie has at last achieved proportion, that balance of sensuality and spirituality idealized in Plato's myth." Renault herself emphasizes that Ralph is finally a pathetic character: "What he feels is the perpetual need to justify himself and his life by being needed and depended on . . . ; and it is Laurie's sense of his pathos which causes Laurie to conceal the fact of having read his suicide note, so as not to wound his pride by the knowledge that he is being taken on out of pity."[6]

Awareness of Renault's lesbian partnership also makes it impossible to understand the ending as primarily the protagonist's personal failure, as Peter Wolfe suggests in his misreading of the novel. Rather, Laurie has made accommodation not by sublimating his sexuality nor by capitulating to the queer underground, the world of gay men that Ralph calls " 'something between a lonely hearts club and an amateur brothel' " (*TC*, 341). Laurie has instead accepted the lover who wants him rather than struggle, perhaps hopelessly, against the general homophobia of British society during the war years, an ostensibly Christian position that causes Andrew to retreat and with which both men would need to contend were they to try to forge a homosexual life together apart from the conventions of a sequestered community. Finally, despite self-awareness and self-knowledge, Laurie has given up independence, autonomy, self-determination, loyalty to his ideals, and truth—the very heroic qualities that Renault will go on to explore in *The Last of the Wine.*

Throughout her first six novels with their modern settings, Renault offered complicated intellectual accounts of the dynamics of her characters' relations with one another and with themselves and simultaneously sought abstract constructs beyond the novels within which to situate their morality. Specifically, she drew on her understanding of her own experiences, using contemporary knowledge of Freudian psychology and developing literary allusions, often elaborated at great length, to suggest a larger framework within which to read the book. By the time she came to write *The Last of the Wine* in 1956, it was as if these frameworks had expanded and overtaken her writing, so that she in fact situated her text (the story) entirely within the context of another text (ancient Greece).

6. Summers, " 'Plain of Truth,' " 170; Renault to Wolfe, January 10, 1970.

Renault's decision to turn to historical fiction seems logical in many ways. She had been drawn from girlhood to the romance of the past, and her early literary efforts had been historical if also fanciful narratives. From the time of her first novel, her increasingly sophisticated use of doubles and parallels, mirroring, layering, and masking had offered her literary strategies whereby she could explore what was not generally known or admitted or spoken, what was socially forbidden. Her use of meticulously researched historical material seems a natural extension of these devices and serves a similar purpose. Additionally, Renault's formal education and independent reading had made clear to her the nature of scholarship and literary excellence, while she was simultaneously aware of her own marginality: a matter of gender, sexuality, and historical circumstance that obstructed her developing her identity as a writer. A seasoned author by the 1950s, Renault had at last the discipline and the means to focus on her work. She also had the physical distance from England and the carefully selected society that allowed her the concentration she required. She could now, too, become the student she had never been. Moreover, the setting of ancient Greece in particular would permit her to write freely about transgressive sexuality as she could not in a contemporary novel; and if she did it well, such historical fiction would allow her to claim a position of traditionally masculine authority denied to female novelists.

When asked to explain why she turned to historical fiction, Renault offered a deceptively simple but convincing and characteristic response: "I wanted to do it. . . . [I]t excited my imagination." She explained her decision further in a letter to Bryher: "[O]ne of the greatest fascinations of historical writing is to compare the dilemmas of the present with those of the past, to try to sort out the universal, basic stuff of human nature from the emphemeridae, sometimes overwhelming in their momentary impact, of the particular society and environment." Aware that she was corresponding with a woman who had traveled in Africa and Greece, who had chosen, like Renault, to write both veiled autobiography and historical fiction, and who had also made lesbian choices, Renault continued, "I feel that the vast populations of the leading nations today present a new situation quite distinct from the technological advances which seem to hypnotise so many writers. It is too soon to assess its full significance."[7]

Aware of Bryher's relationship with H. D., a poet whose reputation was associated with her Hellenism, Renault concluded, relying on Bryher's sympathetic understanding as well as on her ability to read between the lines, "You

7. Renault, *Omnibus* interview; Renault to Bryher, May 26, 1961.

have probably found, as I have, that it is not until one gets among the less 'advanced' peoples of the world that one can begin to understand the past, and the nature of its lessons for the present. Living here [in South Africa], where the situation is so archaic that it might well have happened in fourth-century Sicily, I am often appalled by the encapsulated thought-processes of the British intelligentsia, who have learned nothing from the mistakes of their forebears."[8] Here Renault suggests at least two further reasons for her interest in the historical novel. Analysis of characters in a particular past would allow her, ironically and simultaneously, to focus on the universal in human experience. Through a correlative depiction of a specific historical society, she would also be able to comment politically on the social dynamics of power; she would be able to develop for herself a political and moral position as well as the means to voice it, which the pattern of her own life and society had conspired to deny her.

This letter to Bryher further indicates Renault's understanding, evident throughout her historical novels, that sexuality and relationships could not be isolated from their time and place, that it was society as well as the family that shaped individuals, who are also unique in their own right. In trying to explain to David Sweetman her shift from contemporary to historical fiction, Renault focused explicitly on sexual identity and on the issues she raised in *The Charioteer.* She told him that she felt it was much healthier that sexual matters be given "free play" in the lives of heterosexual, homosexual, and "intermediately-sexed" people, for only then can people "live natural lives, and not be hounded by guilt." She elaborated,

> I think the sort of defensiveness that people put on who feel guilty about their homosexuality is one of the most painful things. I mean, they shouldn't feel any guilt unless they behave badly . . . but just for having an ordinary love relationship with another human being—why should they feel guilty? It's really very bad for public morals that this guilt is forced on them, I think, because it segregates them into . . . a sort of mass which is not homogenous, and they meet all the wrong sort of people who they think they have something in common with. They have nothing in common with them really. . . .

She explained, "I made this point in *The Charioteer.* People who are idealistic and generally well-integrated people are thrown all together in this huddle

8. Renault to Bryher, May 26, 1961.

Mary in the 1950s, Camps Bay, South Africa. Photo courtesy of Julie Mullard.

with really dregs, you know, and they don't belong together in any way, but they have to feel they do because they're made defensive." Renault's development of this moral and political position in *The Charioteer* led her to write about ancient Greece, where homosexuality was an entirely different identity and experience from Laurie's or her own in the England of her time. Most simply, Renault explained to Sweetman, "it was much freer and it had standards, which of course it doesn't have today in the sense of being accepted by society."[9] In having "standards," homosexuality was an identity, not merely a matter of physical attraction or something one did in bed, but a publicly recognized and integral part of one's being—individual, certainly, but also a viable social identity, not forbidden or masked or silenced. It seems no wonder that "standards" fascinated her, excited her imagination.

The Last of the Wine can be understood in part as a rewriting of *The Charioteer*: a recasting of the material that Renault had been exploring up until 1956, and a reworking of her own experiences, knowledge, and literary skills in a new genre, a different setting. This understanding of her first historical novel in no way trivializes Renault's achievement, as did her reviewers when they praised her apparently instant command of a fresh form and attributed to her a supposedly magical awareness of the past. Such attitudes are rooted

9. Renault, *Omnibus* interview.

in the tradition that reserves for men in universities, in museums, and on archeological digs the study of a particular classical past. Such history is the province of not merely any men, but of highly regarded men at European universities, men who went from public schools to Oxbridge and read not just Greek or "Classics" but "Greats," men whose class, erudite training, travel experiences, and work in the field granted them an unquestioned status as authorities whose position and reputation were a result of birth, privilege, and scholarly achievement. One reviewer praised Renault as a "sorceress" whose "incantations" and "imagination" could "breathe life" into the past; another found himself "spellbound . . . by her art." Auberon Waugh attributed Renault's extraordinary success in *The Last of the Wine* to "the literary equivalent of sex appeal" and to the creative powers of "her imagination or historical fancy," while the reviewer for the *Times Literary Supplement* heaped his accolades on her achievement as "masterly."[10] John Guest, her editor at Longmans, referred to her "psychic vision of life in Ancient Greece," while Sweetman followed Bernard Dick in pointing out the responsible scholarship involved in Renault's historical fiction, presenting her achievement as the product of "skill and ingenuity rather than magic,"[11] her cleverness and invention rather than the careful reading of sources and scholarly authority that, beginning with *The Last of the Wine,* both liberated Renault and contributed to the development of her distinctive voice.

The novel opens with Alexias's memory of his father's rejection, his foiled intention to expose him as an infant, which informed the boy's childhood, especially when he was "sick or in trouble, or had been beaten at school."[12] Alexias's identity, his very being, depends on his father's failure to enforce his exposure because of having been called away to repel the Spartans at Athens's gates. Like Laurie, Alexias is raised as an only child, distanced from his father, and forms an intensely affectionate bond with his young stepmother; his boyhood is defined by "the Great War" (*Last,* 11) much as Laurie's is an English childhood following the Great War of 1914–1918. In turn, both boys as young men will come to a mature understanding of themselves in war. Just as Laurie's war in 1940 was in many ways a legacy of the First World War with its unresolved attitudes towards homoerotics, pacifism, and manliness,

10. The quotations are from excerpted reviews used, apparently without any sense of their sexism, to advertise the 1990 New English Library paperback edition of *The Last of the Wine,* 2–3.

11. John Guest, interview by David Sweetman; Sweetman, *Mary Renault,* 156.

12. Mary Renault, *The Last of the Wine,* 11. All further references to this novel (hereafter cited as *Last*) will be included parenthetically in the text.

for Alexias, the conflict, which raises many of the same issues, will be the long-lasting Peloponnesian War between Athens and Sparta.

The public silence about homosexuality that pervades *The Charioteer* and defines Laurie's world is immediately displaced in *The Last of the Wine* by the social acknowledgment of homosexual love in the figures of Alexias's uncle, after whom he is named, and Alexias's noble lover, Philon. Thus Renault replaces the weak and often badly behaved homosexuals of the community forced underground by the English mores of 1940 with the exemplum offered by the two admirable Greek youths: Philon, dying of the plague, "had not called out to anyone to fetch his friend, not wishing to endanger him," but Alexias, hearing of his friend's condition, "went at once to him." When discovered, both young men are dead: "From the way they were lying, it seems that in the hour of Philon's death, Alexias had felt himself sicken; and, knowing the end, had taken hemlock, so that they should make the journey together. The cup was standing on the floor beside him; he had tipped out the dregs, and written PHILON with his finger, as one does after supper in the last of the wine" (*Last,* 12). With this story, Renault rewrites the trope of Plato's charioteer, which had given her last contemporary novel its title, and in parallel fashion takes from it her title for her first historical novel.

This rewriting in fact becomes the pattern for this novel, as Renault recasts not only *The Charioteer* but Plato's fable itself in terms of the relationship between Alexias and Lysis, whose names even echo those of Andrew and Laurie, the potential but thwarted lovers of the earlier novel. While in their respective novels Alexias is the central character and Andrew a secondary one, the parallels suggested by their names are numerous: Both are idealistic young novices inexperienced in sexual matters and in battle; both are finally survivors of ordeals (war, deprivation, social repression, and ostracism) that threaten to compromise their values and their very lives. In turn, Laurie, as *The Charioteer*'s protagonist, shares a great deal with Lysis, Alexias's lover: Both are older, more experienced partners, already initiated into the mysteries of sexuality and the battlefield; both are finally victims (Laurie morally, Lysis physically) of the larger political and social tensions in their culture.

But the issues raised in *The Last of the Wine* are more radically rewritten than these incidental nominal parallels suggest. Renault would explain to Bernard Dick that "*The Charioteer* leads up to *The Last of the Wine.* In the former book the lovers have neither social acceptance nor recognized ethos, in the latter they have both." Responding to Dick's study of her work, she was pleased that he understood "Alexias and Lysis as Ralph and Laurie . . . transposed into a culture where their relationship, being socially acknowledged, was subject to qualitative comparisons. I didn't conceive both books beforehand, the Greek one arose, in fact, out of its predecessor."[13] The body, war, and sexuality persist as matters of primary importance, while Renault's recasting allows her to explore these concerns carried over from her contemporary work but now imagined differently. With this first historical novel, the hospital is erased and replaced with the athletic arena, the bedroom, and the battlefield, where care is given by individuals in a special relationship. The body in Renault's Greek world is thus never anonymous, never medicalized, always personal. The nurse, as often male as female, is more reliable than physicians, priests, or magicians, who, steeped in superstition and dependent on patronage, are generally less knowledgeable, skillful, and trustworthy than the philosopher-scientist or the friend or lover, who is presented as qualified by experience, logical observation, and affection. Renault's specialized medical knowledge invariably informs her portrayal of the body, its physical responses in athletic contests, battle, and love, but now her careful research into historical period enables her to create for herself a new authority and a cultural situation that allow her to be more frank and specific than ever before. The sense of gritty reality that results gives her work an unprecedented power—not sorcery at all but a "vivid and convincing reconstruction of . . . life," an extraordinary achievement in fiction.[14]

The hospital world in *The Charioteer* anticipates these shifts. As an experienced patient, Laurie knows the institutional routine and takes on the role of nurse. In preparation for his final operation, for instance, he shaves his own leg because the hospital is short staffed, taking a bitter pride in the fact that he does the task better than the modest nurse, "who wouldn't shave it far enough up," thinking, "[i]t was a job for an orderly, but the whole place was in a chronic muddle" (*TC*, 34). Similarly, when Charlot, the wounded French soldier, injures his head during a bomb attack, Laurie tends him while Andrew reports to Nurse Sims: "The injured man was lying with his head resting on a towel; Laurie realized that he had vomited on the sheet and pillow, and that was why Andrew needed clean things" (255). When Andrew returns, "they . . . work on Charlot together, changing his pajama jacket and the soiled bed-linen" (257). The simple act of caring for a sick person, without

13. Renault to Dick, January 27, 1970, and September 10, 1972.

14. *Sunday Times* review, quoted on the back of the 1974 paperback edition of *The Last of the Wine.*

revulsion and as if instinctively, binds the two men together in the traditionally feminine acts of cleaning and dressing another, calling into question not only professional roles and conventional responses to the body but gender as well and adumbrating the way in which Renault will treat similar scenes in her historical fiction.

In *The Last of the Wine,* the intimate bond between Alexias and Lysis allows each to serve as the other's best physician in a relationship that is often both medical and erotic. Thus, when after a swim with Lysis near their army camp at Cape Sounion, Alexias cuts his foot while walking out of the water, he remembers that "Lysis knelt and looked at it while I leaned on his shoulder." His friend advises him sensibly to wash the wound well in the sea, then, to avoid contamination from the grit of the shore, Lysis will carry him " 'to a place where a horse can go' " (*Last,* 134):

> I leaned back for him to take hold of me, and fastened my arms round his neck. But he did not carry me; nor did I let him go. We spoke without sound each other's names. A gull screamed over us, an empty sound, to tell us we two were alone upon the shore.
>
> . . . I called upon my soul, but it bled away from me like salt washed back into the ocean. My soul melted and fled; the wound in my foot, which the water had opened, streamed out scarlet over the wet rock.
>
> I lay between sea and sky, stricken by the Hunter; the fiery immortal hounds of Eros, slipped from the leash, dragged at my throat and at my vitals, to bring the quarry in. It seemed to me now that my soul was here, if it was anywhere. . . . He whom I loved knew my mind; perhaps it was his own. We were still, understanding each other. (134–35)

Here Alexias and Lysis resolve the tensions that define Laurie's relationships with Andrew and Ralph, and Renault emphasizes that the Greek lovers have now "exchanged the good" for "the best" (135).

In a parallel scene, Alexias takes care of Lysis after he is brutally injured in the *pankration* at Corinth. Alexias recalls that while looking after his friend in the dressing room, "I thought he would die as I watched him. Someone else's clothes were lying in a corner; I heaped those on him, but he still felt cold, so I added my own, and came in beside him" (*Last,* 190). When finally "Lysis moved, and groaned," Alexias reports that "[h]e felt a little warmer. Presently he tried to sit up, and was sick. As I finished cleaning up, the doctor came in again." The act of caring for one's friend is personal and again eroticized:

"trying to put some life into him," Alexias records that "his mouth felt cold to mine" (191).

Later in the novel Lysis sets Alexias's broken collarbone, bracing back his shoulder with a bandage, "or I should be crooked to this day," while in turn Alexias cares for Lysis, who has suffered an arm wound. Alexias comments that despite the bad conditions—"Most of us found that we did not heal so quickly as at first; the food was bad, and we were tired"—"This was the first time Lysis and I had been wounded together; so we thought it a holiday" (*Last,* 149).

The erasure of the hospital in this ancient Greek context liberates Renault from an ultimately feminine world in which enclosure, passivity, dependence, illness, and nascent rebellion against the status quo are central problems for both patients and medical personnel. Like all of her historical fiction, *The Last of the Wine* explores a predominantly masculine world in which the author's interest in and understanding of the body inform her startling physical descriptions of men as athletes, lovers, and soldiers in war. Thus Renault presents Alexias's initiation into manhood on the battlefield in gruesome detail. Having struck an opponent with his javelin, Alexias finds him "lying on his back with the shaft still sticking in him. . . . Both his hands were clutching the ground beside him, digging down into the dirt; his teeth were clenched, and his lips drawn backward; the whites of his eyes showed and his back was lifted in an arch" (*Last,* 130). Commanded by Lysis to pull the javelin out, "I put my foot on the Spartan's breastplate, and pulled. I could feel the javelin-head tearing out through the sinews and grating on the bone, and heard the breath hissing in the man's throat, either of itself or as he tried not to scream. He gave a great cough, and blood splashed out of his mouth on my arms and on my knees. . . ." Renault's precise observations here attest to her control of the narration, but this is Alexias's first experience of such a death, and he is appalled: "I went off and vomited behind a wall. It was getting dark, and when I came back I don't think anyone noticed I was pale" (131). Alexias may vomit, but Renault herself, like the experienced Lysis, has long ago lost all squeamishness about the body. Her displacement of the site of violence and death from the feminine hospital to the masculine battlefield allows her to exercise a traditionally male authority further supported by her obvious medical knowledge, lack of reticence, and use of the Greek setting—a special past in direct contrast to the realm of contemporary hospital fiction.

War itself, for Renault, is a wide canvas involving territorial, cultural, and moral imperatives: physical combat, the sweep of battle, the technology of violence. At issue is the body, of course, but also the spirit and the society at large. The subject of war, as suggested by its presentation in *The Charioteer* and its looming presence in all of her previous work, will in Renault's Greek novels give her the scope to develop her moral and political views. At the same time that she conveys her characters' sense of the inevitability of war's existence as part of life (pacifism as we find it in Andrew is entirely alien to the ancient world), Renault emphasizes the moral codes, the personal and national sense of honor, that give meaning to violence. When, for example, Alexias encounters two wounded Thebans among the Athenian prisoners, he reveals the principles that determine their behavior: "one could have got away, but had rushed back when he saw the other fall. . . . I brought them some food and drink at night and asked then if they were lovers. They said they were, and that it was a custom of their city to take a vow . . . they always served together in battle, and were put in front to stiffen the line, as being more likely than anyone else to prefer death before dishonour." The Athenians are similarly principled in adhering to standards in war: "Next day we handed them over through the heralds; for it would be long before they fought again, and to dispatch helpless men is always disagreeable, particularly if they have shown courage first" (*Last,* 145). Later, the code of lovers, the personal respect of one man for another, supersedes the rules of war when Alexias is captured by Theban troops. Recognized by one of the Theban pair, he is allowed to go free in memory of the care he gave. The Theban, aware that Lysis and Alexias are lovers, too, explains: " 'He sent us food at night; you brought it. My friend could not sit up to drink, so you raised his head. . . . If you had been rough with him, I would have cut out your heart tonight' " (159).

The athletic field functions as battle's analogue, and with its clearer rules and patterns, its ordered pace and regulated contests, Renault uses it both literally and symbolically to convey a morality that is both Greek and her own. For instance, when Lysis, mauled by his opponent, loses the *pankration,* there is no shame in losing; the disgrace lies in his having been so mismatched. Lysis has trained for the event, but as a soldier-athlete, a citizen with other responsibilities as well and with attention to the aesthetics of performance. He is matched with Sostratos, a "mountain of gross flesh, great muscles like twisted oakwood gnarling his body and arms . . . a man too heavy to leap or run, who would fall dead if he had to make a forced march in armour, and whom no horse could carry, . . . someone worse than a slave, since he had chosen his own condition" (*Last,* 187). The horror of this "monster" is that he has given up of his own volition human wholeness and possible beauty for bestial physical power and distortion. He is reduced to a single function in the wrestling ring and to winning at all costs. We later see that Sostratos is morally as well as physically corrupt: He is concerned that Lysis survive his wounds, but only because if he dies during the games, the winner will be disqualified and lose his crown. Akin to this material greediness is Sostratos's sexuality: He flirts with Alexias over Lysis's exhausted body, urging him lewdly: " '[come] and meet some of the other winners. It is time you and I knew each other better' " (192). Alexias rudely rebuffs him. The young Plato, who has come to know Alexias and Lysis as fellow students in Socrates' circle, voices Renault's concerns explicitly: " 'What does Sostratos think he has got? What good? What pleasure? What did he want?' " (193). Sostratos's freely chosen narrow training and his limited and gross desires (the crown, sex) echo the corruption of the homosexual underground in *The Charioteer:* Material gain, sexual satisfaction divorced from love or principle, and self-chosen limitation in both cases define the human being at the cost of both individuality and moral or spiritual honesty.

For Alexias, Plato's questions also have particular application to his own race. Offered a bribe by the father of one of the other runners, Alexias is told when he refuses that several of the other contestants have already accepted. The moral confusion is intense as Alexias debates whether or not to report the offer to the officials, who may not believe him, or to confront his fellows, who may accuse him of slander, or to seek advise from Lysis, who will then be distracted from concentrating on his own match. Alexias realizes: "It seemed there was no way I could turn with perfect honour, and that I should never be clean again" (*Last,* 178). He can finally only run his best, realizing that he must follow the philosopher's words that he recalls at the start of the contest: " 'Know yourself, Alexias,' I thought, 'and look to what you know' " (182).

War and the games are analogues of each other and in turn both are macrocosms for Renault of the important relationship between two lovers. The significance of either contest is a moral matter, which, by the end of the novel, returns Alexias and his author to the yoked issues of education and philosophy. Throughout the book, Socrates has been presented as the ideal teacher, and, towards the conclusion, Alexias notes, "I came back to philosophy, but differently; feeling it in myself and in those I met in talk, a fever of the blood. I had come to it as a boy from wonder at the visible world; to know the causes of things; and to feel the sinews of my mind, as one feels muscles in the palaestra. But now we searched the nature of the universe, and our own souls, like physicians in time of sickness" (*Last,* 287–288). Alexias's relation to philosophy is even physical here, a matter of sinews and blood as Renault uses corporeal reality to emphasize the moral choices at the novel's core. The Greek world that she reconstructs and animates in her historical novels would finally clarify the central themes and problems of her earlier fiction, but the scholarly research that enabled her to recast *The Charioteer* also required physical experience, and at the end of March 1954 Mary and Julie set out for an extended trip to Greece.

The Last of the Wine had now been in process for nearly two years and would take over another year to finish, and it seemed important for technical reasons as well as atmosphere to visit the geographical terrain and surviving monuments of the culture that the book so specifically evokes. Embarking from Durban, again on an Italian ship, the SS *Africa,* the two women retraced their route of six years earlier, traveling up the east coast of the continent via Zanzibar and the Red Sea, and finally via Trieste to Venice.[15] They carried no guidebooks and were determined to avoid any organized sightseeing; Mary's informed interest in specific archeological and architectural details and sensitivity to art, nature, and mood would determine their itinerary.

A sojourn in Italy served as a prelude to their weeks in Greece itself; they stopped briefly in Venice and then, traveling by train, spent six days in Florence before heading on to Rome. There they were energetic tourists, intent particularly on the ancient city, spending long hours in the Forum. After another rail trip to the port of Brindisi on the east coast, they took the overnight boat across the Ionian Sea and through the Corinth Canal to Piraeus, which Mary insisted on seeing first from the deck in the morning light. Such a particular landscape, the port as perceived from the sea, would be more significant for her than the local people they would meet or the distinctive food and drink that for many tourists define a holiday. Outweighing the privations and exhaustion of travel and eclipsing the amusing and irritating incidents that characterize any long trip from home, such carefully selected planned or serendipitous experiences of geography or art would be for Mary the purpose and meaning of this adventure. These spring months in Greece were a writer's journey, a kind of pilgrimage as much a part of her life's work and her creative process as the uninterrupted solitary hours at her desk.

15. Particular details of this trip are taken from Mullard, interview by Sweetman, tape 12, side B, and tape 13, side A.

Mary and Julie about to board the ship for Greece, 1956. Photo courtesy of Julie Mullard.

Julie remembered Piraeus as a powerful introduction to the land they would explore, for the two women could find no one to change money at the port and "you could feel the suffering and starvation that had gone on, and the feeling was dreadful. You knew that there had been a civil war, and the poverty was immense. People were tremendously reduced. . . . They were so unaccustomed to having visitors that when we got off the ship, only one man got off with us. The others all went on to Israel." When they reached Athens itself, they found bullet holes still noticeable on buildings and became sharply conscious of their situation as single women. Julie recalled that "the tavernas were packed with men, never with women—night after night, all talking politics, and the fact that we were women alone was very strange. There were other women travelling alone, but they were always linked with the university or they were linked with something, or linked with a family, but Mary and I, being on our own, were considered very weird indeed."[16]

With little extra money, Mary and Julie were, by necessity as well as choice, economic travelers. Using their simple boardinghouse in Athens as a base, they explored both the city, most of whose museums were still closed, and the surrounding area, devoting day after day to the Acropolis but also taking bus trips into the hills, climbing Mount Pares overlooking Eleusis, and walking for miles and miles, as they had in the Cotswolds, over land that in the novel would contain Alexias's family farm and the battlesites for many of the Athenians' encounters with the attacking Spartans. Packing picnics, they explored archeological areas not yet roped off from public access. They visited Sounion, where Alexias injures his foot, and behaved with each other throughout "as though there were no book,"[17] Renault remaining very private and Julie respecting the silence, which masked even from her Renault's deep involvement with the rush of experience that would nourish her imagination for the rest of her life.

Greece in April was still chilly, and the wildflowers they found often bloomed amid patches of snow, but they had not come for sun and sea bathing and reveled rather in their independence and freedom. They took a government-sponsored tour of the islands—the only such trip available to them in 1954—stopping at Poros, Mykonons, and Crete, visiting Delos with its three temples to Apollo and seeing Santorini from the sea, but the high point of the excursion for Renault was their brief visit to Knossos, when the boat docked at Heraklion for the day. She was overwhelmed by Sir Arthur Evens's colorful reconstruction of the House of Axe, which would play such a central role in *The King Must Die,* and impressed, too, even by a rushed tour of the museum at Heraklion itself. Another overnight boat from Athens took them to Samos, where they spent several days at a simple hotel, eating every evening at the local restaurant, walking in the island's hills. Returning to the capital, they made industrious forays in May to smaller cities, including train excursions to Marathon and to Olympia, north of Sparta.

Before finally departing by boat for Brindisi once more, Mary and Julie left Athens for six days on Corfu. From pictures, the two women had felt that the island would be "arcadian," providing an experience of "Mediterranean life" they had not yet enjoyed, a restful idyll they both deserved after their

16. Ibid.
17. Ibid., tape 12, side B.

hectic weeks of touring. Corfu fulfilled their expectations. They stayed at the small Swiss Hotel, where they "shared a very nice room at the front with a large window," and Julie remembered especially vividly the tranquility of these last evocative days, during which they walked along the beach "as far as the place where the Duke of Edinburgh was born and was an infant. And it was absolutely wonderful: it was still spring with the tall grass and masses of wild flowers and not a soul around. And we lay in the grass and looked through the baby oak leaves at the sky."[18] From Italy they boarded the liner to South Africa, which headed back again through the Red Sea, returning to Durban in late June.

Both women found the trip exhilarating. The months in Italy and Greece stimulated Renault's imagination and her research, anchoring both in the landscape, art, and architecture that had filled their weeks away. The trip had been essentially a solitary one as well, a variation of their other, shorter, more conventional holidays together in Britain and France. Greece had yet to be invaded by tourists, bringing with them all of the comfortable, materialistic, and superficial conveniences of the modern world. The Italy and Greece that Mary and Julie visited in 1954 were countries still recovering from the war and from the civil unrest that had followed in Greece. As two Englishwomen traveling alone in Mediterranean areas unused as yet to huge numbers of foreign visitors, Mary and Julie had a special and occasionally suspect status in which most of the time they delighted. They were together in the lands they had both known from childhood through books; they were on their own in their own favorite company; Mary was in charge of the intellectual shape of their journey, its historical content, its aesthetic joys, while Julie took care, as always, of the practical details, maintaining the domestic balance that had been part of their life together from the start. Although roles were somewhat reversed when Julie became ill before leaving Corfu, Mary was a competent nurse, and both women rested from their exhausting pace on the long voyage home to South Africa.

They quickly settled back into life in Durban, where they were welcomed by their circle of friends in a country that was clearly now their home. Julie returned to her nursing position and Mary worked on *The Last of the Wine.* By the time it appeared to rave reviews, she had already begun to write the first of her two novels about Theseus: *The King Must Die* appeared in the summer of 1958; the second book, *The Bull from the Sea,* followed early in 1962. With

18. Ibid.

these three historical novels, Renault secured her particular fictional territory, defining her voice and developing her artistic confidence. South African life beyond her desk and library, however, was becoming increasingly unstable and turbulent.

The polarizing issue of apartheid had a direct effect on their daily life through Julie's hospital where separation of nurses and patients by color was rapidly politicizing the staff. Julie's own position of peaceful protest with the support of some of her fellow nurses was perceived as radical indeed in the late 1950s, and by the end of the decade difficulties at the hospital brought about her resignation. Mitigated only slightly by the fact that Mary was now earning a very comfortable living from her successful novels, Julie's disappointment and frustration were intense; she realized that "It was the end of my career. It meant I would never nurse again in South Africa. It was an absolute body blow. It was staggering."[19] In late 1958, Mary and Julie decided to move to Cape Town, which had long seemed to them a more sympathetic location than the increasingly commercial Durban. They bought and renovated a cottage by the sea in Camps Bay; they would call it "Delos."

Mary described their situation in 1959 in a letter to Kathleen Abbott; after the war, she wrote, "I grew restless and wanted to see the world. Now I seem to need some to-and-fro of people and talk as well as space and air. In this country of few people and big spaces you can manage both; here in Cape Town you can side-step the dull smart social life and gather a manageable circle of people you really like and can talk to." Mary and Julie would be financially secure for the rest of their lives and settled now into a pattern of controlled work and carefully selected society that in many ways suited them both and certainly suited Mary. Julie would never formally nurse again within the racist institutions of their adopted country. She would go on to write periodically for SABC radio, but she would lose her daily contact with people who needed her highly trained professional skills. Her job would be to care for the house and for Mary, to support Mary domestically and emotionally, and to help even more than in the past with the onerous practical, secretarial, and intellectual tasks of proofreading, typing, and correspondence. Such a partnership would place particular pressures on Julie, but with the move to Cape Town, both women felt liberated and privileged, recapitulating their feelings on having left England for South Africa over a decade before. Julie reflected, "We were constantly in a state of wonder that life should have been so good to us," and

19. Ibid., tape 3, side A.

Mary on vacation near Mombassa, mid-1950s. Photo courtesy of Julie Mullard.

put into words what Mary herself felt at the time: " 'After all, I'm doing what I like doing best, and I get paid for it, and I still can't believe it. I'm living in this house by the sea, and I've got all the things that I've ever wanted, and I can't believe it's real or that I should be so lucky.' "[20]

Turning from *The Last of the Wine* to the myth of Theseus, Renault preserved a continuity with the ancient Greek world but left history for myth. In doing so, she maintained her allegiance to the geography and artifacts of the classical past, but she now had to work with fewer established facts and without the written accounts and familiar historical figures that had contributed so much to her narrative of the fictional Alexias. With Theseus,

20. Renault to Abbott, September 13, 1959; Mullard, interview by Sweetman, tape 14, side B.

she had two basic stories to tell: that of the "bull-leaper," the youth who went to Crete and returned to rule Athens; and that of the mature king and his marriage first to the Amazon Hippolyta and then to Phaedra. Renault's own practical and scientific training contributed to her approach as she attempted to treat the myth as history, to explain motivation and apparently fantastic phenomena (the Minotaur, the centaurs, the Amazons) in rational terms.

The first critical moment in her understanding of her material came when she posited the displacement of matriarchy: "Suddenly everything fell into place. I could begin to guess at the way Theseus' mind was furnished, the kind of beliefs and aspirations and responsibilities which might have determined his actions; the tensions between victorious patriarchy and lately defeated, still powerful matriarchy, which could have underlain the love-conflict element in his legendary relations with women."[21] She thus located the prehistoric world of these two novels at a pivotal moment in the past when political, religious, and sexual power had shifted. Theseus and his "companions," friendship, and especially kingship are the subjects of these books, but a larger subject is gendered power both at the level of the state and at the level of personal relations. Her women on the verge of disenfranchisement (Ariadne, Medea, and Phaedra) are often angry, resentful, and ruthless, driven to subterfuge and manipulation, with the exception of Hippolyta who, as an Amazon, a Lesbian, is at once woman and not-woman. Theseus is both male and heterosexual, yet he must come to understand himself as an unconventional man. He is ironically revolutionary in overthrowing matriarchal rule and its vestiges in patriarchy in order to establish his own kingship, and he is equally unusual in disregarding traditional boundaries of gender, class, and race (frequently portrayed as a matter of color) in his new order.

The meritocracy Theseus advocates and demonstrates in his own being depends on the individual, on distinctive physical, mental, and moral qualities. A good example occurs early in the novel when Theseus, who understands himself as semidivine, perhaps a god's son, and certainly in a special relation to Poseidon, must accept his body as human and ordinary in size. He initially thinks he will be a large and very strong man, a veritable Hercules, a legend made flesh, but his uncle instructs him: " 'Why can't you take yourself as you are? . . . You will make a warrior, if you go on as you are; you're not frightened, you are quick, and you've a grip like a grown man's. If you are sensible and get to know yourself, you'll seldom come away from the games without two

21. Mary Renault, "Notes on *The King Must Die*," 83.

or three prizes. . . . It's time you stopped fretting your heart out, and wasting time, over contests where only weight will do. You will never make a wrestler, Theseus. Face it once for all.' "[22]

Ironically, as she began to write *The King Must Die,* Renault herself did not at first realize the extent to which her protagonist would need to be different from the conventional male hero, the extent to which she could only come to understand and portray this heterosexual man as a kind of self-projection, an alter ego. Her conception of his body suggests the complexity of her radical presentation of gender and sexuality by the late 1950s.

Renault mentions another "crucial turning-point" in her composition: The story continued to resist her until she realized that she was having a problem with her hero's body. Having initially made him a "six-foot-three warrior," she found that he was "unreal":

> Suddenly I saw Theseus as the kind of man his conditioning might produce, if his mind and aspirations had been those of a Helladic prince, but his body that of a bull-leaper; a body not of his own conquering race (and there was a mystery about his birth) but of the conquered Palasgians. A constant element of the Theseus legend, I remembered, was that he had invented the science of wrestling. Why should a big man need to do that? It would much likelier be the resource of an intelligent lightweight. . . . [T]he real Theseus was a man who had made an asset of his liabilities, as so many real-life heroes do.[23]

The hero at the center of these two novels thus becomes at one level an intimate projection of the author herself, and his short stature and wiry body suggest her physical distinctiveness, her female gender. The tensions between female power (the artistic gifts Renault realizes in her own writing) and male power (the forces of patriarchy that work against female expression) underlie Renault's own "love-conflict," her own struggles with sexual identity and with her calling as a writer. Further, "a big man," a male academic, for example, would not need to invent "the science of wrestling," would not need to write historical novels—such an invention, such a creative response, would more likely be "the resource of an intelligent lightweight," the choice of a gifted female. Like Theseus, Renault makes "an asset" of "liabilities," art from her femaleness.

22. Mary Renault, *The King Must Die,* 24–25. All further references to this novel (hereafter cited as *King*) will be included parenthetically in the text.

23. Renault, "Notes on *The King Must Die,*" 84.

The process was not an easy one, as her career indicates, and Renault notes that in this particular instance, as a result of her understanding of Theseus's body, "Obviously, there was now no alternative but to re-write from the beginning."[24] Such rewriting results in an extraordinary emphasis on the body as a defining fact and image throughout *The King Must Die.* Because of his body-build, the young Theseus must rely on his wits to win at wrestling and to raise the stone that hides the secret of his patrimony and his royal destiny. Setting out from Troizen for Athens, he must use first his wrestling skill and then his cleverness and strength of character to overthrow the matriarchal power at Eleusis, with its annual ritual murder of a captive man. In the process, Theseus develops a group of "companions," male friends bonded to him by shared gender and sociopolitical interests, whose support is vital and on whom he depends, feeling "that something joined us, like a birth-cord filled with common blood" (*King,* 119).

Theseus no sooner claims his kinship with King Aigeus than he volunteers for moral reasons to go to Crete with the young men and women chosen by lot as tribute. This group, under Theseus's leadership, becomes Renault's clearest illustration of an ideal society: a special band, performers who name themselves "The Cranes," whose power depends on physical and mental skills rather than on gender or race or color or birth or cultural tradition, whose equal number of men and women participate together for the common and the individual's good, a meritocracy of "bull-leapers," whose sexual orientation is an accepted and personal matter. Renault's rewriting thus involves not only a revision of Theseus's body from Schwarzenegger to "normal" dimensions, but also a fresh understanding in this revised context of both heroism and power. The novel that results is of course just the sort of work the mature Renault would want to write; *The King Must Die,* despite all of its conventional and romantic elements and the suspenseful narrative that develops with such drama and apparent ease, is an account not of Theseus as a sort of Hercules but of Theseus as a philosopher-king who is as concerned with morality as he is with the body.

His heterosexuality also defines his personality, but particularly in *The Bull from the Sea,* which becomes an account of his two marriages, his traditional maleness allows Renault a doubly transgressive position. First, her hero, as an ideal man, permits her, a female author, to focus her novels on historically male situations (physical contests, affairs of state) and issues (power and

24. Ibid.

specifically kingship). Second, as the novels are also told in the first person from Theseus's point of view, his heterosexuality allows Renault to voice what is in fact lesbian desire and to describe not only the male but the female body. For instance, the opening scene of *The King Must Die* concerns the animal sacrifice in which Theseus identifies himself with the beautiful doomed horse, who mesmerizes him with his delicate lips "softer than my mother's breast" (*King,* 6). Breasts reappear throughout the story to signal female eroticism, the erotics of the female body, while Theseus himself comes to an easy and early acceptance of female sexuality. His attitudes result in part from his own experiences with lusty girls and from his understanding of his own birth, which he cannot accept as an aspect of his mother's possible rape, reflecting at one stage that "I could have forgiven a man she had taken for her pleasure, but not one who had taken her for his, and gone away" (41).

Renault offers voluptuous descriptions now of the female body, as a source of pleasure for the woman herself as well as for her partner. Theseus is aroused by the Eleusinian Queen—"Her deep breasts looked gold and rosy, bloomed like the cheeks of peaches . . ." (*King,* 60)—and learns from her in "one night" more than he had "in three whole years from the girls of Troizen" (66). Realizing on Crete that Ariadne is not a goddess but a woman, Theseus is also drawn to her body: "Her hair was fine and dark, with a soft burnish on it; a curling lock had fallen down over her breast; I could see tiny creases in the gilded nipple" (167). He is particularly attracted to "Amazon girls from Pontos, proud-faced and slim, free-striding, with slender fingers hard from the bow and spear, who looked you in the eyes as cool and measuring as young princes at war. . . . Whenever I saw such a girl, my heart would stir and quicken, I could not tell why" (190). Even Phaedra, at the age of nine, appears to Theseus indisputably female and physically attractive, with a body "as delicate to touch as a fresh lily-flower, and her breasts . . . just beginning" (199).

Theseus's heterosexual desire reaches its most erotic expression in his love for the Lesbian (and lesbian but also heterosexual, in fact bisexual) Hippolyta. When he first meets her in *The Bull from the Sea,* she is naked, plunging through the waves towards her attackers in defense of her community, and he is immediately overwhelmed: "The lift of her breast to her back-bent arm, the curve of her neck with its strong and tender cord drawn like the bow-string, shot me clean through like a shaft of flame. She stood to aim, all gold and silver touched with rose."[25] The ensuing struggle becomes both a battle of physical

25. Mary Renault, *The Bull from the Sea,* 84. All further references to this novel (hereafter cited as *Bull*) will be included parenthetically in the text.

strength (in which Hippolyta loses) and an eroticized contest (in which a sort of truce eventually results). The "arrow" directed towards Theseus is both the literal arrow of war and the "shaft of flame" that is Cupid's arrow; the "lift of her breast" and "the curve of her neck" are themselves the "shaft," at once the sign of her femaleness and the phallic "shaft" of traditionally male power. At first, Theseus does not see Hippolyta as Lesbian, does not see his attraction to her as other than conventional, assuming, for example, that in order to win her, he will need to battle a man (her father, brother, or even boyfriend or husband). When his friend Pirithoos points out to him that she is an "Amazon," Theseus is stunned—"I had not thought of it. . . . She had seemed only herself, without kind or peer." Once he understands Hippolyta as Lesbian, he accepts her own authority over herself; she is no unique aberration, but an independent woman, a "king" in her own right, his political equal, and he realizes, "I had met the warrior I must win her from" (*Bull,* 86). But kingship and not lesbian love, however encoded, is finally at the center of these two novels, and the denouement of *The Bull from the Sea,* with its account of Theseus's marriage to Phaedra and her ill-fated desire for her stepson Hippolytus, obscures Renault's more original and interesting treatment of sexuality, gender, and power in the relationship between Theseus and Hippolyta.

The conclusion of *The Bull From the Sea* left Renault up in the air. *The Charioteer* had lead easily to *The Last of the Wine,* while the myth of Theseus that followed was also two stories: that of his mission to Crete and the prelude to kingship, and that of his rule itself, with the two narratives neatly portraying Theseus's life from birth to death. The homosexuality at the center of the first two books was displaced by the ostensible heterosexuality of the central characters and the gendered power at issue in the political systems examined in the Theseus novels. The work that would follow would bring Renault increasingly closer to home, to personal issues significant for her in her own life as a bisexual woman in a lesbian partnership and as an expatriate writer, but these more difficult matters would lie in abeyance as she returned to Greece in 1962, to the physical world in which she had now anchored her imaginative life.

The circumstances of this second trip to Greece were different indeed from those that had shaped the first visit eight years earlier. Renault had finished her two books about Theseus but had yet to begin *The Mask of Apollo;* absent was the clear focus of the first trip, occurring as it did in the middle of the composition of *The Last of the Wine.* Having established herself as a historical novelist with a large audience including gay readers as well as admiring scholars, Renault found herself arranging to meet people with whom she had up until now only corresponded, as well as acquaintances and friends willing to fly out from England to see her. The solitude and calm that she and Julie had enjoyed together at simple establishments was now impossible: Tourists were flocking to Greece in increasing numbers and the nation was responding with tacky apartment complexes and restaurants catering to a flush international clientele.

At the end of March 1962, Mary and Julie set out from Cape Town on a Portuguese ship, following the west coast of Africa, stopping in ports that seemed to them "terribly depressing, rotten-smelling," docking briefly in Madiera before disembarking in Lisbon. The trip had not even begun well: Just before their departure, Mary had slipped and fallen, bruising her throat on a table edge. The brief swelling was unnerving, but the injury continued to be painful, forcing her to whisper throughout the voyage, muting her in effect and precluding the torrent of social experiences that she had anticipated. The train across the breadth of Spain to Madrid was tiring and the weather gray, compensated for only by the long hours they spent in the Prado.

In mid-April the two women, again by train, left Madrid for Barcelona, where they departed by ship for Naples. There they were met by Cedric Messina, a good friend from their earliest days in Durban, one of the many people in the art world to whom Jack and Peter had introduced them soon after their arrival. For years he had worked as a drama producer with SABC radio, but since 1956 he had been working for the BBC in London. With Messina they toured both the beautifully preserved Greek temples at Paestum and the ruined Roman city of Pompeii, before setting off by boat once more to Greece. Docking at Piraeus, they were surprised by the immediately apparent changes. Beachfront apartments and commercial improvements for the tourist trade had transformed the port, forcing one "to dodge the busloads in order to have quiet," but Mary was "pleased to see the growing prosperity, remembering the terrible and almost universal poverty before."[26] The city was, however, no cleaner than it had been under more primitive conditions, and Mary promptly came down with a forty-eight-hour intestinal upset that sharply curtailed her sightseeing. The group moved the next day to the El Greco Hotel in Athens, which, like the simple boarding house they had discovered in 1956, would serve on this visit as their touring base.

Mary and Julie left the capital in late April for an overnight car trip to Delphi, where Mary was charmed by "the mountain smells, huge spaces full

26. Renault to Abbott, July 25, 1962.

of moonlight falling away to the sea below, and the soft-harsh tinkle of the donkey bells, sometimes across the mountain and sometimes right under your window, sounding as they move about and graze."[27] In May they toured the islands of Aegina and Hydra and made a trip to the Peloponnisos to visit Corinth and Epidaurus with its famous theater. These were rewarding journeys, but their energy this time was expended primarily in the capital, where their days and evenings were heavily booked with social engagements. One of Renault's correspondents, the scholar Kimon Friar, was a lively companion, escorting Mary to the Acropolis museum, where he arranged for her to see art not yet on display to the general public. She saw the Blond Ephebe and was especially delighted with the Apollo of Piraeus. Accompanied by Friar to a formal museum reception, Renault met the American poet James Merrill, one of several writers who turned up during her weeks in Athens. John Guest, her editor at Longmans, made a trip out from England especially to see her, and through him she met Colin Spencer, who was traveling in Greece with his current lover, and the English novelist Robert Liddell, then head of the English department at the University of Athens. Messina also continued to be an intrusive presence, and it was problematic for the two women that he was "moving over from being gay to being heterosexual."[28]

Above an undercurrent of homosexual tensions, party seemed to follow party: Renault was introduced to the English authors Barbara Pym and Elizabeth Taylor at one gathering, to Sinclair Hood, director of the British School of Archeology, at another. The social round was occasionally stimulating but quickly became an infringement on Mary's time and interests. She had not come to Greece for the entertainment or the gay nightlife nor for contact with the English-speaking literary world. Renault had her own agenda, even if she was not now reading Greece as a direct gloss on a novel-in-process, while at home in Cape Town she had a carefully selected society of friends as well as regular access to lively productions of drama and dance. Finally, she preferred her correspondents to remain as correspondents, distanced colleagues with whom she was ultimately more comfortable through the medium of the written word.

It was something of a relief as well as a disappointment when Mary and Julie sailed for Italy in the first week of June. They spent several days in Venice, but again were not on their own. Here, as previously arranged, they met Naomi

27. Renault to Williams, June 30, 1962.
28. Mullard, interview by Sweetman, tape 12, side B.

Burton, Renault's agent at Curtis Brown, and the three women toured the city together before Mary and Julie departed once more for South Africa, this time via Suez and the east coast. It took weeks to settle back into a routine, but they were glad to be home, back at "Delos" with their dogs and cat and the peaceful view over the beach below the house.

Despite the enduring joy she felt in the art she had seen and in the landscape she would continue to write about for the next twenty years, Mary would always have mixed feeling about this last trip to Greece. Looking back, Julie would explain that Mary had not felt well the entire time; her throat had continued to bother her and her stomach from the start had been sensitive to local germs as well as to the wine. Yet it was the social whirl that had been most debilitating, and Mary's physical distress seems to have been in part a reaction to these other pressures. Julie explained that Mary "wasn't made for that sort of thing," the constant round of engagements, insisting that "It was really because of things like this that it was unbearable for Mary to travel, because a situation like that would throw her for days. . . . It certainly settled us that we would never go again. But every year, at least once a year, sometimes twice a year, we would say, 'Well, I think we ought to.' And we'd sit down all over again and say that if we go, we'd have to go here, and we'd have to see so-and-so and so-and-so—and we'd say, 'No, forget it.' " After their return, Mary wrote to Kathleen Abbott about the trip as an exquisite pleasure; however, she concluded that "In spite of Greece and Italy, the Cape in winter still seems as beautiful as anywhere one could actually *live* without being overwhelmed." But, she added finally, "If I couldn't live here I think I could live in Hydra."[29]

29. Ibid.; Renault to Abbott, July 25, 1962.

s e v e n

Politics 1962–1970

The physical isolation that Mary chose at "Delos," in its beautiful setting on Camps Bay at the edge of Cape Town, was necessary for her writing, but she could not avoid engagement with the political problems that permeated life in South Africa by the 1960s. This socially turbulent decade and her own sensitivity to moral issues would make her involvement inevitable, although political activity and specific causes would invariably be at odds with her own personality and priorities.

Mary had come to political consciousness slowly. As a girl, she had adopted, apparently without reflection, her parents' conservatism, confessing that even in the 1930s, "The only thing I felt strongly about . . . was [Edward VIII] at the time of the Abdication. I would have gone out with a banner . . . on Edward's side." She continued: "I had just enough sense of history at the time of the Spanish Civil War to know that both sides were committing the most horrible barbarities and I couldn't identify with either of them."[1] Identification was a vital element for Mary; she sympathized with Edward, championing his love for Mrs. Simpson, because the personal moved her, the romantic, the erotic, the specific. In contrast, the body politic seemed alien, uncomfortable, even immoral to her, as any group would be that was prone to absorbing and obscuring the individual.

In retrospect, her youthful political ignorance could amuse her, although she was not above also feeling nostalgic for a sensibility that could afford to respond primarily to romance or beauty. She wrote to John Guest about her attitudes in the 1920s and 1930s, recalling "the credulous innocence with

1. Renault, *Omnibus* interview.

which one kept *joining* things." She reported "that for a brief period I joined simultaneously the League of Nations and the British Union of Fascists, which I thought was a society for being romantically patriotic." Even when she received "some of their literature and read all the anti-semitic part," she did not realize "it could lead to wickedness—none of that had happened; on the other hand, I didn't *believe* any of it. I just thought I had strayed into a dotty sort of cult like the British Israelites who think everything can be read in the Great Pyramid, and I dropped it, keeping the badge to use as a safety pin, since I seldom sewed. It is hard to think oneself back into such naivety today. The League of Nations badge, I remember, was very much prettier, in fact the nicest badge I have ever seen around, a blue-and-silver world surrounded with little silver stars. I kept that for years."[2]

Mary's experiences during the Second World War, once the "wickedness" in fact "had happened," raised her political consciousness and confirmed her lifelong distrust of groups and dedication to individuality. Asked in a 1970s radio interview what was the most alarming or frustrating thing to have happened to her, Mary responded characteristically: "In common with a few million other people, I have sat in a shelter while overhead a planeful of young men, perfect strangers who never saw me in their lives, were deciding on whether to drop a bomb on where I was, or where someone else was, simply because governments and propagandists had labelled us with certain labels." She was well aware by 1942 that only "[a] few hundred miles away, millions of individuals with every kind of character and potentiality were being disposed of like garbage because they had been labelled 'Jew.' Ever since then, this urge to mass-label people has seemed to me one of the most dangerous of mental and moral aberrations." She elaborated, "What disgusts me about it is the flabby self-indulgence and mental cowardice in it. People get a sort of instant, dehydrated self-esteem which they have done nothing to earn; not by thinking, even, that they have earned it, but simply by thinking 'that lot over there is worse.' "[3] What horrifies Renault about this experience, what alarms and frustrates her, is the contrast between the anonymous "planeful of . . . perfect strangers," acting on behalf of "governments and propagandists," and the "individuals with every kind of character and potentiality," at risk because their individuality is erased by labels that force them together as a despised

2. Renault to Guest, May 2, 1978.

3. Renault, *What Life Has Taught Me* interview. It seems likely that Watling gave Renault the questions ahead of time and that she first wrote and later read out her answers.

group. In this case, the group comprises not homosexuals, as depicted in *The Charioteer,* but Jews or the millions of Britons, including Mary herself, who were to the German bombers during the Blitz merely the enemy. Her outrage is not only or perhaps at all personal: she conveys not fear for her own life but disgust with "self-indulgence and mental cowardice"—mass prejudice, power abused.

Such a political understanding certainly informs all of Renault's novels after her departure from England in 1948, but she did not bring with her to Durban any sophisticated sense of South Africa's particular situation. Rather, her attitudes and expectations were rooted in her passion for romance and in a personal optimism about what might be possible in her own career and in the life she hoped to forge with Julie. Interviewed by Sue MacGregor, Mary confessed that the reason she chose South Africa—besides the fact that it was a sterling area and therefore a practical choice—was that "[t]his to me was the country of Rider Haggard and Kipling and all the writers who wrote the boys' adventure stories of my childhood—and the present political situation of course hadn't even developed." In retrospect, Julie would describe herself and Mary in the 1940s as "not political," although they were definitely "pacifists." In the flurry of activity during the six weeks between the time of their decision to leave England and the moment of their departure, they were, Julie remembered, aware of some problems with "Afrikaaners," but figured that they lived on farms, and the two women were not going to live on farms. Their impressions were formed most immediately on the basis of their acquaintance with a few South Africans, who were "nice," and, Julie admitted, "The fact was, we had the money to go, and we could always come back."[4]

Once they settled in Durban, they became aware of political realities. At first, everything in Africa seemed new, beyond anything they had ever experienced, and, being uninformed and unprejudiced, they were without "race feelings." During these early days, Mary recalled, she "mixed with all the other expatriates" who were reveling in the sun, and "it took a long time before one really took in the country apart from its beauty and its tropicality." Because of apartheid, however, Julie confessed that they were "deeply ashamed to be British within months" of their arrival.[5] By the 1960s, Mary was acutely conscious of the country's difficulties and had defined her

4. Renault, *Kaleidoscope* interview; Mullard, interview by Sweetman, tape 4, side B.
5. Renault, *Omnibus* interview; Mullard, interview by Sweetman, tape 1, sides A and B.

own political position not only with respect to racial issues but more broadly. Group membership and mass action would continue to be uncongenial, but she and Julie marched in Cape Town in protest over the Sharpeville killings in the middle of the decade and Mary took radical political stands within the organizations that she felt morally compelled to join: the Progressive Party, "Black Sash," and P.E.N., the international society of poets, playwrights, editors, essayists, and novelists.

The Progressive Party, formed in 1959 as a more liberal but gradualist offshoot of the opposition United Party, immediately gained Mary's and Julie's support. On its behalf, they canvassed door to door, distributed pamphlets, and met with others to raise money, but Mary's active participation intensified her awareness of the differences between individual and group interests. The problem for her was moral as well as personal. She wrote to Kathleen Abbott in 1961, "I don't know what the answer is about politics. They seem such a mixture of good and bad. If no well-meaning or honest people take an interest, corruption or tyranny take over and one would feel one had failed one's fellow-men, as well as having to suffer the effects oneself." She had no doubts at that time about the decency and justice of the Progressive Party's policy, yet she found that "there is so much bickering and baseness, people get so petty, so prone to think of their fellow humans as group members instead of individuals, one cannot immerse oneself in it for long without wondering if one is doing harm, just by pushing the machine along. It is like the theatre which has produced such irreplaceable works of art and yet is (and I expect always has been) a sink of bitchery and corruption, where only the strongest personalities can survive untainted." The personal dimension of the problem became one of painfully divided loyalties. Mary voiced her dilemma clearly, again in a letter to Abbott: "Here, naturally, one often has to choose between creative and political or social work. Though of course I turn out with the protest marches . . . on important occasions, rightly or wrongly I mostly opt for sitting at my desk. I do try to exercise some moral responsibility in what I write, and I suppose there is room in the world for people who try to address themselves to what man *is* as well as what he does. Yet the divided pull is always there. . . ." Both Julie and Mary soon came to see the Progressive Party as weak, too willing to compromise, insufficiently committed, and too conservative; in the midsixties, they resigned their membership.[6]

6. Renault to Abbott, October 7, 1961, and August 7, 1962; Mullard, interview by Sweetman, tape 15, side A.

The Women's Defense of the Constitution League, popularly known as "Black Sash" because of the dark bands its members wore when demonstrating, posed a more complicated problem. Mary and Julie joined this organization shortly after it was formed in May 1956 in protest against parliamentary efforts to disenfranchise the "coloured" population. The group's attraction lay in its ostensible commitment to the country's constitution, to abstract principles whose violation it pledged to challenge. The difficulties, however, were threefold. First, Black Sash protests invariably involved marches and stands, meetings and speeches—all time-consuming activities that took Mary away from her writing. Second, the group consisted primarily of middle-class white women—the irony of whose privilege was not lost on Mary—whose traditional, feminine gatherings offended her as an independent professional committed to work at her desk. Third, the league's interpretation of constitutional civil rights was narrow and focused exclusively on race; Mary was committed to civil rights more broadly and personally conceived, broad enough to include matters of gender and sexual identity.

Julie, emphasizing that "in South Africa it is impossible not to become involved in politics," generalized about Mary's simultaneous involvement and disengagement: "Mary had a firm sense of principle. She was not aggressive, but she could be assertive, she not only spoke her mind clearly, but she also wrote letters [to friends and acquaintances; to newspaper editors] giving her opinions without fear or favour. Mary summed up politics by saying they were like drains, unpleasant but necessary." Because she was a "name," Mary was frequently asked to speak, but although she had enjoyed acting, she was not a natural speaker, and her refusals caused a great deal of disappointment. Yet, Julie pointed out, "what really upset people was the fact that she would never attend women's meetings held in rich drawing rooms with masses of cream cakes and going on all morning when she was longing to get to her typewriter."[7]

Because Mary's understanding of civil rights was based on principle and not merely on opposition to racism, she found Black Sash, like the Progressive Party, insufficiently radical. A purist in a political arena in which compromise was an essential element, she was frustrated, for example, when in 1968 the league refused to protest impending laws against homosexuality. Julie summarized Mary's disillusion: "If they had said in the beginning that we are here just to fight apartheid . . . but that wasn't their aim to begin with, and Mary was very strict about that sort of thing: if you say a thing, you must stick

7. Mullard, letter to author, November 20, 1996.

to that; you must not go off on a tangent and think or do what it suits you at the time."[8]

Mary found herself awkwardly and painfully caught between morality and expediency, between principles and compromise. Her involvement in two other local issues reveals her predicament. When the large Nico Malan Theatre opened in Cape Town in 1970, a polarizing furor erupted. In need of funds, the board had accepted support on the condition that the theater be open only to whites. The artistic community was divided: Some argued for a boycott in support of the African leaders of the antiapartheid movement; others argued against it, feeling that to keep out Western, European culture merely achieved the ends of the Nationalist government. Mary objected to the segregation but refused to give up attending performances. She delineated her position to Bryher: " . . . there has been a lot of protest about the new theatre, and I am one of a great many people who have protested in print. But now someone has got up a move to boycott it, and with this I will have nothing to do. . . . it will just be a question of killing something which should be kept alive for the ultimate good of all." Confident in the power of art to influence and even eventually to effect social change, Renault felt strongly that the issue here was finally one of censorship. For personal as well as moral reasons, she was convinced that freedom of expression was an absolute necessity both for society at large and for the individual artist. Writing to Cedric and Ruth Messina, she explained her commitment: "who does and doesn't go to the Nico Malan is a great issue; some very nice people go, some very nice people don't, together, in both cases, with some proper stinkers. We go, because it's not the actors' fault they need a theatre to do their thing in, and I know very well that if my books were to be banned to non-whites I would naturally protest, but I could not leave off writing."[9]

Mary's commitments created a more difficult situation when her involvement with P.E.N. brought her into direct conflict with Nadine Gordimer, raising the issue of censorship again, this time in the context of standards and the artist's responsibilities. In 1960 the international literary society founded a South African chapter with Cape Town as its first center. In 1964, the group chose Renault as its president, a position she held until 1981. This center,

8. Mullard, interview by Sweetman, tape 12, side A.

9. Renault to Bryher, December 27, 1970; Renault to Ruth and Cedric Messina, March 13, 1972.

meeting monthly, focused its political energies on protest against censorship in all forms. Its relations with the other South African P.E.N. center, in Johannesburg, were cordial, although this group, often led by Gordimer, developed a more specific concern with supporting the work and careers of black and "coloured" writers. Mary was disposed to be friendly. When Gordimer visited Cape Town in 1972, she addressed the P.E.N. club with a talk entitled "The Position of the Writer in South Africa." Renault was impressed, despite the differences in their personalities, and wrote the Messinas that she had enjoyed the presentation, "though I'd hoped she would talk about her experiences in America, simply because I know she would be very informative about it. She wore a beautiful Kaftan of some kind of African batik, and looked most handsome. Her husband flew down from Joburg specially to hear her, and it is nice to hear of a marriage being so devoted. She seemed somehow warmer and more outgoing than she used to be long ago, and I expect this has a lot to do with it."[10]

Having adopted the tenets of the English charter, the Cape Town P.E.N. required two published books in order for an author to qualify for membership. In the late 1970s, many had come to view this rule as a European imposition by white writers with little understanding of the literary problems of the developing world. The Johannesburg center advocated relaxing this standard in order to admit black members, who often had difficulty getting their work into print in their racist country. The differences between the two centers came to a head when Gordimer, serving as an international vice president, raised the issue not with Renault, nor with the Cape Town center, but at the annual meeting of P.E.N. in Stockholm in 1977. She specifically criticized Cape Town for having few black members and for not making specific efforts to recruit more, implying that the center's attitudes and those of its president were, if not blatantly racist, at least unfair and reactionary. Several delegations from other countries then called for Cape Town's expulsion.

The immediate problem was resolved when Gerald Gordon, a lawyer and founding member of the Cape Town P.E.N., was sent to Holland to defend the center. His account of the realities of the situation gained applause and an acquittal, but Gordimer persisted in her criticism, which continued to be insidious and bitter. Interviewed by a French journalist in 1979, Gordimer reiterated her position in terms that would futher antagonize Renault. "We recently held our first conference in Johannesburg," Gordimer declared. "We

10. Renault to Ruth and Cedric Messina, March 13, 1972.

had among us some young blacks, 18 or 19 years old, who had published a few poems in a small, mimeographed journal. We were accused of not being selective enough in our recruitment of members. But we don't care. What is essential lies elsewhere: we have a different set of goals."[11]

Mary saw the difficulty in part as a function of personality. After Gordimer gratuitously wrote a vitriolic review of a colleague's life's work, Renault wrote to Kathleen Abbott that she found Gordimer "an extraordinary person," even "malicious": "With her very considerable talent you'd think she would have neither time nor patience for this sort of thing. There's hardly anyone who knows her and likes her, and instead of ever asking herself if this can possibly be because she is a bit of a bitch, she always attributes it to political martyrdom." Renault concluded, "Alan Paton has been every bit as outspoken as she has, and everyone respects *him*. I could write you chronicles about her, the only writer I've ever known to go in for calculated intrigue in the world of letters."[12]

But Renault was also aware that for her the issue was finally one of principle. When Peter Elstob, P.E.N.'s international secretary, visited South Africa in February 1979, he suggested explicitly that the Cape Town chapter lower its membership requirements for blacks; Renault was shocked and refused. Her position was a moral one and as such had complex implications that went beyond anyone's specific desire to include black members in South African P.E.N. chapters. She would not compromise, reduce to merely political what she understood as an ethical matter. She repeatedly tried to explain her view in correspondence, writing to Elstob as late as 1980 that "A double standard is essentially patronising, and is recognised as such by serious writers of any race or sex. Until fairly recent decades it was often extended to women, but I never knew a self-respecting woman writer who wished to exchange self-criticism for the facile self-esteem it offers. I would expect an ambitious black writer to reject it equally."[13] The problem of P.E.N. membership was finally impossible to resolve, reflecting in microcosm not only the complex racial difficulties of a nation but also, for Renault at least, larger issues of history and gender, including, more broadly, questions about class and power—precisely the issues she would explore in her novels.

11. Nadine Gordimer, interview by Claude Servan-Schreiber, November 1979 (trans. Nancy Topping Bazin), in Nancy Topping Bazin and Marilyn Dallman Seymour, eds., *Conversations with Nadine Gordimer,* 115–16.

12. Renault to Abbott, September 21, 1978.

13. Renault to Peter Elstob, March 4, 1980.

Renault was well aware that her position would be understood as elitist, but she had always believed in a meritocracy. Optimistic about what she saw as a scientific process, she was also confident that such a world could best be understood through reasoned examination. Indeed, it is its rationality that in large measure drew her to classical thought. She would tell Cyril Watling that "The essential virtue of the Greek philosophers, which we are in need of today as much as any age of history, is that they thought straight. They took it for granted one would reach one's conclusions by the use of reason." Addressing from this perspective the issue of equality, including, incidentally, that of racial or sexual differences, she explained to John Guest that, however uncomfortable it might be to accept, she saw evolution as essentially "elitist." Further, she insisted, "Nothing can really be said to be 'unnatural' which exists in nature, whether good or bad. The one thing which can be so called because it *doesn't* exist in nature, is equality. I'm not talking about race because differences within races are always greater than between them. But half the hatred and envy infesting the world today comes from people being sold the idea that they have a right to be as good as everyone else, and if not someone else should pay for it."[14]

Two additional matters that Renault raises here were extremely important to her throughout her mature life. She invariably emphasized what is rationally so, both existential and mundane facts, drawing attention in all of her work to the significance of telling the truth. She also felt strongly about "hatred and envy" of the sort she describes to Guest. A desire to make "someone else . . . pay" for individual "inequality" or difference repelled her, and political protest or action to this end was alien to her. Rather, she strove in her own writing never to complain while simultaneously to present the world as she found it—such a representation of reality being in itself a political act, the one to which she felt most called and an integral part of her own art.

Truth as historical accuracy, fidelity to the reality of the past, becomes the hallmark of her later work, though Laurie's lying to Ralph at the end of *The Charioteer* is a particularly poignant moral failure in being a strategic, even political accommodation. Renault wrote to Williams that as early as the 1930s when she first read the *Communist Manifesto,* she "received a moral shock I have never got over yet" in the discovery that "if one accepts this [document], one can justify oneself in telling any lie, in doing *anything* to *anyone.* . . . This is wickedness and a true sin against the Holy Ghost." Reflecting more generally

14. Renault, *What Life Has Taught Me* interview; Renault to Guest, June 15, 1977.

on politicians' propensity to lie, Renault declared that in her experience Communists revealed in their distortion of truth a moral transgression of the utmost seriousness, for "[o]nce having crossed that river, conscience has no more meaning; honour, friendship and kindness all become sins."[15]

Another form of lying, of suppressing truth, is censorship, and protesting against it was for the Cape Town P.E.N. a commitment that logically earned Renault's allegiance. In her own work, however, the issue arose when directly or indirectly her subject matter was called into question, when she felt challenged in her decision to write about the classical past instead of about racism in South Africa. Such a judgment pitted her once more against Gordimer and privileged those writers, white and black, who chose to write topical and explicitly political fiction. When Sweetman criticized Renault on this point in an early draft of his biography, Julie was outraged. Irritated by the inaccuracies she discovered in this version, she sent him an extensive list of corrections, but her real ire was reserved for his misunderstanding: "Why Mary should be expected to write about the political situation in South Africa simply because she lived there, I do not know. . . . The reason she did not is she was not inspired to do so."[16]

Renault herself developed her position in a long letter to the editor of the *Cape Times*. She contended that it is necessary for an artist to choose "whatever subject makes a natural appeal to his imagination. Any refusal of this instinct, whether for commercial or political objects, is a betrayal of his soul." She continued to describe the kind of artist she admired: "[T]he writer with any moral concern for human beings . . . can address himself to the individual, in the belief that society is made up of individuals, that reading is a solitary act, and that political behaviour is only one aspect of a man's total life-style. . . . The proper work of the artist therefore is to appeal from self to self, and this can be done regardless of the age in which his tale is set." She heartily rejected "the 'committed' writer" whose principles are those "of the advertising copywriter: not positively to lie, but negatively to cut out any aspects of truth which reduce acceptance of the product." Renault concluded by referring to the artist's responsibility in South African politics:

> No field of human existence has been more exploited in the world today by the committed writer, whether of the left or right, than has South

15. Renault to Williams, July 30, 1968, and June 18, 1966.
16. Mullard to Sweetman, May 30, 1991.

> Africa. A point has been reached when the refusal to write propaganda is itself received by opinion-formers as a propagandist act. If merely courage were needed to turn the tide, there are, I am sure, many writers who would have it. The block [against writing about present-day South Africa] goes deeper: a kind of nausea of the imagination, which causes it to reject, unassimilated, a theme which has acquired a corrupt and tainted smell. A creative artist cannot transform himself at will into a one-man sanitary squad. He turns to the food he can absorb, receive stimulus from, and use.[17]

Renault was an eloquent leader of Cape Town P.E.N., and it is no wonder from such a letter as this that the members chose her as their president. It was a considerable understatement when Julie noted that "Mary always said her best weapon was the pen—or the typewriter."[18]

In so much as sexuality—an issue more personally important than race in her own experience—was a political matter, Renault was courageously ready throughout her career to express her own ideas in writing, while also invariably careful to separate public discussion from her private life. Drawing on her experience of friendship with gay men, Renault voluntarily wrote in 1968 to the Immorality Act (Amendment) Commission of the South African House of Representatives to protest the commission's hearings on homosexuality. She feared that testimony would be given primarily by those who had nothing to lose, by "[t]he promiscuous homosexual, who, like the equivalent type of heterosexual, relies for his sex life on casual or mercenary contacts" rather than by "[t]he respectable and domesticated homosexual . . . likely to have found himself a permanent companion, with whom he lives, often without mixing at all in an exclusively homosexual set." While offering her own "testimony," she is sharply aware that, as a bisexual woman in a lesbian relationship, she had indeed a great deal to lose, had she widened the debate to include female as well as male homosexuality, had she introduced her own life as evidence. She concluded with characteristic discretion: "Since I have no personal information to offer the Committee, I do not suppose that any useful purpose could be served by my appearing before it. I have nothing to add to the above, which I submit for the Committee's consideration."[19]

17. Quoted from Renault's file copy of this letter, dated August 7, 1968.
18. Mullard, interview by Sweetman, tape 14, side A.
19. Quoted from Renault's file copy of this letter, dated May 9, 1968.

Sexual politics, both the personal politics of intimate sexual relationships and the politics of institutionally gendered power and homophobia, are at the center of all of Renault's work, although in retrospect she generally wished to distance herself from the sometimes awkwardly developed or inconsistent ideas daringly explored in her contemporary fiction. For example, Renault seldom commented in interviews or letters on her early novels. She routinely dismissed them as boring, making exceptions only for *Purposes of Love* and *The Charioteer.* The impression she conveys is that they are juvenile efforts, hackwork of a sort, books that would have been aesthetically better had she spent longer on them, had she not been distracted by her necessary commitment to nursing and the war effort, by the pressure from her editors to publish, and by her need to make money. She thus protectively deflects attention from texts that are more clearly autobiographical than her historically displaced narratives of the classical world and avoids explicitly voicing the political, even feminist implications of her early work.

When she agreed shortly before her death to write an afterword to Virago's reissue of *The Friendly Young Ladies,* Renault found herself in an extremely uncomfortable position. She felt she was expected to extol the virtues of the novel's lesbian relationship, to support a feminist party line, as it were, by admitting that she would have been more frank, more "lesbian," had she not been restricted by the social pressures of the early 1940s. She felt she was being asked to confess to a moral cowardice, which she heartily rejects in her short essay. She writes: "I have sometimes been asked whether I would have written this book more explicitly in a more permissive decade. No; I have always been as explicit as I wanted to be. . . ." But Renault is also aware that "Inch-by-inch physical descriptions" (afterword to *FYL,* 283) were not exactly what her inquisitors were after.

Her essay is muddled by sections that do not logically cohere as she struggles to sidestep the central feminist and lesbian concerns of visibility and political commitment to sexual freedom. She writes instead about "what caused it to be written," describing the circumstances during which she read *The Well of Loneliness* while "staying with a friend in the small hotel of a French fishing village" (afterword to *FYL,* 281). Renault does not name Julie nor does she reveal that friendship as lesbian. She implies that *The Friendly Young Ladies* is somehow a response to both Hall's novel and to Compton Mackenzies's satiric portrait of lesbians in *Extraordinary Women* (1928) rather than a complex study of bisexuality based in large measure on her own experience characteristically and artfully transformed, masked, split, and doubled.

Renault uses the essay finally to emphasize three central points, two moral and one psychological. First, she wants to make clear her objection to the "needless fuss and bellyaching" about the "tribulation" of homosexual orientation, which she denominates as "a slight deviation of the sex urge." In the context of war and poverty, for example, and the pain and havoc they create in individual human lives, she finds that "defensive stridency [about women's liberation or homosexual rights] is not, on the whole, much more attractive than self-pity" (afterword to *FYL*, 282, 283). Defensive again of privacy, she rejects public demonstration, implicitly and problematically suggesting that art is a more viable and responsible vehicle for effecting social change.

But, moving on to her second point, Renault also stresses her conviction that writers must never "cook their books for good causes" (afterword to *FYL*, 284). She refers the reader expressly to Joe's opinion of political literature. Anticipating the war and his own participation " 'at the front, up to the knees in muck and stink' " (*FYL*, 160), Joe reveals his own and Renault's literary principles. He and Leo have already discussed the war "from the political angle"; now he tells her that he will not write a " 'war book' " until " 'Four or five years after it's over—just about the time the reading public's sick of the subject' " and, as Leo notes with sardonic understanding, " 'When it's too late to cash in on the action or the reaction' " (*FYL*, 159).

Joe then describes his own creative approach, distinguishing it from that of other writers: " 'Good books will be written [during wartime]. . . . There's no virtue in being unable to handle your stuff till it's cooled. It's just a matter of knowing your limitations. But if you do work cold, it imposes certain obligations. . . ." Much may be excused perhaps when work is written in the heat of conflict; literature written "cold," from a perspective of reflection and reason, requires above all honesty and dedication to the truth, for "it doesn't take much to damn your soul. Just leave out a little something, and shift the high-lights somewhere else, and change a bit that would never do for something that will do at a pinch. Well, it's all right if you can take to it, I suppose. I'd sooner go to bed with a woman for money" (*FYL*, 159–60).

Joe's speech in *The Friendly Young Ladies* makes clear that, long before settling in South Africa, Renault was aware of the political content in her own writing. She would refrain from writing her own "war book" until 1953, and *The Charioteer* would examine war and peace by focusing on individual homosexuals and their homophobic society in a novel whose political implications were finally subsumed by moral concerns. War itself would continue to be an important topic in all of her historical novels, and

Renault would treat political problems with increasing explicitness, but her own approach and convictions would invariably be those she attributed to Joe: to write "cold," from the responsible distance created by time, and to be scrupulously honest and truthful, never prostituting one's talents, not even "for good causes"—such as antiapartheid in South Africa or, in this afterword, gay or women's rights. Specifically, Renault is unwilling to write an essay that will complain that earlier oppression prevented her from saying what she wanted to say; she is unwilling, nearly forty years later, to contend that her novel is in fact an argument for lesbian sexuality. The problem she wrestles with is a moral issue twice over: Renault will not confess to having written less than the truth in her treatment of lesbian characters in 1944; she will not confess to having written more than the truth in her presentation of Helen's and Leo's heterosexual relationships.

Beyond these two moral issues—she was right in refusing to "fuss" and she told the truth—is the psychological matter of the novel's apparently happy conclusion. "Reader, I married him" has been the convention, especially in women's fiction, since at least Charlotte Brontë's time, but Renault admits to having been "naïve" in presenting Joe's and Leo's future together as a satisfying possibility; in retrospect, what strikes her most about *The Friendly Young Ladies* is "the silliness of the ending" (afterword to *FYL*, 281). Renault will go so far as to retract as highly unlikely the suggestion that the heterosexual lovers have a happy future ahead of them, but the heterosexual union that displaces Helen's and Leo's partnership is real indeed, and although she obviously feels she is being asked for political reasons to do so in her afterword, Renault will not recant it.

Her most explicit study of politics, a theme that plays an important role in all of her historical fiction, is *The Mask of Apollo*, in which the actor Nikeratos, who filters the narrative, recounts both his own life in the theater and the story of Plato's failure to transform the corrupt state of Syracuse into his ideal democracy. Renault was well aware that the political drama, even specifically anchored as it was in the established events of the fourth century B.C.E., had relevance as a gloss on modern political problems, but she in no way wanted the novel to be seen as an allegory of particular local difficulties in South Africa. She was typically outraged with the reviewer who "apparently thought I had invented Plutarch's entire narrative [in *The Mask of Apollo*] as insidious propaganda against self-government for the under-developed nations!"[20] Her

20. Renault to Cedric Messina, November 10, 1966.

artistic purpose was larger than such a reductive reading, and she insisted in her author's note that "No true parallel exists between this passage in Syracusan history and the affairs of any present-day state." But Renault was not ingenuous, and drawing attention to the "real value of history," which "lies in considering this endlessly varied play between the essence and the accidents," she wrote a book that offers both historical particulars and insight into political life as it transcends the boundaries of a specific time and place.[21] It is finally the human weaknesses in Renault's characters that work against the realization of Plato's ideal state, and Nikeratos concludes: "Perhaps it is impossible for a philosopher to be a king; at any rate, to be both at once. . . . We are weary of ourselves and have dreamed a king. If now the gods have sent us one, let us not ask him to be more than mortal" (*Mask,* 290).

Unlike Plato but like her protagonist, Renault is a realist in her view of politics, but the novel is finally less concerned with the government of a community than with morality, an individual matter. For instance, when Axiothea, passing as a boy to participate in Plato's academy, reveals her identity to Nikeratos, he wonders at Plato's acceptance of a woman and asks if the philosopher has given her " 'equality with the rest.' " Axiothea is shocked and reveals an attitude that is precisely her author's: " 'Equality! I hope I need never sink so low. That poppy-syrup! Does the soldier ask to be equal to every other? No, to prove himself. The philosopher? No, to know himself. I had rather be least of Plato's school, knowing the good and taking my own measure of it, than run back to Philos where I could command what praise I chose. Equality! No, indeed, Plato doesn't so insult me. People whom such things concern you'll find at the schools of rhetoric. They don't come here' " (*Mask,* 75). Situating the soldier in the field—the individual seeking recognition on the basis of merit—within the realm of the moral, Axiothea distinguishes between those who study philosophy and those who apply themselves to rhetoric, between those concerned with morality and those whose focus is political. Nikeratos immediately apologizes, realizing that as an actor it is on the basis of merit that he, too, wishes to be appreciated: " 'An artist should have known better' " (76). Plato's error in the novel is confusing the two realms, in failing to have the artist's insight.

After the fall of Dion's corrupt democracy and after Plato's death, the novel ends with the example of Nikeratos, the moral actor, and with the promise

21. Mary Renault, author's note to *The Mask of Apollo,* 377. All further references to this novel (hereafter cited as *Mask*) will be included parenthetically in the text.

of Alexander, the statesman who understands art. Nikeratos leaves Syracuse with the aging Ariston, the down-and-out colleague who "had been kind when kindness or cruelty had power to shape my soul." The younger actor resolves to "see he did not die hungry, or alone," concluding "That . . . is as much as most men can hope to bring away from the march of history, when all is said" (*Mask,* 364). Salvaging the intimacy of friendship from the politics of Syracuse, Nikeratos survives as a morally admirable figure. Renault concludes, however, with the young Alexander, who glows as an extraordinary man, gifted in politics and sensitive to art. He treats Nikeratos with the respect due a great actor, but their relationship is profoundly personal: From Alexander, Nikeratos learns what the voice of Achilles must have been; from Nikeratos, Alexander gains insight into Homer. Alexander contributes to the actor's art; Nikeratos, through his art, contributes to Alexander's greatness. Characteristically, Renault signifies this exchange in intimate, physical terms when Alexander kisses Nikeratos, who reflects that he and his actor companion "will follow this golden daimon, wherever he calls us to show him gods and heroes, kindling our art at his dreams and his dreams at our art" (372–73).

Renault makes clear that Dion has failed Plato, that self-interest has compromised moral standards, but she suggests that Alexander would not have failed the philosopher; in his case, it is the philosopher, in the person of his tutor, Aristotle, who fails him. We see Aristotle in *The Mask of Apollo* as a "small, dapper, thin-legged man . . . with the beard of a philosopher," a teacher of limited authority and petty passions who approximates Plato but is not his equal. Nikeratos adumbrates the trilogy that will follow this volume by reflecting on tragedy both in art and in life: "All tragedies deal with fated meetings," but "[n]o one will ever make a tragedy—and that is as well, for one could not bear it—whose grief is that the principals never meet" (*Mask,* 373). Alexander never meets Plato and, in Renault's account, is ultimately betrayed by Aristotle's selfish political machinations. The story of Alexander's life and its aftermath assumes in her trilogy a tragic sweep and power. There is the illusion that it is history, a factual past revivified in the novels, which is tragic, but of course it is Renault herself who has shaped her material into art, who has made through her fictional recreation of the past a tragedy "whose grief is that the principals never meet." Politics causes Alexander's death and the downfall of his empire; the pain for Renault is that others' abuse of power destroys Alexander the individual man, the leader, the lover; that politics wins out over morality, the public triumphing over the personal.

A meritocracy, as illustrated in Theseus's Cranes on Crete, was invariably Renault's ideal community. Her Alexander strove to create one in his empire, and race, the defining issue in South Africa's political life, displaces sexuality as a central political issue in Renault's historical novels. In her two novels about Theseus, the narrative is informed by racial tensions—between the hirsute "Shore People," with their matriarchal religion, and the patriarchal Hellenes, between the dark Cretans and the light Athenians. A matter of stock and color, race persists as an issue in *The Mask of Apollo.* Here, for example, the Sicilian actor Menekrates is stigmatized by his family because he is dark, the product of a " 'Numidian strain' " (*Mask,* 116). He calls Nikeratos's attention to his character, which is principled and not " 'savage,' " and points out that people " 'do not look beneath the skin.' " Art, however, transcends this social problem, rises above prejudice, refuses difference as a negative feature, erases otherness. As Menekrates remarks, " 'it's all one in the theatre, under the mask' " (117).

For Alexander, the racial issue finally configures itself both in the tensions between the dark and hairy Macedonians and the lighter southern Greeks, who shave their faces, and between the Greeks, both dark and light, and the Persians, with their almond eyes and yellow skin, with their different religious and cultural practices. Alexander's political success depends in part on his lack of prejudice, on his willingness to adapt to a different culture, to learn a new language, to incorporate into his personal and court life local ways of dress and manner. Renault illustrates his potential early in *Fire from Heaven,* when she links his open-mindedness about race with his attitudes towards class. As a small boy, Alexander kindles a friendship with Lambaros, a Thracian prince held hostage in the Macedonian court. Despite his rank, Lambaros, with his red hair and blue tattoos, is regarded by King Philip as a "savage," racially alien, marked by his visible differences.[22] Philip also finds the friendship particularly repellant in that Alexander could have chosen as his playmate any "boy of decent birth in Pella" (109); Lambaros is beneath Alexander because of both race and "birth," class. However, the young Macedonian astutely makes a lifelong ally of his Thracian friend, and he seals their pledge with a ritual kiss, which, as a sign of loyalty among equals, outrages Philip.

Class and race also mingle with gender as issues that divide King Philip and Queen Olympias: He is Macedonian while she is Hellenic; his power

22. Mary Renault, *Fire from Heaven,* 108. All further references to this novel (hereafter cited as *Fire*) will be included parenthetically in the text.

derives from his status as a soldier and a man, while hers depends on female subterfuge and her reputation as a witch. As king and queen, male and female, Macedonian and Greek, Alexander's parents struggle to define him, to force him to choose between them, between two parts of himself. For Renault, one source of his greatness lies in his refusal ultimately to take sides, in his combination in one person of the strengths of both father and mother, male and female. His psychological situation is fraught, but the sexual politics of Alexander's childhood, both the politics of sex and gendered politics on the scale of the state, contribute to his understanding of the nature of power as he learns to use it by example. His future relationships with women are informed by his sense of them as dangerous opponents as well as useful friends from whom, in both cases, it is best to maintain a controlled distance. His future relationships with men reflect his awareness of love as an intimate bond between individuals (as in his relationships with Hephaistion and with Bagoas, the Persian boy) and between a leader and his subjects, his troops, be they Macedonian, Greek, or Persian.

Alexander's ability to combine the opposites so vivid in his parents makes him a romantic figure whose attraction depends on his personal charisma as well as on his education, knowledge, experience, and intelligence. Renault makes important distinctions here: One's worth ought not to depend on class, race, gender, or sexuality. Merit is linked to chance (to personality, to being in the right place at the right time), but it is especially a matter of effort, of experience in the field (in court, in battle, in art, in sex), of learning, understanding, and temperance. Culture shapes the individual, and any particular society delineates the relative significance of class, race, gender, and sexual behavior and inclinations. Yet despite her concern with historical accuracy and her commitment to presenting the past on its own terms, Renault's values emerge clearly in her depiction of iconoclastic characters, courageous individuals who dare to do the forbidden, figures whose respect for individual merit transcends the attitudes of their specific culture.

Her personal view of class provides as much a case in point as her attitudes towards apartheid expressed in her daily life in South Africa. Julie recounted with amusement a revealing anecdote. In the early 1940s, when Mary was first developing a reputation as a writer, she was "beginning to get fans. . . . People wanted to visit her. . . . We both had this weird idea that they must always visit here [at the Leckford flat in Oxford], and she must do the hostess and I mustn't be here." The two women conspired to mask their relationship, to create a particular impression that would, for casual others, erase their lesbian partnership. Both women were consciously acting, but when Julie proposed to go further and borrow a uniform in order to play "the maid," Mary drew the line: she "would never say yes. I would have absolutely loved it . . . but Mary always wanted us to be equal, which only in certain ways we were, of course."[23] In Alexander's case, his view of class and race distinguishes him from those with more conventional attitudes. His friendship with Lambaros, which erases the boundaries of race and class, foreshadows his later love for the eunuch Bagoas, which crosses the boundaries not only of race and class but of sex and gender.

Logically, Alexander's vision of the future in *The Persian Boy* includes a multiracial band, achieved through intermarriage, which will bring about "harmony between Macedonians and Persians."[24] Even such eugenics, however, cannot achieve the "harmony" Alexander prays for; he and his empire are doomed by political forces beyond his control. In *The Praise Singer*—the novel that interrupts her Alexander trilogy, intervening between *The Persian Boy* and *Funeral Games,* between the tragedy of Alexander's death and the tragedy of his empire's dissolution—Renault will contend that it is not individual societies but art that endures, the artist, not the politician, who can maintain an ethical position and call for morality in others through his (or her) life and work. The political alternative is a travesty made particularly poignant for Renault's readers in that *Funeral Games,* with all of its horrors—and not *The Praise Singer,* her most tender novel—is the book that concludes her writing career.

The artist for Renault was of necessity and by definition above politics, beyond compromise. Alexander succeeds as a great man insomuch as he has the sensibility and the morality of the artist; he fails as a politician insomuch as he is unable to modify his principles, to connive with one group against another, to recognize the depth of human corruption and self-interest. Renault's values and achievements are well described in the anonymous commentary that at the time of her death appeared in the *Cape Times,* a newspaper to which she regularly submitted letters, often about political matters:

23. Mullard, interview by Sweetman, tape 4, side B.

24. Mary Renault, *The Persian Boy,* 361. All further references to this novel (hereafter cited as *PB*) will be included parenthetically in the text.

> She had a well-trained mind, sharpened by impatience with cant and tempered with humanity. In her many contributions to discussions on public issues, she was at pains to maintain a tone of civilized toleration. . . . [S]he showed an acute sense of the intricacy of human and artistic problems of the country, never succumbing to the narrow view that these problems were without parallel.
>
> Most of all, she had sympathy for the problems of cultivating the arts in a land where severe criticism and indulgence alike might damage new buds. From this sympathy flowed her indefatigable opposition to censorship. As president of the P.E.N. Club of Southern Africa . . . , she did much to focus public attention on the harm that was being done to South Africa's burgeoning literature by censorship. Younger writers, finding themselves in a more enlightened climate, have much to thank her for.
>
> She was, in the sense of her beloved Greeks, a good citizen. She left the quality of life in South Africa, especially in Cape Town, improved by her life and she used her art well. . . . [25]

Censorship was the issue at the heart of her commitment to P.E.N. and, broadly interpreted as a variant of denial, silence, and erasure, at the core of her understanding of art and of herself as an individual writer. Asked by the SABC radio journalist Cyril Watling what an artist requires, Renault responded: "It is necessary, for happiness, to be free from anxiety and want." She pointed out that artists vary tremendously in the amount of money or material prosperity they may need: "A married man with dependents can be in the red where a bachelor man or woman would be free as air. Any serious artist who is able to do so should keep his overheads down, not get caught up in time-wasting social nonsense nor cultivate expensive tastes. His savings are his freedom, that is their real value—freedom to write what he chooses, not what someone offers to pay him for." Julie elaborated on Renault's commitment to what she herself called "standards," the moral principles that might inform political positions but that transcended the specific politics of any particular time and place. Especially in writing about sexuality, Renault had known from the beginning that she was taking risks, both personal and professional: "She would point out that she had no dependents; she was very fortunate. Had she been a man with a family, she might not dare take the chance. . . ." As an artist, Mary felt compelled to present the world as she found it: " 'If I start being

25. "Mary Renault," *Cape Times*, December 14, 1983.

afraid of writing what I know I must write, I may as well give up. My books have not been banned; I don't expect them to be banned, but if they are, so be it. You can't sit up being frightened.' "[26] Having the courage of her convictions, Renault's challenge was not to involve herself in any direct political activity but to develop the artistic strategies to express what she knew she must, to readers often unprepared or unwilling to understand.

26. Renault, *What Life Has Taught Me* interview; Mullard, interview by Sweetman, tape 12, side A.

e i g h t

Art
1970–1975

Long before *Purposes of Love,* even before she began to train as a nurse, Mary had known that she and her writing might be misunderstood. Her childhood had not made her feel particularly loved or accepted, and part of the problem was that her parents had failed to understand the little girl who refused to be conventionally feminine, the child who liked to act and write, the young woman who wanted first university and then independence. Indeed, her parents would *misread* her because they had no knowledge of what it meant to be a writer, to be the sort of author their daughter would become, to be a bisexual woman who would choose to live in a lesbian relationship. Additionally, they had no desire to know these things; they were in fact determined to impose upon Mary an identity, a career, a life defined by conventional expectations. Renault's reception has been shaped by these two sorts of misreading—the one naive, the other patriarchal—as well as by the problem her identity poses for an audience that has had trouble reading an author who was both woman and writer, both female and sexual, both lesbian and attracted to men, both nurse and intellectual, an artist in fact whose identity often seemed a paradox (she could not be both) and an impossibility (she must be one or the other—or neither, something altogether "other").

Charlotte Georgi is typical in her positive review of the first American edition of *The Charioteer* in 1959. She recommends the novel but begins her discussion by pointing out that "this is an odd subject for a woman author." Another positive reviewer, Siegfried Mandel, felt obligated to emphasize that, despite her insight into Laurie's character, Renault was "working against the inevitable odds of deviational material"; while Hubert Saal was distinctly uncomfortable, concluding that "Miss Renault asks more of us than we can give. As well as sympathy, she demands identification. But Odell's world is so alien that its conflicts are internecine; we watch bemused, like anthropologists at a native fertility rite that seems to bear some faint connection to our culture." Gore Vidal is finally more hopeful than accurate when he asserts in his review of *The Persian Boy* in 1973 that Renault had forced "even the dullest of bookchat writers to recognize that bisexuality was once our culture's norm," but even while praising Renault, Vidal confesses, "I cannot think how Renault has managed to do what she has done."[1]

One of the results of this apparent conundrum is that readers, at once curious and threatened, male for the most part—gay, bisexual, and straight—speculated from the very beginning of her career that Renault must be a man. In 1939, Robert Wilson reviewed her first novel for *St. Mary's Hospital Gazette*. Focusing on her treatment of love, with which he was favorably impressed, Wilson condemned most books on this subject as foolish, attributing such wrong-thinking to their frequently female authors. His misogyny surfaces explicitly at the end of his first paragraph: "There are few things more terrible than half-educated women with no sharp lines in their minds." Wilson then began to discuss the novel: "It is therefore a considerable pleasure to come across a book about love written by a woman (unless Mary Renault is a deceitful pseudonym) who has plenty of sharp lines in her mind and who realizes the many-sidedness of the thing called love." Thirty-five years later (although before the current understanding that all gender is a matter of performance), the modernist scholar Hugh Kenner, reflecting on her then six classical novels, labeled Renault a "male impersonator." Such patriarchal posturing and the impulse to claim Renault as other than she is—an unconventional woman and therefore not a woman, an imposter, in fact a man—indicate misreadings more distorted than those she might have anticipated. Referring primarily to her historical novels, even Bernard Dick, one her most sympathetic readers, noted "her unique ability to inhabit male characters with such conviction that I—and others—originally thought 'Mary Renault' was a pseudonym for a male."[2]

1. Charlotte Georgi, *Library Journal*, June 1, 1959, 1921; Siegfried Mandel, *New York Times*, May 10, 1959, 6; Hubert Saal, *Saturday Review*, May 16, 1959, 30; Gore Vidal, *New York Review of Books*, May 31, 1973, 15.

2. Robert Wilson, "Review of Books," *St. Mary's Hospital Gazette*, 61; Hugh Kenner, "Mary Renault and Her Various Personas," *New York Times Book Review*, 15; Dick, letter to author, November 28, 1992.

The impulse to mask or unmask Renault as a male author suggests the real difficulties that readers have in understanding the rich and confusing relation she sets up between writer and subject, between the reader and both writer and protagonist. If Mary Renault, whose name was revealed as a pseudonym early in her career (although not at the time of her first novel; Wilson is merely precocious, making his claim even more suggestive of the problem indicated here), is in reality or attitudes a man, then the serious reader of serious fiction, who is either male or, following Judith Fetterley, is probably even today reading as a man, can identify with her/him and share a position of authority from which to understand (and speak about) the sexuality at the core of her/his novels. Further, if the author is male and the reader can assume his values, then one can more easily impose a patriarchal reading on the novels, one could indeed more easily misread the texts and dismiss or condemn the transgressive sexual elements.

In fact, this is exactly what frequently happens in readers' responses to Renault's fiction. Thus Peter Wolfe declares that the author of *The Charioteer* "is unmistakably addressing a heterosexual audience," producing a text, in other words, that would be unreadable by its creator as well as by male homosexuals who have, beginning with this novel, seen Renault's work as addressed especially to gay readers. Sweetman emphasizes that following the publication of *The Last of the Wine* in 1956, "Mary's correspondence was dominated by letters from men, thanking her for explaining their own feelings to them" (184). He adds that in the 1950s and 1960s, "Gay bookshops in San Francisco had prominent 'Renault' sections" as, today, does the London bookshop Gay's the Word, belying Mary Beard's contention that "Gone are the days when . . . a copy of *The Last of the Wine,* tucked casually under the arm, would be taken as a badge of homosexuality, a barely coded sign of support for the 'Greek love' that the novel itself appeared to celebrate." Renault would finally be infuriated by Wolfe's misreading. Contending that Laurie's friendship with Nurse Adrian promises him hope of a "normal" heterosexual future, Wolfe concluded that "Renault convinces us that, by age twenty-three, Laurie has trained himself to ignore girls"; his homosexual experiences up until the end of the book encourage him by stages to assume what Wolfe calls "the male role," through which he could achieve "the psychic balance and self-acceptance to enjoy heterosexual love, a more distant goal, at a later time." Accordingly, Laurie's friendship with Nurse Adrian "constitutes one of those rare chances that can change the entire substance and direction of one's life." This may indeed be what a heterosexual and homophobic male reader might wish, but it is not the author's position; heterosexual marriage for Laurie is impossible. When Laurie confronts the duplicity in continuing his relationship with Nurse Adrian, he realizes that "he was already beginning to exploit her" and to compromise himself not only sexually but morally (*TC*, 273). Focusing first on Wolfe's treatment of her historical fiction and then on his more general failures, Renault shared her irritation with Kathleen Abbott: "I sat clutching my hair as I read his involved [Freudian] theories accounting for the presence of simple well-authenticated historic, social or archeological facts which he supposed I had *invented*. . . . Not only did he know no history but he didn't know what I meant, sometimes, in the whole intention of a book, so that in fact anyone reading him would know less about me than before they started."[3]

In contrast, Renault was especially pleased by the responses of two sorts of readers. First there were the personal reactions of gay men and occasionally lesbian women to her treatment of characters who, at least by twentieth-century standards, led sexually transgressive lives. Jeannette Foster, whose ground-breaking *Sex Variant Women in Literature* drew attention to the variety of fictional lesbians, is typical in having felt a deep sympathy with Renault. Knowing her only through her work and through correspondence, Foster would call Renault "my remote-control friend." Renault was also delighted with a second sort of reader: the man or woman who was influenced by her historical novels to pursue a scholarly career. Toward the end of her life, she revealed to John Guest her sense of responsibility to these young people as well as her pride in having inspired them: "This week I had a letter from a girl who said that entirely owing to having read my books she had decided to become an archeologist and has already started at a university. When one thinks her whole life, her marriage and children maybe, will be determined by her career, it does give one a solemn feeling. It isn't the first time either, though it is classics as a rule."[4]

In contrast, Renault was particularly irritated by ignorant readers who failed to realize or respect her meticulous efforts to ground her work in historical evidence. Responding to a negative review of *The Mask of Apollo*

3. Peter Wolfe, *Mary Renault,* 104, 107, 112; Sweetman, *Mary Renault,* 184, 273; Mary Beard, "The Classic Paradox," 13; Renault to Abbott, September 12, 1972.

4. Jeannette Foster to Margaret Anderson, June 8, 1960, published in Mathilda M. Hills's edition of Anderson's novel *Forbidden Fires,* 159. In a letter to me (February 5, 1997), Julie Mullard confirms that "Jeannette Foster and Mary corresponded for years." Renault to Guest, May 2, 1978.

in the *Sunday Times,* she wrote, again to John Guest, that "What staggered me . . . was not so much its venom, since it's an occupational hazard to get a reviewer who just hates one's smell; but the fact that in a paper of that standing it was possible to fill the summary with flat, downright lies about the narrative, characters and plot, and actually to base the criticism on them. There are not less than four gross historical errors in the summary, which would stick out a mile to anyone who knows the period . . . none of which are in the book, which in fact says the exact opposite." Renault concluded, "What I can't understand is why this kind of thing, which if practiced on a straight biography would get the reviewer shot down in flames, is allowed in reviewing a historical novel. Anybody has the right to say he hates a book; but surely no one should get away with saying, untruthfully, that it is full of historical howlers of the most elementary kind. . . ."[5] Renault is generous in respecting difference—here differences of opinion or taste—while insisting, typically, on "the truth," in this instance on the inviolability of both historical evidence and the evidence of what she herself has actually written.

Renault also distinguishes in this letter between biography and the novel, between the record of a life and fiction. She was invariably faithful in her historical writing to the evidence of particular lives (for example, to recorded facts about Socrates, Plato, and Aristotle as well as Alexander and Simonides), but she was simultaneously suspicious of the tendency to place a work in the context of the author's life, defensive of her own privacy and wary of intrusive readers. When at Bryher's request her friend, the American academic Norman Holmes Pearson, sent to "Delos" copies of H. D.'s *Helen in Egypt* and *Selected Poems,* Renault was somewhat discomforted at his having included in the packet copies of his interview with H. D. and biographical notes he had made. She even admitted to not really having liked the interview with its direct probing of the author's intentions, although she did find "the biographical notes extremely interesting, and was glad to have read them." Renault admitted: "I am probably a bit prejudiced against explication, by the work of certain critics who have set out to explicate me, and have failed in the most essential respects to grasp what I was driving at, though ordinary readers (I mean readers with no literary apparatus) seem to have understood it perfectly." Many literary critics and scholars, she complained, "seem to be under the delusion that creative work is mathematical instead of organic; that one starts with some elaborate equation worked out down to the last

5. Renault to Guest, October 23, 1966.

x = y, knowing at Chapter I precisely what you will say in Chapter XX, all complete with carefully patterned sets of conscious symbolism. In this zest for schematisation, they seem unable even to grasp that when history says that something happened, you have to say it too; it does not symbolise anything, it is just a fact."[6]

Renault is rather disingenuous in denying the symbolic value of "a fact," whose inclusion she was well aware was a matter of selection and more largely of the general subject's capturing the writer's imagination, but she defends herself here against readers' tendencies to impose upon her work reductive and rigid Freudian interpretations that often ignored the evidence as well as the spirit of her writing. Like Simonides in *The Praise Singer,* she knew that there is praise that "makes one wonder what one did wrong, to have caught the fancy of such a fool" (*PS,* 102). Thus she wrote to a doctoral student, who had sent her a list of queries, that she could not encourage his thesis and condemned such academic studies as Peter Wolfe's: "He got everything wrong, including the whole development of Alexias in *The Last of the Wine.*"[7] She objected specifically to Wolfe's Freudian analysis and lack of concern with history, her scholarship, and factual accuracy. She angrily deflected interest in her life as irrelevant, insisting that the important context for reading her books was the historical context of their settings. Renault obviously felt that the student's questions were impertinent as well as an invasion of her privacy and an encroachment on her time, but she was also clearly aware that twentieth-century English history and the personal experiences of her own life, which she so carefully sequestered from public scrutiny, provided, as in the case of H. D., another vital context for her literary achievement.

One of the reasons both for this interest in Renault's life and for these misreadings of her work is the nature of the writing itself. Partly intentionally, because of a conscious desire for self-protection and her own sense of the complexity of sexuality, and partly inadvertently, as a result of her own ambivalence and bisexuality, Renault encouraged readers' struggles and confusions. Understanding that her readers included people like her characters Elsie, who would refuse to see what she was driving at; Peter, who would insist on conventional interpretations regardless of evidence to the contrary; and Laurie, who would be eager for external validation of his sexually transgressive

6. Renault to Bryher, February 9, 1971.

7. Renault to "Mr. Dole," January 19, 1977. Mr. Dole's letter to Renault has apparently not survived.

identity, she presented her audience with material that was difficult to read. Throughout her career, Renault was interested in fluidity and instability, in liminal individuals and experiences—all elements that both fascinated and confused her readers. In her contemporary novels, for example, she emphasizes her characters' marginality: Vivian is a student nurse; Mic, who had hoped to become a doctor, is displaced, working as a lab technician; Kit contemplates a divorce, which would force him to give up medicine; Leo's cowboy novels may be popular, but they are not, as she is well aware, serious art; Hilary depends on local regard to maintain her practice; Neil is emotionally as well as literally dislocated in Devon, having left both his marriage and his teaching career. Further, Renault's contemporary characters are frequently deprived of or give up their professional authority. Vivian leaves nursing before she completes her training; Hilary quits brain surgery for a provincial practice; Julian refuses to take up professional acting opportunities; Laurie's injury, which makes him physically unstable, prevents his continuing as a soldier.

In a similar vein, her Greek novels are frequently narratives about the struggle to attain positions of power and the struggle to maintain power once achieved. Her protagonists are consistently threatened; they are often outsiders who depend for their status on patronage, complicated diplomacy, and a fickle audience or constituency; they are in danger from their own families, their wives, parents, and children. They are often divided or ambiguous beings, whose identity is nearly always bisexual. Theseus is heterosexual, but his relationships with men are strongly homoerotic. Alexias is homosexual—*The Last of the Wine* is an account of his love for Lysis—but he marries and has children, and we are lead to believe he is fulfilled in the roles of husband and father and grandfather. Alexander is homosexual, but sexual desire is not strong in him, despite his tremendous need for love. He marries and fathers two children, yet he finds little physical pleasure or emotional satisfaction in erotic relationships with women. Instead it is his homosexual friendship with Hephaistion that is central to his life, although he also has deep affection and erotic feeling for Bagoas. The Persian boy himself is an anomaly: As a eunuch, he is neither woman nor man; he is mutilated to serve the needs of others, and his own sexuality becomes impossible to determine—had he heterosexual inclinations, he would be unable to consummate them in any conventional way; with a male partner, his role is to give pleasure, not to receive it. His adoration of Alexander is expressed in numerous domestic acts as well as sexual service, and it inspires in the Persian youth jealousy, dedication, reverence, and enduring loyalty, but while Renault can be erotic in her descriptions of their intimacy, Bagoas's love is not finally a function of sexual desire. Only Simonides, the praise singer, the artist, is exclusively heterosexual, yet despite or because of his long partnership with his affectionate servant, the illegitimate Dorothea, he fulfills his sexuality with hetairas and never marries, never begets children of his own.

From the very beginning of her literary career, Renault would not only portray her characters' sexual identities as fluid but would present herself ambiguously to her readers, veiled by her pseudonym. She would tell Sweetman that even the pronunciation of her pen name was a flexible and individual matter. Asked whether the final letters in her chosen surname were to be articulated or silenced, she responded: "It's optional. I always think of it as 'RenauLT' because . . . so many French words have been anglicized, but of course practically everyone calls it 'Ren-O,' and of course they're quite right."[8] In other words, her public identity is indefinite, changeable, a matter of a particular reader's pronunciation (or reading)—incidental and shifting.

Renault chose a number of pseudonyms before settling on the one by which she is now known. Long before Mary and Julie met, Renault was playing with alternative names under which she might write, trial identities that she explored like an actor trying out roles. Julie recalled that "She used all manner of names. Mary Martin was one. . . . This is before she started nursing. . . . She was forever thinking up different names. Mary Rutland was one, but I don't think she ever used it." "Mary Radcliffe" was another possibility, connecting the writer with her nursing self, but she quickly rejected it as too much like "Radclyffe Hall"[9]— too closely identified with lesbian authorship and subject matter, with what to some extent her chosen pseudonym was intended to conceal. Always an individual, Mary was also in search of something distinctive, something "other."

There were immediately pressing reasons to publish under a name that was not her own. Julie confessed that "Mary . . . didn't dare sign her own name to her own work, apart from people knowing at the hospital, she knew her parents wouldn't have liked it." Together, they "thought of hundreds of names. And she chose Renault because it was a name she had used for something she had written earlier but never attempted to have published." This "something she had written earlier" was her medieval romance whose narrative, like

8. Renault, *Omnibus* interview.
9. Mullard, interview by Sweetman, tape 3, side B, and tape 5, side A.

its pseudonym, may well have had its roots in Thomas Otway's play *Venice Preserved* (1682), in which one of the conspirators is called "Renault." Since Otway's traitor, while perhaps admirable in his desire to overthrow the corrupt Senate, is also despicable in his attempted rape of the central female character Belvidera, Mary's choice of his name may seem the result of youthful caprice or even of careless misreading. It seems likely, however, that Mary chose *Renault* at least in part for its pleasant and even foreign sound rather than because of any clear significance called up by an ambiguous character in an ambiguous play, and it also seems possible that this very ambiguity may have attracted her. Later, Mary would merely emphasize the strategic importance of choosing a pseudonym for the publication of her first novel, indicating that in 1939, "I couldn't have gone and written it under my own name and stayed on [in nursing], and of course it was essential that I should go on being able to get nursing jobs because I had no idea I'd ever be able to live on writing."[10]

The pseudonym of "Renault" thus masked her identity as both nurse and her parents' daughter, but as "Mary Renault," it was also a revelation, a sort of coming out. Most obviously, it was an identity that she had consciously fashioned for herself, her identity as an artist, and "under" this name she not only wrote *Purposes of Love* and all her subsequent work, but she firmly inscribed herself for her readers. Further, from her first days at Headington in 1933 until she left nursing thirteen years later, Mary would be known to her medical colleagues by her surname alone or as "Nurse Challans," a relative anonymity that was at once empowering, denoting her clear professional status, and diminishing, as it denied her personality, her individuality, and her identity as a writer. Choosing for herself the name *Mary Renault,* she stressed the difference between the military "Challans" and the creative author, the cloistered nurse in the service of her calling and the iconoclastic young writer.

No matter which of the "hundreds" of pseudonyms she considered, however, she invariably kept the name of Mary, which was, after all, her own name, but also a chosen identity. In being neither *Eileen,* her given name, which she had always felt was rather silly, nor *Molly,* the childhood name associated with home and her years at school and university, *Mary* was her adult name, the fixed name of her familiar and enduring self that transcended the boundaries between private and public.

Mary spent years choosing the right pseudonym, but she seems to have been convinced from the start that a pseudonym would be necessary. The decision

10. Ibid., tape 1, side B; Renault, *Omnibus* interview.

to write as "Mary Renault" resolved the problem of her professional name, but exactly who Mary Renault was remained a more open matter. Mary Renault was defined by the books she wrote, by the fact of having written them; what the books in turn meant might be quite unclear to many of her readers, but her name indisputably established her as their author. When Watling asked her if she were satisfied with the person she had become, she responded by addressing this matter explicitly: "What depths of fatuous self-delusion I'd need for that. My patron saint is Socrates, who spent most of his working life trying to save people from being satisfied with what they thought and were." Renault continued, "As for potential selves, I can imagine myself, if I try, into an extroverted, adventure-seeking person or even a contemplative one, but what has really determined my life, for better or worse, has been the instinct to write, which I've had ever since I was old enough to grasp the fact that books are written by people. Art is limiting."[11] Art was indeed limiting. In Mary's case, it defined her, set limits on what she could be, and forced her to make choices, but she was always clear that she did not regret these choices and in most cases felt enriched by them, as she always felt affirmed in her identity as a writer.

Mary would develop firm views about the nature of writing and would continue to reflect on the creation and the interpretation of art, including literature, throughout her life. Her conviction that art should be not without political implications, but above and beyond politics, informed her sense of artistic responsibility. Prompted by the controversy surrounding attendance at the Nico Malan Theatre, Renault wrote to Colin Spencer that "if a writer thinks he can do more good by suppressing his work than propagating it, no matter to whom, he has signed off as an artist and had better make an honest living selling nylons or something. Shakespeare was put on by people who were burning Catholics alive for nothing but being Catholics, and if he'd said no, there'd be no Shakespeare today." Most simply, a writer's job is to write, to speak his or her mind come what may. Renault was well aware of the potential risks of such expression, and aware, too, that this sort of writing implied an intimate relationship between the author and the work, between the mind and life creating the text and the text itself. Confronted with the political and personal content of her novels, however, Renault could become defensive and self-protective. When Sweetman asked if she saw herself as "a pioneer" in writing about homosexuality in *The Charioteer*, she prickled: "I

11. Renault, *What Life Has Taught Me* interview.

just felt it was a book that needed to be written and it was a book I wanted to write, and that was it." When pushed to comment on why she chose to write about one subject rather than another, about Greece rather than South Africa, she was deceptively simplistic as well as truthful: "One doesn't decide what not to write about, one decides what to write about. . . . [As] Keats said, you know the truth of the heart's imagination. You do what grips you." When encouraged to talk about her choice of controversial sexual material, she dissembled: "I never really think when I am going to write a book of what people are going to do, if they are going to be shocked or anything like that. I just write what I think it should be."[12]

Asked generally about the role of autobiography in writing, Renault responded more revealingly: "I think it's extremely difficult to sort it out. . . . [O]ne hardly knows oneself because what you get, I think, as a result of your childhood is not so much definitely streaks of autobiography that you have to write out of your system (although some authors, of course, do that). . . . [A]ll you have is probably some bias in your character which has been caused by that [past], but which you yourself very likely don't know [about consciously]. . . . You may have inherited it; it may have been calculated." The specific role of autobiography in her own writing was something else again. She discussed the creative process with Rowland Hilder in early 1947: "Rather than retreat from one's psychological limitations into art, I suppose the alternative is to regard them as a problem in construction, the way a Chinese carver does with a fissure in the quartz." She continued, "As for the psychological source of art, that's formidable, far beyond me. The primitive elements, either graphic or poetic, seem to have been wishful conjuration, and worship. Modern psychologists seem to by-pass the latter, but without it I don't know how they explain the desire for truth, order and solution. All that leaves out so much, though, the pleasure of technique and the self-protective element. . . ."[13]

This significant "self-protective element" is a strategy at the core of her work, suggesting her need to encode, to mask and unmask, literally to displace while invariably struggling as well to reveal "truth, order and solution" in ways carefully negotiated aesthetically and psychically. Both Mary and Julie were careful to sidestep any imputation that Renault's novels were anchored in their personal lives. Except for the most obvious elements (for instance, the hospital world in *Purposes of Love* and the homosexual underground

12. Renault to Spencer, June 27, 1965; Renault, *Omnibus* interview.
13. Renault, *Omnibus* interview; Renault to Hilder, undated.

in *The Charioteer*), both women would understandably volunteer very little decoding, very little deconstructive interpretation. Julie, years after Mary's death, would gloss many bits and pieces in Renault's contemporary novels and offer reductive readings of the historical fiction—stating, for instance, that the two male lovers in *The Last of the Wine* were based on "us"—yet declaring that *The Praise Singer,* with a poet at its center, contains no autobiographical material. Renault, in her insistence on the facticity of her later work, would deflect attention from the complicated relation between her historical fiction and her own experience and artistic strategies. Revealing as much as she concealed, she would maintain that "the best way to know a writer is from the books because they really tell you more than they [writers themselves directly] ever can or than they probably even know themselves." Writing to Kathleen Abbott about the significance of delineating life and art, the importance of writing at all costs if one is called to it, and the necessity of avoiding distraction, Renault would also indicate the uncontrollable interpenetration of the two spheres. Encouraging her friend to continue to write poetry, she insisted that "one is not given these talents for nothing. Life and art are meant to be symbiotic, to nourish and support each other, neither of them to swallow the other up. But no two artists need them in just the same proportions—few poets, for instance, could assimilate Byron's masses of doses of life and retain all that creative vigour. It's vital to preserve the delicate balance and not, if you are a contemplative, to clog your system with practicalities and people."[14]

In her own life, Renault would eventually succeed in carefully sequestering her writing from the daily trivia that earlier in her career had "clogged her system." By the time she had settled in Durban and focused her energies on *The Charioteer,* her own approach to her art and her methods of working had developed a pattern to which she adhered until her death. She described the process in detail:

> I always start in pencil on a scribbling pad, and I have an India rubber, and I go over everything . . . till I have roughed out some sort of a sentence. Then I can rub it all out and start again. I don't do very much of that at a time because I usually can't read my own writing if I have left it for too long. As long as I can remember most of it, I can make out the rest, and then I put that on the typewriter, and of course I do a lot of tightening up

14. Mullard, interview by Sweetman, tape 16, side B; Renault, *Omnibus* interview; Renault to Abbott, August 7, 1962.

> in the process. There is something about typing which gives you a tidier mind than when you are just scribbling, and I do that and maybe I see something and alter it—and then I go on and do the next bit the same way. I don't do usually more than a few hundred words a day. Then, when I have got the whole thing together and I have looked back and found a few things that won't do and I have re-written those, then I re-write the entire thing again from beginning to end, and that's the fair copy. . . . I cut vast quantities; I love cutting. I always think I know how I can make it tighter, how I can take this padding out, this bit where I have said the same thing twice over. Cutting is tremendous fun. . . . I usually take out a quarter at least when I am doing the fair copy, and then that's it. The fair copy is the last of it.[15]

Emphasizing the genuine pleasure she so obviously took in technique, Renault also reveals here how much of her art depended on rubbing out, altering, cutting, revising, rewriting. Such careful craft contributed to the elegance of her phrasing and the pace of her narratives, but it also suggests the effort involved in constructing a text in which "the self-protective element" played an important part.

Additionally, this kind of writing required intense concentration in order to achieve the "fair copy," the finished novel, the book that in each case required on average three or more years of work. This fierce attention for Renault involved the "delicate balance" that she mentioned to Kathleen Abbott as well as the creative "pleasure"; her writing would inevitably be a matter both of joy and frustration, of exhilaration and compulsion. The process was complicated by Renault's commitment to historical fiction, a genre that would serve her as acting served Nikeratos in *The Mask of Apollo,* allowing him to assume a strategically masked role for an aesthetic and moral purpose. Significantly, Nikeratos rejects "easy" roles, however "safe" they might be, because "I could have got the effects in my sleep." Instead he seeks a play's most difficult part "because it was something new for me; it was testing; I had thoughts about it; in a word, I had pleased myself. If I was not to break faith . . . and throw my chance away, I had better be good" (*Mask,* 87–88).

Beyond setting a high standard, historical fiction made tremendous demands on Renault, requiring meticulous research as well as a consistently maintained and carefully fashioned public self. Allowing her both a degree

15. Renault, *Omnibus* interview.

of self-protection and the freedom to speak what was otherwise unspeakable, her choice to be this sort of author meant preserving a sharp demarcation between the private self and the literary persona signified by the pseudonym *Mary Renault.* In the novel's terms, a mask is necessary to the artist, because "to strip one's own face to the crowd, as if it were all happening to one's self instead of to Oidipos or Priam; one would need a front of brass to bear it. One knows, as one plays, that behind the mask one's face is speaking, as it must if one feels at all; but that's one's own secret. . . ." (*Mask,* 99–100).

By the 1950s, Renault had developed the scholarly approach that would anchor her writing historically and allow her the independence and creativity she also needed. At some distance from the archives on which the academic classicist might need to rely, she developed the methods her fiction required, although she could make the "hard work" seem easier than it of course was. "As far as research is concerned," she told Sweetman, "one is lucky with books about Greece because practically anything of any importance is available. You don't have to go ferreting about getting medieval manuscripts and incunabulae and so on; you can just get the Loeb edition, and practically everything is in it. Apart, of course, from the ancillary things about art and archeology, . . . you don't have to go to a library, and I just gradually bought [books] as I needed them and built my library up." Indeed, she confessed, "I can never work by going to a library and scribbling down a lot of notes. It's all the details that matter—the way somebody spoke, all the little things about personality—that's what you have to have. I mean, facts by themselves are just no good at all."[16]

Here Renault vividly echoes what Virginia Woolf emphasized about the gendered nature of scholarship, the "truth" she discusses in *A Room of One's Own.* Men, especially those trained at Oxbridge, could easily scribble copious notes in libraries, mining the "ore" of dusty tomes in order to extract the "nugget" of "pure" knowledge at their core, then display it for public admiration "on the mantelpiece forever." But such truth or knowledge was dry and sterile, an exercise in formulaic scholarship of just the sort that Renault deplored in her own formal education. In contrast, it is the important details of human experience that Woolf's narrator and Renault are after, details that they—as self-educated women—are perhaps particularly well qualified to discover. Such research makes use of both public and, especially, private libraries but must also rely on direct observation and the evidence of one's

16. Ibid.

own life, be this information gathered at Oxbridge meals or in Chloe's and Olivia's laboratory, at English hospitals or from one's own relationships. Only through such investigation can one discover the significance of the Manx cat or "the little things about personality."[17]

Renault would have had Woolf's full support for her statement that "facts by themselves are just no good at all," and logically visual evidence was as important for Renault as literary material. The written record, she insisted, "tells you in a very large way what was going on, what motivated people, what kind of people even they were, but for how they lived you have to go to quite other sources." She emphasized that all Greek art was tremendously important to her, but vase painting was most useful. Greek sculpture was heroic, even if "emotion wasn't ever depicted until later in the Hellenistic era," but "every single detail of their daily lives practically you find in a vase painting. This is absolutely invaluable: you know the places they washed in; you know the fountains, the kind of vessels they used, the wine cups they drank from. Since you know roughly the period of any vase, you know . . . the right time." For example, Renault pointed out that, in *The Praise Singer,* "I had this fashionable hetaira, and I found that at this period, they all had their hair done up in little turbans . . . made of embroidery, and they would at other times have their hair hanging down. All these little details are fascinating."[18]

In these descriptions of her working methods, Renault reveals her unmistakable joy in discovering "all the details that matter," her exhilaration in finding out about "the places they washed in," "the kind of vessels they used, the wine cups they drank from," and the "little turbans," but such intense research and writing took their emotional toll. They made Renault's self-imposed seclusion and concentration all the more necessary. Rewriting was not only a matter of fine-tuning a sentence; it often involved the wholesale destruction of first chapters and necessitated beginning all over again and approaching her material from a different angle. To Cecil Roberts, an older writer of historical fiction whose work she admired, Renault confessed her need to focus all of her energy when writing, for "I work so slowly, and am so easily thrown off by interruption."[19]

It was in large measure because of this commitment to her work that, after the second trip to Greece, Julie and Mary would take very few holidays

17. Ibid.; Virginia Woolf, *A Room of One's Own,* 3–4, 28, 11, 13.

18. Renault, *Omnibus* interview.

19. Renault to Cecil Roberts, February 1, 1976, quoted by permission of the Archive Centre at Churchill College, Cambridge University

and none far from South Africa. Julie described the situation: "Mary was full of what she had to get done. . . . She had this tremendous feeling and frustration about the time she had wasted. . . ." Mary even came to feel that she had wasted time, over a decade, while nursing. Julie continued: "I could feel in her all the time the phrase, 'I must get on.' 'I must get on' was on her lips all the time." There were occasions, of course, when Mary enjoyed relaxing, reading, going to the theater, but she was also driven to write, going downstairs to her study to write a bit more even after returning, exhausted, from an evening out.[20]

Writing had not initially seemed such a demanding vocation, and as far back as she could remember, Mary had thought of herself as a writer. She had always imagined she would earn her own living, and "wanted to be a writer," although it took her "a long time to realise that you could actually be paid for writing." This transition from fantasy to reality, from desire to practice, from imagined to actualized self, is reflected in the development of her work from girlhood to maturity. Her earliest stories and poems were at once original efforts and conventional narratives derived from her reading and dependent on the principles she had learned at school. In a letter to Colin Spencer, Mary addressed the problem of the tension between the artist's vision and social restrictions. Just as "Christ was passionately concerned with elementary survival rules for the soul, and would be exasperated beyond words by the pettifogging by-laws which have been fathered off on him by bureaucratic minds," the artist, too, must struggle against institutional repression. Thus "a painter has to receive his visual impressions as a little child, before he starts to organise," grounding art in "that absolute freshness of perception" that Jesus demanded of his followers when he asked them to seek the kingdom of God like little children, not naively, but with "the concentration children bring to experience before habit drugs them, and their amazingly direct recognition of justice, kindness, honesty, and of course their converses." Here Renault opposes the artistic impulse—which is unique, moral, fresh, and concentrated if also unorganized—to the social conventions that work against creativity. Her literary development reflects her struggle to defy such institutional expectations and to achieve expression that was both mature and a reflection of the moral self, the soul. This moral element was intimately related for Renault to the problem of self-expression, which required complex literary strategies, among them her choice of the historical novel, with its apparent

20. Mullard, interview by Sweetman, tape 15, side A, and tape 17, side A.

distance between author and subject. Thus she responded characteristically to the news that Bryher was writing her war memoirs: "I don't think I would ever have the courage to write mine. Not I mean that they would reveal, however complete, anything sensational, but the effort of judging oneself must be so great."[21]

Renault's earliest literary efforts were romantic fantasies, "very soppy sorts of things . . . fairy stories and things like that." She used to write in a small notebook in a loft over an unused stable at the back of her house, and the first completed narrative she recalled was a western written when she was eight years old. Here are the roots of Leo as the author of pulp fiction, the young woman who writes to escape reality, who produces "the sort of thing a lively but unintellectual man might write for boys" (*FYL,* 89). This type of popular, formulaic narrative erases the self, fulfilling a convention that Renault had carefully learned. Discussing style with Bryher, she wondered, " . . . were you taught at school never to start a letter with 'I'? I was; it now strikes me as a notable example of neglecting the spirit for the letter." Mary had been taught to write well by particular standards and simultaneously to behave herself properly (as a child, as a girl, as a woman) through public self-effacement. Brought up on traditional writers like Kipling, she had no desire to write like Joyce; like Leo, she had read boys' adventure stories: "I always identified with the boys and I always thought the girls are always somehow tagging on. . . ."[22] But she would become a writer like Joe nonetheless, a writer who thinks and prepares carefully before beginning because she " 'feels too strongly about things at the time to get them fair,' " a writer whose success would depend in part on her ability to draw on her own experiences (*FYL,* 104, 134, 257).

The process of writing longhand, then revising on the typewriter—rewriting and retyping towards the final "fair copy"—began as early as her days at St. Hugh's when she acquired a secondhand typewriter from a university classmate, but her contemporary novels, with the exception of *Purposes of Love* and *The Charioteer,* seemed less than satisfactory when she looked back on them. For one thing, they had not received the attention they deserved. She confessed to Sue MacGregor that she thought "the books I wrote during the war were all a bit superficial because I didn't have the time to sit down and think or, of course, even to consider doing research for anything historical

21. Renault, *Woman's Hour* interview; Renault to Spencer, April 3, 1963; Renault to Bryher, December 22, 1969.

22. Renault, *Omnibus* interview; Renault to Bryher, December 27, 1970.

because that's about a year's work before you start to write." Renault added, "I don't think I was writing as well as I could have done if I had had my time to myself." There were other problems as well, and she repeatedly dismissed these novels as "boring," even going so far as to call *Return to Night* "pure escapism." Julie would be more specific: By the time she had found her voice as a historical novelist, "that whole situation, those boy-girl situations bored her."[23]

The Charioteer would be a transitional novel not only in subject matter, historical setting, and Platonic allusions but also in technique. In her earlier fiction Renault had shaped her plots in a limited present, relying on flashbacks and on information provided through characters' conversations after the fact in order to elucidate confusion and create dramatic tension. Previously Renault had suggested some mystery, often implied as sexual, just beneath the surface, about her characters' backgrounds. Frequently there were two mysteries, two characters with unusual pasts, one male, one female. The plot then became twofold: How would each character confront his or her own past and deal with it? And how would the other character accept the past and heal his or her counterpart? Plot, in other words, became a sort of trick, as the author withheld information from the reader and perhaps also from her characters' own conscious awareness and certainly from other characters. The denouement became one of revelation, confrontation, acceptance, and affirmation. In contrast, in *The Charioteer* she approached her subject as she would in all her later books, as a *Bildungsroman,* a biography, and began with Laurie's boyhood. This structure focuses the novel immediately and securely on a central character, solving the problem of vacillating or confused focus recurrent in her earlier work while forcing the author to consider point-of-view as an important issue.

From the start, Renault's books also depended on narrative, a strong and exciting story line through which she explores her ideas. This emphasis on narrative occasionally results, particularly in her early novels but even in such a fine work as *The Charioteer,* in creaky plots and stagy coincidences or conventions, yet it is invariably narrative that saves her work from becoming a static study of psychological angst (in which her early characters are especially prone to engage) and from the philosophical stasis of authorial intrusion or problematic irresolution. Strong narrative is an obvious element that links the contemporary and historical novels. The blatant material explicitly

23. Mullard to Sweetman, December 19, 1990; Renault *Woman's Hour* interview; Renault, *Omnibus* interview; Mullard, interview by Sweetman, tape 10, side A.

struggled with in the early novels anticipates the achievement of the later novels, in which so much is transformed, displaced, and masked, but all of Renault's books recount in some measure love stories that depend on romantic relationships between characters who strive to discover and adhere to worthy ideals and to realize their own identities.

She also develops, over the course of her career, her own coded universe, evident in the techniques that link all of her novels, suggesting that indeed there is less of a split between the two modes than one might think. For example, from the time of *Purposes of Love,* "my dear," used between men, signals homosexual revelation, self-declaration, and intimacy and functions in this way in *The Charioteer* and even in her Greek novels in which, amid otherwise credible and natural conversation, the term stands out as especially modern and English, typical of Renault. Thus in *The Last of the Wine,* Lysis calls Alexias "my dear" as he reassures him about his confused affection towards his stepmother and again when he counsels him to drink less wine as they compete in play after dinner, then turn serious and resolve their differences in physical love (*Last,* 103, 224). Later, having survived a serious naval defeat, Alexias and Lysis discuss the inevitability of death, the passage of time, and the duration of war. Finally, Lysis quotes "a certain phrase, recalling a personal matter between us" and suggests to the younger man, calling him "my dear," that individual perceptions shape one's experience (284). Still later, comforting and distracting Alexias in mourning for his father, Lysis holds out his hand and urges him to leave for Thebes: "Come, my dear . . ." (355). The endearment serves in this novel to indicate the lovers' intimacy as well Lysis's status as the older and wiser partner, but it is primarily a signal of homosexual relationship. For instance, the gay sculptor Chremon, tight with money and offensively familiar with his male models, positions Alexias by taking his waist "between his thick hands," calling him "my dear" as he instructs him (313).

Many of these implications are called up and extended by the same phrase as it occurs in *The Mask of Apollo.* Thus Nikeratos as the more able actor addresses the flamboyant Anaxis as "my dear," reminding him of their shared profession and sexual orientation in a effort to restrain him (*Mask,* 86, 89). Similarly, in a spirit of camaraderie, Nikeratos speaks to his fellow actors when they lose a commission because of their patron's death, " 'Well, my dears. That's the theatre' " (104). Nikeratos regularly calls his lesser colleague Menekrates "my dear" (120, 196, 198, 204), and in gay repartee the gregarious Theodoros, for whom "No one in the business had a bad word," enthuses to Nikeratos after a performance, " 'My dear! Superb! It killed me to miss the end, I was almost too late to dress. . . . I sat there, my dear, . . . quite hating you for having that lovely role and knowing what to do with it. But I had to give in like all the rest. . . . May I come to your party? A married woman, dear, even though forsaken. A girl from the country needs a chaperon, among all these horrid men.' " Such camp effusion is both playfully affectionate and carefully encoded communication; Nikeratos comments: "I knew enough to be honoured by this foolery. His dignity could be freezing; he stood no nonsense from the richest of sponsors, nor, I believe, from kings. He kept this kind of thing for equals" (220). Between lovers, the endearment indicates arch loftiness, amused posing, sincere affection. When the gifted younger actor Thettalos, Nikeratos's lover, begs to accompany him to Syracuse—" 'Please, Niko, take me to Sicily' " he pleads, with his arm across the older man's knees—their exchange is at once serious and playful, and Nikeratos counsels his friends, " 'Don't tempt me, my dear' " (250–51), before inevitably conceding. Again, it is in part through his employment of "my dear" that Nikeratos sensibly instructs the misguided Thettalos not to play the role of Thersites sympathetically (269). When later, despite evidence to the contrary, Nikeratos tries to maintain his delusion that Dion is heroic, it is the more realistic Thettalos, protecting and enlightening his lover, who turns the tables and calls him "my dear" (351).

Having invested this phrase with such a variety of meanings—indicating affection, power relations, and both serious playfulness and playful seriousness—Renault can use it as a code for revealing the complex and multiple sexual transgression going on when, during the civil chaos after the fall of Syracuse, Axiothea agrees to flee with Nikeratos under the guise of being his boyfriend. She has reached Sicily by masquerading as a male youth, but then, as the crew sprouted beards, "they had taken her for a eunuch, which she had had to confirm and bear the sailors' jokes." On shipboard, her sex could not be biologically determined and her gender depended not on her sex nor on her choice of cultural signifiers (hair, clothing, mannerisms, language) but on the imputation of despised others on whose misperceptions she needed to rely for her own safely. Once on land again, she is alone and understandably frightened amid "the soldiers, the beggars, the young drunks coming from the wine-shops, the agents who canvassed her for their factions, the pimps offering her girls or boys," expecting "to be caught out and stoned" for her erasure of her female sex, her feminine status. When she meets Nikeratos, her identity shifts once more, for she is as glad to see him "as a friendless child its mother"; she is the ungendered child while Nikeratos becomes female, "its mother."

Apprising her of the unstable political and social situation, Nikeratos calls her "my dear," as if they were both gay men, and when Axiothea apparently confirms their relation by referring to him as " 'dear Niko,' " he responds, as if their sexual relationship were now settled and clear (which, of course, it is not), " 'That's better. You never called me that before' " (*Mask,* 318–19). If their relationship is erotically charged (as indeed it is), they will not be two gay men, older actor and youthful boyfriend (the parts they choose here, the roles in which they will appear to others, the relationship they at first think they have established), but they will become heterosexual lovers, biologically defined in heterosexual intercourse despite their respective homosexual orientations.

When Nikeratos and Thettalos meet in Pella towards the end of *Fire from Heaven,* their relationship is immediately recalled and reestablished for the reader when Thettalos, confessing his shock at Philip's cruelty and his pity for the young Alexander, says to his lover with a sincerity embedded in camp and effeminate exaggeration, " 'My dear, I bled for the boy' " (*Fire,* 367). The phrase continues to have a special significance: In *The Persian Boy,* Alexander calls Bagoas "my dear" (*PB,* 140, 152, 156) or even "my dear boy" (160), while in contrast Hephaistion calls Alexander "my love" (153). It is through Anakreon's use of "my dear" when speaking to Simonides in *The Praise Singer* that he at once signals his own homosexuality and their shared integrity (*PS,* 59, 223, 238). Reflecting on his worthy colleague, Simonides reveals the depth of respect in their friendship: "But different men as we were and different artists, we had some things in common. I have never come to want in my calling, I am glad to say; but I have gone where my work was liked as I chose to do it. Neither he nor I were like robe-makers to whom anyone can say, 'Cut it this size and trim it so' " (60). Such a deceptively minor element as this endearment thus indicates the overriding unity of Renault's work, the continuities in the human experience she explored; it is an insider's cue to the fictional world that stretches from Mic to Anakreon, from Vivian through Axiothea.

Renault's art, while unified, continues to develop after she establishes her identity as a historical novelist. Art itself as a subject grows increasingly central, eventually surpassing even sexuality as an important issue in the late work. For example, *The Last of the Wine* is not only Renault's first "Greek" novel, but the first in which she uses a first-person narrator, and Alexias is finally a writer, the protagonist who tells his own story in his own voice. Alexias carefully and consciously filters his narrative, drawing our attention to his control of the record, emphasizing his role as the artist who selects for a purpose. Thus "authorial" intrusion often interrupts the story, for instance at the end of a chapter ("This is all I have to relate of the Isthmian festival . . ." [*Last,* 195]), or when Alexias censors his account, refusing "out of respect to the dead" to set down his father's rude remarks about Socrates (205) or, from a sense of decorum based on gender, to reveal details of Thalia's later life (373). Renault finally stresses Alexias's role as writer when she employs the effective if rather hackneyed device of disclosing at the end of the novel, in the voice of yet another writer, that the account was a book "found among the papers of my father Myron, . . . the work of my grandfather Alexias . . ." (382).

In Bagoas, who tells his own but primarily Alexander's story in *The Persian Boy,* Renault offers us a more complex first-person narrator who is both insider and outsider, court intimate and Persian, Alexander's lover and a eunuch. Bagoas's documentary record, the most personal account that history might have had of Alexander, is spurious, is in fact Renault's own creation (Renault gives Bagoas a voice and is to a degree herself the Persian boy, the author of Alexander's life as recounted in this novel). But in her author's note, Renault logically suggests that Curtius, one of her most useful sources, may have drawn upon a firsthand account, no longer extant, written "it is reasonable to suppose by Bagoas himself," which, she surmises, "must have been known to all Alexander's contemporary historians" (*PB,* 409).

All of Renault's subsequent books would be first-person accounts except for *Fire from Heaven* and *Funeral Games.* While the huge cast of characters, broad geographical sweep, and episodic structure of the last novel in the Alexander trilogy probably determined her choice of a third-person omniscient point of view for this book, nevertheless her final emphasis even here is on Ptolemy's record, on Ptolemy as writer, on the problem of inscribing history, on biography, the known life, in which what is unwritten becomes ephemeral and what is written endures as the truth. Thus her last chapter is set in King Ptolemy's "book-room" overlooking the harbor at Alexandria, at the moment when the monarch, nearly the only one of Alexander's boyhood friends still alive, has just finished his history. The novel's final image is of the aging writer, gathering "the new tablets together with shaky but determined hands," and setting them "neatly in order" for the scribes.[24]

In many ways, Simonides, the first and last of Renault's protagonists to be explicitly and above all an artist, is of all her characters the one who comes closest to her writing self. Nikeratos, with his charm and gay vivacity, is an

24. Mary Renault, *Funeral Games,* 271. Hereafter all references to this novel will be cited parenthetically in the text as *FG.*

actor, not a playwright; an artist-interpreter, not the original creator of the figures he portrays. While he takes pride in his creativity, in the "fact" that a skillful player who believes in his performance "can make an audience see nearly anything" (*Mask,* 24), he is aware of his limitations. Impressed by his first experience of Delphi, he confesses his inadequacy: "Ask some poet to describe the awe of Delphi, and some philosopher to explain it. I work with the words of other men" (35). Like Renault in her choice of the historical novel, Nikeratos is dependent on his sources, a performer speaking from a mask, defined by the texts through which he is represented, but Renault is finally much more than an actor; drawing on her research, her language is always her own, never "the words of other men." Simonides, as one of the last Greek poets to work primarily in an oral tradition, links the past with the present of the narrative through his prodigious memory of Homer and other poets, other "praise singers," while through the inscription of his verse by his protégé, the young Bacchylides, Simonides' own poetry is preserved for the future. More personally, the novel is Simonides' memory, recounted through his own voice in old age, of his life—from his boyhood on the island of Keos through his achievement as court poet in late-sixth- and early-fifth-century Athens to his retirement in Sicily at the age of eighty-three. Sweetman wondered at Renault's choice of protagonist, finding it "odd," since Simonides was, in contrast to Alexander, both heterosexual and ugly, and "even stranger" since "the ancient poets were essentially singers," while all of Renault's friends agreed that "she was not musical."[25] But *The Praise Singer* is not about musical composition; it is about creativity, verbal expression, audience, the selection of subject matter, and the development of literary technique, and it tells the life of a man Renault identifies in her list of characters as a "Heroic, dithyrambic and lyric poet," an "Author" (*PS,* 292). Through his voice, the voice of a man who loved women, whose artistic achievement does not depend on his physical attributes or his appearance, whose subject matter is both contemporary life and the past, including myth and history, Renault ironically came closer to speaking in her own voice than in any of her other books.

The novel begins with Simonides at the moment when he has just finished a poem. He muses: "A good song, I think. . . . The boy will need to write it, I suppose, as well as hear it. Trusting to the pen. . . . So what can I do, unless I'm to be remembered only by what's carved in marble?" (*PS,* 3). When Themistokles wondered if he had "a secret art of memory," Simonides

25. Sweetman, *Mary Renault,* 282.

responded much as did Renault herself when asked by trivializing interviewers how she came to know such a great deal about the ancient world: "Practice, practice, that's all; but who wants to hear nowadays about hard work?" (4). His discovery of a possible public future for his poetic gifts echoes Renault's own account of her slow realization not that she was a writer (she and Simonides have both known their creative natures since their solitary childhoods) but that she might make a career as an author. At the Apollo festival, at the age of "nine or ten," Simonides hears poets reciting and notes, "For the first time, I knew that my secret joy was a thing grown men could make a life of, even a living" (7). Like Renault, Simonides comes from a family who cannot understand his desire to be a poet; his father especially disapproves, wanting him to become a traditional farmer. Simonides needs instruction and is blessed with a good teacher in Kleobis, but like Renault he must serve a rough apprenticeship, doing menial labor (carrying the lyre and the baggage of the troubadour through the countryside) and caring physically for his master's first helper and later for his master himself. Simonides, like Renault, is a skilled and knowledgeable nurse, warning Kleobis against poison berries as a cure for fever (22) and throughout his life trusting from experience not in doctors with their arbitrary rules but in his own good sense and "the local wise woman" (28). When his nephew is bitten by a scorpion, Simonides notes that "weeping in pain," he "would let no one touch it, only asking for me. He was right, in that ignorant village; I nicked the wound and sucked it, bound it with a cloth wrung out in hot water mixed with myrrh, as a Euboian herb-wife had taught me" (235).

As a young man, Simonides feels awkward about his sexuality, seeing himself as uniquely unlikable because he is dark and hairy, reflecting in words with which Renault must have sympathized, "In those years, I hardly knew I was made like other men. I had married my art. . . ." Simonides is ashamed of his appearance and has no need to "master" his desires (*PS*, 34); fear of rejection and scorn keep him chaste until he is liberated by finally losing his virginity with an affirming hetaira, "a true Ephesian, heavy-breasted, with a skin like thickened cream" (43). The physical unattractiveness that makes the adolescent self-conscious recalls the discomfort Mic and Laurie, for instance, feel about their transgressive sexuality, the discomfort Renault as a young woman may have felt about her lesbian desires. But Simonides' difficulty is resolved in the mature poet, who comes to accept his appearance as he fulfills himself with individual female partners. As a result of developing her protagonist as a psychologically well-adjusted heterosexual man, Renault is able to deemphasize (homo)sexuality as an issue and to focus on art as this novel's central subject. Further, as in the case of Theseus, the voice of the heterosexual Simonides also allows Renault to describe female bodies erotically, and we follow him into bed with Dorothea and with his favorite mistress, the hetaira Lyra. Through Simonides Renault will offer her readers some of her most intimate love scenes, which, while occasionally explicit, derive their charm from the affectionate conversations that occur over wine and among the cushions.

In fact, art in this novel is insistently female, as in the metaphor Renault attributes to the sculptor Theodoros's apprentice, who says about the casting of a figure: " 'It's like childbirth. . . . You know what went in at the start, but you don't know what will come out' " (*PS,* 69). In turn, Lyra's name itself suggests the lyre, the instrument and symbol of the praise singer's art, to which Simonides is indeed "married." Simonides echoes Joe's view of art, which is also Renault's—"Praise-singing is like love. . . . You do it from the heart or you're a whore" (95)—and he amplifies, in words Renault might well have used in defense of her own subject matter: "Like every poet, I have sold my praises, in the sense that I've been paid for them; but, like Lyra with her lovers, I want freedom to pick and choose" (239).

Above all, Renault uses this novel to convey her artistic ideals. Thus she contrasts the admirable Anakreon with the offensive Hipponax, the abusive satirist who despises women and whose work is inspired by envy, whose negative example teaches Simonides that "All men seek esteem; the best by lifting themselves, which is hard to do, the rest by shoving others down, which is much easier" (*PS,* 39–40). Here again Renault privileges art that is "hard" over that which is "easy" and people who succeed on their own merits over those whose success depends on the denigration of others. Firmly situating art within a moral realm, Simonides insists that, unlike artists, "Politicians always prefer the useful to the true" (206), and declares, in words that resonate poignantly in the context of Renault's own life, that artists cannot work in an oppressive society: "Tell a man what he may not sing, and he is still half free; even all free, if he never wanted to sing it. But tell him what he *must* sing, take up his time with it so that his true voice cannot sound even in secret—there, I have seen, is slavery" (60).

The overarching mood of *The Praise Singer* ultimately derives from the tenderness of memory as Simonides looks back over his life as an artist, repeatedly interrupting the narrative so that the reader is always conscious of the gifted old man whose active work, like his passionate love life, are behind him. For example, remembering his jealousy of a "javelin-thrower" who slept with Lyra after a particularly impressive athletic display, Simonides remarks that at the time, "I lay awake; he was a handsome fellow, whom I knew she wanted; I guessed he was learning more about the management of his javelin than he'd ever known." Then the elderly poet intrudes: "Well, it is all gone by. Aphrodite herself could not raise my old spear now, and I can scarcely recall the rage of that wakeful night. Yet her beauty lives for me as clear as ever, her room with its treasures, her laugh, her friendship. Often, still, I find myself thinking, I must tell Lyra that" (*PS*, 183). Lyra is physically but not mentally absent, actually dead but emotionally alive as the ideal audience for Simonides' words, gone from the world but eternally present in his (Renault's) narrative. Finally, art endures, not only one's individual art, but the vast historical sweep of human artistic expression of which any singular work is an inextricable part. Art, in other words, is anchored in time, both a product of its unique maker at a particular time and a text that transcends that time to speak to any present audience. Thus, speaking of Homer, Simonides explains that "He is for all time. . . . But only his own time could have begotten him. He is a god to me, yet my own time made me otherwise; and time has taught me that I have my own things to say" (175). Conscious that she, too, had her "own things to say," Renault would use her historical material not only to comment on the past but to speak about her own time, her own experience, her own art.

n i n e

Women 1975–1983

When Renault finished *The Praise Singer* in 1978, she was seventy-three years old, still energetic and actively writing; ahead of her lay the powerful conclusion of the Alexander trilogy, *Funeral Games,* as well as the untitled novel that she began in 1981, on which she would work for the rest of her life. But important changes in the tenor of her world in Camps Bay had occurred since the return from Greece in 1962. Not only had racial tensions in South Africa made political problems an issue in her daily life as well as in her work, but also a number of incidents closer to home had made her acutely conscious of her own mortality and of the vulnerability of her partnership with Julie.

Illnesses and accidents reminded the two women of their aging bodies in poignant ways. As trained nurses, they were accustomed to taking such matters in stride, familiar with doctors and hospitals and medication, but to deal with the body in personal terms was rather different for both of them. When Mary was hit by a motorbike while crossing the street in April 1967, she described the experience to a range of correspondents in varying degrees of physical detail but in each case with humor and detachment, insisting on her own resilience while also revealing her concern for Julie. She recounted the "drama" three weeks later to Jay Williams. She and Julie had gone to get their hair done, but Mary had gone off on her own for a bit because "I can spend hours buying clothes, while Julie loses patience and gives it up if she can't find what she wants in 5 minutes." She recalled being about to cross the road, but "The rest is amnesia with glimpses, like a Venetian blind. I remember a violent physical shock, not painful but astonishing. Then I was lying in the road and saw some gaping faces, and thought, 'I have been in an accident';

quite flatly, without apprehension or anything. Someone took my hand and held it kindly. . . ." She recalled thinking " 'This is important' " and described telling one of the people helping her "which hair-dresser's Julie would be at, and her name, and asking him to ring them." Then she remembered being taken to "some surgery and then being X-rayed. Of course I knew it was an X-ray room because I've seen so many. . . . There was a pad all soaked in blood under my head, and I thought how messy I'd made my hand. And I remember telling the radiographer who was doing me that I knew about head injuries, I'd done them in the war, and I might be passing out presently with intra-cranial bleeding . . . so before this happened would she mind taking a name and an address for me, and gave them her all over again. I felt very practical about all this." Suffering from a concussion and a cracked rib, Mary waited for treatment, but " . . . my nose kept running and I wondered if it was cerebro-spinal fluid running away, which is the sort of thing that would occur only to someone who'd worked on a neuro-surgical ward. Then I felt in my ears, which of course were full of blood, but only from the scalp-wound, only I couldn't tell that. . . . I thought 'Perhaps I shall die,' but the thought did not move me." Then "Julie appeared and I was awfully pleased to see her." Mary finally concluded, "Poor Julie, *she* had had the drive out there not knowing what she'd find, and when she did get let in to see me they'd not cleaned me up and I was bloody all over under a heap of gray blanket."[1]

A month later, Mary recounted her "odd sort of time" to Kathleen Abbott, stressing again her dislocation and professional understanding as well as reiterating her feelings for Julie: "I was able to feel the greatest pleasure at seeing her. . . . Poor Julie, she really had the worst of it. . . . Of course she kept quite calm and was wonderful, and it made all the difference having her there." Because Julie was a trained nurse, the hospital released Mary in her care. The severe dizziness soon passed as did her aches and bruises, but the cracked rib would bother her for several weeks, and she had to keep it "well bound up by buying those awful 'long-line' bras which grip you down to the middle, meant to give waists to ladies with spare tyres."[2] Mary's sense of humor, her medical practicality, and her calm acceptance of physical distress as well as the inevitable (whatever it might be) are all characteristic elements in her response to her injury; her narrative also reveals, however, her simultaneous concern for "Poor Julie."

1. Renault to Williams, May 18, 1967.
2. Renault to Abbott, June 17, 1967.

When Julie developed a tumor in her breast later the same year, the two women were understandably troubled but accepted medical intervention as a matter of course. Julie discovered the lump on Christmas Eve and, as Mary wrote Kathleen Abbott, " . . . of course we knew there are various kinds of benign tumor you can have there, and the signs pointed to this being one; but it was a horrible shock, even to us who know plenty of women who actually did have cancer, running about quite well many years later after a timely operation." Unable to arrange surgery until after the holiday, they went ahead with a large party they had planned, that "did distract our minds quite a lot from the impending operation, which was of course a certainty whether it was benign or not; such things always have to come out." Fortunately, the biopsy revealed that the tumor "was quite innocent, which was a huge relief," and the doctor "was able to leave most of the breast intact with a very small scar which we'll hardly notice."[3] This aesthetic detail, shared with a female friend to whom she had felt comfortable mentioning, in a less solemn way, a long-line bra, was obviously important to her as well as to Julie.

More serious than Julie's benign lump was Mary's situation in April 1970. Julie wrote to Kathleen Abbott in May to explain that Mary had just had a hysterectomy: "She was perfectly fit and well one day, saw her doctor the next, and by good luck and clever management had her operation twenty four hours later. I am very glad indeed that she had it right away, it would be horrible having to sit around waiting for it." Julie insisted that Mary was "making a wonderful recovery. She can walk well, does full knee bend and all that. In fact she is fine, but she does get very easily tired. . . . To my great surprise she is not worrying about work or writing letters. This is a great relief to me as letter writing is just the sort of concentration that can quickly wear you out. . . . Oh, I forgot to tell you, the reason for the operation was that she had three fibroids." Here Julie reveals her own state as much as Mary's, who is "fine" although "tired" three weeks after her surgery. Julie had anticipated a "horrible" wait; she is surprised and greatly relieved that Mary is not worrying about work; she is forgetful in her explanation. Mary herself described the operation as "this bit of trouble," "just a precautionary job," although she experienced the postoperative tiredness and lethargy for a considerable period, writing even five months later that she was "enjoying the feeling of feeling daily less tired; fatigue for some months is the regular thing after a hysterectomy, everyone warned me to expect it; but the most tiresome thing is that it's not only physical

3. Renault to Abbott, January 10, 1968.

but mental, and in the first month or two one gets the dispiriting impression that one will never summon up the necessary concentration to write again." Mary also stressed to friends that Julie "looked after me wonderfully when I got home."[4]

Actually, the situation was more grave than Mary knew. When she had suddenly started to bleed profusely while walking the dogs on the beach with Julie, it was obvious that she would need immediate treatment. During the operation, the doctors discovered a malignant tumor, but Julie decided not to inform Mary, whose persistent fatigue was due as much to the drugs that she needed to take for nearly a year as to the surgery itself. Julie's decision forced her into a position of protecting Mary not only from knowing about the cancer but from recognizing the nature of the pills and injections that followed. Mary apparently thought they were only—as some of them must have been—hormone replacement therapy, while Julie carefully hid packets and wrappers and struggled emotionally with her solitary knowledge of Mary's health and with the subterfuge her secrecy entailed.[5]

By 1971, Mary felt much better. In April of that year she wrote to Jay Williams that after months of general tiredness and mental malaise about starting to work again, "suddenly the impetus came back with a rush, combined with a frightful sense of all the time I'd wasted; I dashed into it headlong, to the exclusion of nearly everything else. . . ." Then, in early October 1974, she fell on the hillside above "Delos" and broke her ankle quite badly, a situation finally more difficult for Julie than for Mary. The break itself was a compound fracture in five places and required over three months in a cast. Three weeks after the injury, she was not yet able to return to her desk and wrote longhand to Bernard Dick about the "unimaginable disorganization of one's life" that follows such an immobilizing accident. In November she was finally able to type a letter to Kathleen Abbott to say that she was "marooned in delightful surroundings but still marooned, for another 8 weeks or so; and poor Julie more or less marooned with me, because it's not a walking plaster, and the difficulties of doing the simplest things have to be experienced to be believed. . . . I navigate on my typing stool [with swivel castors], which is a most handy means of locomotion, especially if one goes backwards, pushing

4. Mullard to Abbott, May 22, 1970; Renault to Abbott, June 15, 1970; Renault to Williams, July 1, 1970; Renault to Abbott, October 5, 1970, and May 15, 1970.

5. Julie mentions several times her deception and her distress about it in her interviews with David Sweetman, tape 9, side B; and tapes 12, 13, and 14.

with the good foot." By February 1975, Mary was beginning to move about on her own, but recovery was long and awkward. She wrote to Jay Williams about her frustration: "The bone is all right, but after that long immobilisation the muscles take a lot of working into shape again. . . . I have progressed via crutches and two sticks to one stick, but pottering about on that makes me feel about 90."[6]

Julie had nursed Mary conscientiously while continuing to worry secretly about Mary's health. The broken ankle and its slow healing meant that Julie was now not only seeing to the routine domestic business of their life but insistently taking on additional secretarial chores, often serving as Mary's amanuensis as well as fetching and carrying for her less mobile friend. By April, Julie was clearly taking on too much and had become seriously depressed. Mary was naturally very concerned and, as Sweetman recounts, their family doctor arranged to have Julie admitted to a private clinic for a course of electric shock treatments. Julie would experience "occasional relapses, but they were now forewarned, and at the outset of a bout of depression Julie could quickly enter the clinic for medication and psychiatric care, which helped shorten the attacks, even though it did not prevent them."[7] From this point on, physical and psychic health would become a real concern for both women.

Mary and Julie had the support of a small circle of close friends developed over the years since they had settled in Africa. While Mary was more or less cut off from an intellectual literary circle, her extensive correspondence with other authors partially compensated. Yet Mary had never sought out a literary set; even in Oxford in the late thirties, Julie would stress that Mary had little contact with "other people" beyond her hospital coworkers and "knew no other writers." Renault herself revealed to Sweetman in 1982 that she did not belong to any sort of literary community in Cape Town; she was, by choice and by chance, isolated from other serious writers.[8]

Their friends accepted them on their own terms, most of them now recognizing their lesbian partnership without question, although some people saw it as an unconventional union beyond their direct experience. John MacGregor's response was typical. As an Oxford physician on the Radcliffe staff, he had come to know both women in the early 1940s. He recalled a

6. Renault to Williams, April 13, 1971; Renault to Dick, October 28, 1974; Renault to Abbott, November 9, 1974; Renault to Williams, February 21, 1975.

7. Sweetman, *Mary Renault,* 278.

8. Mullard, interview by Sweetman, tape 6, side A; Renault, *Omnibus* interview.

"splendid good-humoured friendliness that made them both so different from the usual run of sisters and staff nurses." But the two remained defined by their professional status, and MacGregor confessed, "We knew nothing about Mary being a writer, and I don't think we realised how close a friendship there was between Mary and Julie—they were just jolly good sorts. . . ." When he met them again socially in Cape Town in the late 1950s, circumstances had changed: "There they often gave cocktail parties for their friends, and as Mary's Greek novels were coming out with great success, these soirées became a gathering point for writers, artists, anyone to do with the stage or ballet, journalists and Hellenophiles. Many a time my wife and I came away saying that we felt that we were almost the only two 'normals' there." Yet MacGregor was careful to point out that "there was no flavour of decadence: the atmosphere was one of robust good-will and the devil take what one's private life might be. . . . At these parties Mary was usually the hostess and the centre of attraction, while Julie acted as an umbrageous soubrette. . . . Julie was always happy to play second fiddle to Mary: she looked on her as the leader and was content to do anything at all that would help Mary. She was a truly good and self-sacrificing friend." With obvious sensitivity and careful observation, the conventional MacGregor struggled to describe a situation he found difficult to read: "Mary was always very modest about her writings. . . . [I]n her life she seemed to have solved the problem of sexual ambivalence by the way she and Julie lived—they were obviously warm and affectionate comrades. They both had a great sense of humour which helped to blunt the sharp stings of criticism that some directed at them. No one who saw how these two women lived together and acted for each other could have used the usual pejorative expressions that are so often directed at such a situation."[9]

Indeed, neither Mary nor Julie ever thought of themselves as lesbians. Both women had strong erotic feelings for men, which complicated any conventional definition of their identity. Additionally, without "role models," without lesbian acquaintances or knowledge of sympathetic contemporaries like themselves, they had had at first no ready language for their friendship. Julie emphasized, "We were bisexual. We never thought of ourselves as . . . lesbians. What we thought was: our feeling about sex was unique. . . . We had no idea that there were people like us all over." She pointed out succinctly,

9. Mullard, interview by Sweetman, tape 17, side B; John MacGregor to Sweetman, December 4, 1991.

"Between Sappho and Radclyffe Hall there's a pretty wide gap." Further, neither woman had any other lesbian relationship before or after they met in 1934, although in retrospect Julie could see previous friendships as having been lesbian, at least as far as the other woman was concerned: "When we met we both had a number of women friends none of whom were, as far as we knew, specially interested in members of their own sex. However, in no time there were several scenes of jealousy which, being young and heartless, we either ignored or secretly laughed about." Julie recalled, "In all the years before the war there was usually some woman who was warning one of us against the other. We both had a few very good long-lasting friendships with women, none of them lesbian. Looking back we realised that many of the girls and women we had known were lesbian or bisexual, but no one talked about these things. We thought we had invented it. . . ."[10]

Mary and Julie had briefly met a lesbian couple while on holiday in Devon after the war, but in large measure the two women had already established the dynamics of their friendship, so it is not surprising that they did not identify with the lesbians they encountered then or later. Julie commented that "One way and another we found them rather frightening; we continued to feel that way. . . . Apart from [the South African actress] Judy Henderson . . . we've never had a lesbian friend." Not until their last few weeks in England did they meet anyone who openly admitted to being lesbian. Then, Julie reported, they were invited to a party in London "where there were about twenty lesbians; we found it all very curious. The party broke up about nine o'clock and the guests went off in small groups to look for what they called 'talent.' With our hosts and two other young women we went off to a pub near the Middlesex Hospital, which we found was a 'picking up' area. That night there were no other women there but several sailors. When they heard that Mary and I were off to South Africa, they told us about Durban and Cape Town. That was the first time we realised that we did not fit in in the company of lesbians." Julie emphasized, "So it has always been. We both worked well and happily with women in hospital; in fact I can say that we were both quite popular. Here, in South Africa, things are always years behind civilised countries: only the really flamboyant types will admit to being lesbian, very unattractive. To-day we would be expected to carry a torch for Women's Lib."[11]

10. Mullard, interview by Sweetman, tape 3, side B and tape 4, side A; Mullard to Sweetman, October 12, 1990; Mullard, letter to author, November 20, 1996.

11. Mullard to Sweetman, October 12, 1990, Mullard, letter to author, November 20, 1996.

Julie repeatedly stressed their bisexuality—"We were both attracted to men and women"—while making clear that lesbian feeling was confined to and defined for them by their relationship—"once we met, neither of us ever looked at another woman." For her part, Renault declared, "I think a lot of people are intermediately sexed . . . it's like something shading from white to black, and all sorts of grays in the middle." Julie would even insist that in her work Mary "was always trying to say that people can be bisexual. To be bisexual is not necessarily a bad thing. It can be painful and difficult to live with and whatever, but it exists." And, in fact, their bisexuality presented difficulties that overshadowed the issue of lesbian desire or identity. Esther Rothblum has pointed out that "Very few women have had exclusively same-gender sexual experiences" and discusses the range of expression in lesbian relationships and the uncharted territory to be negotiated, even now, by two women committed to each other in an important friendship.[12] Thus Mary and Julie had to work out for themselves, with each other and separately, who they were sexually. It would seem that while Julie may have had erotic friendships with other women before meeting Mary, Mary did not have such relationships. In fact, before 1935, her intense, perhaps even sexual friendships seem to have been with men. Further, even after Mary and Julie began the intimate relationship that allowed them to perceive themselves as a couple and, by the 1940s, to present themselves as a couple to others, they both had "affairs" with men.

Once settled in Africa, however, their closest friends were primarily homosexual men, many of them couples, like the dancers David Poole and his companion Owen Murray, who were interesting, expressive, artistic, theatrical, professional—and "out." The women in their lives appear for the most part to have been either servants, neighbors, or Julie's coworkers at the various hospitals where she nursed, but Mary did not seem to feel the relative isolation as a disadvantage. She was less social, less extroverted than Julie, and she seems never to have needed female friendship beyond her domestic partnership. Once in South Africa, there was never any more question of their fidelity to each other nor any sexual or emotional wandering from the primacy of their partnership. Julie would declare that "From the time we left England neither of us felt anything stronger than friendship for anyone

12. Mullard, interview by Sweetman, tape 4, side A, and tape 5, side A; Renault, *Omnibus* interview; Esther D. Rothblum, "Transforming Lesbian Sexuality," 630.

else."[13] Expatriate life confirmed and strengthened their relationship, defining it exclusively, monogamously, for the first time. Thus their homosexual friends made possible, in a way, their own lesbianism. Bisexuality—or at least its physical expression in heterosexual relationships—was after 1948 no longer even a potential issue for either of them personally.

Parallel to this understanding of themselves as a couple was Renault's flowering as a writer, beginning with *The Charioteer.* It was as if she could finally write freely and clearly about (homo)sexuality because the issue was no longer confusing for her in her own feelings for others or in her own heterosexual behavior. Ironically, it was not homosexuality or lesbianism that encouraged her settlement away from England, but rather her own bisexuality, her "heterosexual tendencies." In England, her nursing—a social profession that brought her into daily contact with other interesting people, many of them men—had diffused her relationship with Julie and posed a constant if unclear potential threat to their partnership and even to her writing. Just as her writing and her identity as an artist were threatened by her profession as a nurse, by the war, which defined her life, and by English expectations of what a woman ought to be (a girlfriend, a wife, a mother), so her sexual identity as a bisexual lesbian, as Julie's partner, was threatened by her nursing, by the war, and by the Englishmen who came into her life and to whom she was attracted sexually as well as intellectually and emotionally.

Julie also figured in this negotiation of identity. That is, she, too, was attracted to men in numerous ways, including sexually, and while the war might not have allowed her to advance in her career as she wanted, it did indeed confirm her identity as a nurse and, as Mary struggled with her own identity as a writer, the war also confirmed for Julie her importance in Mary's life. In other words, when Mary became frustrated or discouraged in her struggle to maintain her status as an active author, Julie saw her role as a supporting partner become more important and defined. When Mary developed an intense relationship with a man in London in the last years of the war, Julie's feelings of jealousy and worry about their friendship further defined for her their lesbian partnership.

For Mary, the matter of sexual identity was less clear. The early years in Durban settled matters, however, for there Mary soon established herself as a writer as Julie returned to nursing. A previously unknown stability came into their lives as they fell into what Nadine Gordimer has called "a solid lesbian

13. Mullard, letter to author, November 16, 1995.

marriage,"[14] with Julie working outside the home and Mary writing within it, with Julie also playing the role of "wife" in her assumption of domestic duties, while Mary took on the conventional male role of the classical scholar.

By the 1960s, Renault had developed a sophisticated understanding of social attitudes toward homosexuality in men and women as well as a recognition of the invisibility of lesbians. She wrote frankly to Colin Spencer, expressing her own view that "the 'normal' men who are most anti-queer are those who have an anxiety-neurosis about their potency. They think being anti somehow makes them more virile. Silly asses. Normal women do, observably, get on the whole much less steamed up about Lesbians, and often don't even notice them, seeing only a couple of old maids who have shared a house for company, unless of course they more or less live in drag." She realized perceptively that men were more bothered by lesbians "because they resent a woman's not being available to them even if they don't want her. I have noticed though that some of the nicest normal men don't mind at all, so the other is probably insecurity too." Throughout her life, she remained wary, however, of seeing others in terms of their sexuality at the cost of seeing them more generally as human beings whose worthiness is a question not of sexuality but of morality. Thus, for example, she responded to a Cape Town performance of *The Killing of Sister George,* objecting to "a general feeling among the critics that the name part was played too unsympathetically; [as if to say] Lesbians are like that, poor things, and one should be tolerant. My own view is that George is a simply bloody woman and deserved all she got. Fundamentally, it is a dishonest play, full of psychological inconsistencies dragged in for dramatic effect. In order to exploit the Laurel and Hardy costumes, the two are supposed to be going to a drag ball. Therefore they belong to a Lesbian set. . . . It just doesn't hang together. Anything for a giggle."[15]

Renault could be very hard on other women, for she disliked the cattiness, the pettiness, and the failures of mind and spirit that she saw in many conventional women; she did not "care for women who live in a huddle of domestic life," yet she was always clear in her admiration for particular women. Thus, responding to a woman who had sent her a questionnaire for her historical novel magazine, Renault called Marguerite Yourcenar "a really great writer," but she also declared, "I don't write 'women's fiction' and judging by my mail the majority of my readers are men." She concluded:

14. Nadine Gordimer, letter to author, November 13, 1992.
15. Renault to Spencer, September 29, 1967, and October 11, 1966.

"I have a feeling I should be out of place in the sort of magazine you have in mind, and that the type of publicity offered would not help my books." Renault was in fact outraged that she had been asked, "Who is your favourite writer of romantic fiction?": "May I, please, make it clear that I do not write or read romantic fiction?" Renault resented certain qualities in people that were socially accepted, even valued in many women, for instance, ignorance, and the tendency to gossip and live life at leisure. She bristled against such women, often relying on Julie to keep them at bay. On one occasion she wrote to Bryher about Julie as her "watchdog," a defending "dragon": "Not so long ago, Julie staved off from me one of these dreadful American women journalists doing an around-the-world-in-8-days and sounding off on their return with a book written with brassy self-confidence and a factual error to every page." Renault felt justified in her resentment of this intrusive woman because when Julie saw her book in a shop, "One glance revealed that it was written too badly to bring into the house, but turning to the S. African episode she found the information that the lady . . . had tried to contact Mary Renault but was informed 'by a female dragon that she could not spare the time as she was writing a book.' As if to say, what excuse could be thinner than *that?* Up with dragons."[16] Here Renault's female solidarity with Julie protects her against a woman outside of that union, a brassy American sort who is intellectually irresponsible as well as insensitive to what art really is or involves.

Throughout her career in hospitals and boarding schools, Renault had, of course, cared for women as well as for men, and she was not hard on women without good cause. In fact, just the reverse is true. When Cedric Messina left South Africa for a post at the BBC in London, he had initially thought of the appointment as short term, and asked Mary and Julie if they would keep an eyes on his aging mother in his absence. By training and, like Julie, by inclination, Mary felt a personal as well as medical obligation to care for others and accepted this task as a friend. Mrs. Messina soon became unable to manage on her own, and Mary and Julie oversaw her entrance into a nursing home, but when, for a series of reasons, the facility could no longer cope with her withdrawn behavior, above and beyond the call of their friendship with Cedric Messina, they made the decision to take his mother into their own home. Messina never did return to South Africa to live, and the curious situation—in which Mary and Julie cared for a woman unrelated to them

16. Mullard to Michael Wilson, May 10, 1993; Renault to Kathryn Falk, September 12, 1980; Renault to Bryher, January 9, 1972.

and for whom they felt no special friendship—went on until Mrs. Messina's death ten years later. During this period, Julie was working full time, and the burden often fell on Mary, who seems to have taken on the obligation as a matter of course and without complaint, indeed, with great kindness.

In contrast to her feelings about intrusive women, Renault was generous in revealing her admiration for women artists and responsive to their individual and distinctive achievements. She admired Bryher's work and was impressed with H. D.'s poetry, writing to Bryher about H. D.'s epic poem *Helen in Egypt* that "Even if the world were not so full today as it is of writers who fly from nobility of mind as mediaeval schoolmen might have done from some deadly heresy—even in a richer time these poems would lose none of their stature, the excitement of their achieved affirmation and their perfect imagery. She is able to create heroic and numinous figures because she can enter the religious instincts of the past and reproduce their aura, a rare gift ever, and especially today." When Kathleen Abbott sent Renault a copy of Sylvia Plath's *Ariel* for her sixtieth birthday, she reacted to the poetry and to the woman with insight and understanding:

> I did not know Sylvia Plath's poetry at all. It has great impact, a most individual voice. Some I responded to at once, like those about the bay with their beautifully sharp, astringent tenderness; and the bees, the yew trees and the moon. Some I find very difficult, others impenetrable. I liked very much the ones about being in hospital and "Gulliver"; so much what one wants to say to any worthwhile person trapped into the personal-publicity racket, though I'm not sure if that is what is meant. The one about her father ["Daddy"] is very frightening. It is just a cry, not really meant, I suppose, to be understood. What a loss that she died so young. I wonder if she would have gone on, or back. Marriage and children do often seem to swallow up other creation. We have got a most beautiful picture by a young woman who after she married scarcely ever painted again. People who know a lot about art exclaim in admiration and ask who did it; when they are told they have never heard of her. I always hope that when we go to the annual Cape Salon that she will have something in it; but she never has now.[17]

Renault similarly admired the South African artist Cecil Higgs, and writing again to Kathleen Abbott, responded to her work with great sensitivity: "A

17. Renault to Bryher, February 9, 1971; Renault to Abbott, September 12, 1965.

friend of ours, a painter called Cecil Higgs (a woman, and not at all mannish, she must have been christened with the name), is about to hold one of her rather rare exhibitions. I do wish you could see her work, because her painting has in so many ways the quality of your poetry." Renault went on to describe Higgs's "beautiful sense of colour and organic form, which sometimes she abstracts to a sort of Platonic idea; but unlike all those sterile, trivial abstracts there are about, hers are simply irradiated with the Idea and you can live with them forever seeing something new." Indeed, Mary and Julie had two of her paintings, one of a small bowl of roses "delicious enough to eat, with a thick swirling technique, but no more abstract than Fatin-Latour," and another of forms that "simply suggest water, spray, rocks, bubbles and clear light beyond a cave-mouth, the outer parts being dark, solid and shadowy and the centre luminous, spinning, floating; it is a picture you can see on two planes, being also a sort of interior landscape with something light and pure visiting, or being born." Mary emphasized that Higgs "is one of the most highly thought of artists in South Africa among people who take painting seriously, and I am sure could have a great success in England if she would leave off painting long enough to do all the necessary pushing and shoving; but she just likes to paint, her output is very high in spite of its quality because she lives in and for it, and as every show she gives more or less sells out she has no need to do more." Mary concluded, "If she were different, she wouldn't be the artist she is; but I should like more people to enjoy her work in more places, including, especially, you. She has a very bold, strong technique, but when one meets her first she looks like a very quiet, retired schoolmistress with a quiet, precise voice. In actual fact no one could be less hidebound, and we love meeting her when she can leave off painting long enough to see anyone. I wish that you and she could meet, I'm sure you would understand each other."[18]

Despite obvious admiration for such women, despite her pleasure in sharing her feelings about them with her female friends, even despite her understanding of the plight of the female artist—who was subject to disenfranchisement specifically by marriage and children and more generally by patriarchal expectations—Renault was characteristically hostile to what she called "Women's Lib." She was aware of the problems that prompted feminist protest, but she characteristically refused association with any organized feminist movement, with any activist group. Thus, when Renault was interviewed by Sue MacGregor for the radio program *The Woman's Hour,* she commented

18. Renault to Abbott, February 25, 1963.

that "one could even switch on without realising it *was* the woman's hour, which I regard as high praise." She explicitly distanced herself from active feminists, writing to Bryher about a cartoon she had enjoyed in *The Spectator* "of a gang boss addressing his mob: 'As from next week you will refer to yourself as gunpersons.' If you have followed the antics of the extreme Women's Libbers this is rather good. I hope if ever a publisher accepts anything of mine because he has to fulfill his quota of women, I shall have the elementary self-respect to throw his contract in his face." In a similar vein, when Cyril Watling asked for her views on the women's movement, she emphasized that women are no better as a group than men: "God save us from the sex war! . . . What governments need is more people with the courage to be individuals."[19]

As an individual, however, Renault often took feminist positions, understanding from experience the dynamics of patriarchy. For instance, she admitted to John Guest that "[i]n the field of actual writing, I've never felt disadvantaged by being a woman; but when it comes down to hard business, there is no doubt one gets pushed around." She understood the linguistic trivialization of women, and Julie noted that, although "gunpersons" went ridiculously overboard, "Mary disliked all words with 'ess' or 'ette' attached—'poetess,' 'authoress,' 'undergraduette' and so on. Why not 'doctorette' or 'busdriveress'?"[20] But while Renault insisted on the limitations of any imposed classification and rejected the categories of identity politics no matter who imposed them, she often created for herself an extremely problematic position, as revealed by a letter she wrote in 1959 to the American lesbian journal the *Ladder.*

Responding to a discussion of her work occasioned in part by the recent publication of *The Charioteer* in the United States, Renault objected to the reviewer's statement that the subject of *The Last of the Wine* was "male homosexuality, transferred to an ancient Greek setting." She insisted that the book was in fact "a portrayal of Athens during the Peloponnesian Wars, and of some members of the Socratic circle." She emphasized that the novel's "love-relationship . . . is one characteristic of that society rather than our own; not only because of its recognised public standing, but because the two young men are, like most classical Greeks, fully bisexual." Taking the moral high ground, she struggled to position herself beyond the issue of sexual

19. Renault to Cedric and Ruth Messina, April 12, 1967; Renault to Bryher, January 2, 1970; Renault, *What Life Has Taught Me* interview.

20. Renault to Guest, June 5, 1980; Mullard to Sweetman, October 15, 1992.

identity. Insisting that in her view the historical novelist's primary duty was "to make his characters people of their era," she claimed that "[t]he writer who exploits a period setting for propaganda purposes, drawing fallacious parallels with his own society, at once sacrifices his integrity not less than by commercial vulgarising." In her final paragraph, she stated that "the first loyalty of any artist must be to his basic humanity and to his sense of man's place in the universe. . . . Asked 'What are you?' his spontaneous answer will be 'a writer.' " She concluded, "If in the practice of his craft he cannot learn maturity enough to raise his sights above mere self-expression, or concern for the public status of his own group, or even social reform, he submits to a castration of his creative self for which both as artist and human being he will be the poorer all his life."[21]

Distancing herself personally from issues central to the journal at the time, Renault here suggests the complex subtext, the contradictions at the core of her foreword to *The Friendly Young Ladies* more than twenty years later. She was, it would appear, a regular reader of the *Ladder*, but even if the review had been drawn to her attention by someone else, she is clearly aware of writing for a journal whose editors and audience were self-identified as sexually transgressive, raising the question of what she was doing in writing for such a publication at all. Sidestepping this issue, Renault elides the reception of her novel (contemporary readers' responses) with her own intentions, insisting on overreading (overriding) the autonomy of the text, the very independence of the text itself, which she stresses as so important to her. In the name of being a writer, she eschews self-expression; she argues in a circular fashion that she wrote as she did because her material required it— diverting attention from her choice of her material. This point is especially interesting since, despite having previously published six novels with contemporary settings, her first two historical novels, *The Last of the Wine* and *The King Must Die,* seem to have brought with them a fully realized public literary identity more potent, Renault argues here, than any sexual or gender identity. Thus Renault speaks of the "primary duty of the historical novelist" as if she is this entity, has always been this entity, as if the role or identity or calling of "the historical novelist" displaces or subsumes or erases any other possible "personal" or sexual or lesbian identity. As a writer, she insists she will not exploit, propagandize, falsify, sacrifice integrity, commercialize, or vulgarize: the writer is above such things, a member of a special elite and beyond politics. Her final paragraph,

21. Renault's letter appeared in the *Ladder,* November 1959, 20–21.

rife with masculine pronouns, shouts at the modern reader who is sensitive to the issue of gender-inclusive or gender-free language, but, even in Renault's day, one must wonder at a female writer in a lesbian journal insisting on such male words (fourteen instances of "he" or "his" occur in the last five sentences), insisting on moral compromise as a "castration" of the self, indeed an autocastration. Curiously, much of this posturing, this assuming of a moral high ground, obscures what may have been for Renault the most personal element in her letter: her emphasis on what she calls the bisexuality of "most Greeks." In fact, she stresses that most Greeks were "fully bisexual"; that is, fully sexual and fully "bi." If she had "come out" in this letter and taken a position on her own sexual identity, her own view of herself as a woman, it would have been this one: that she was not only fully sexual (and therefore transgressing midcentury ideas of femaleness) but fully bisexual, an "identity" that perhaps only very recent, turn-of-the-millennium "queer" readings of experience have made it possible to voice.

Renault's rejection of any collective identity—for example, as a lesbian, but also as a woman, as a white South African, and as a progressive or a conservative within the culture of the Britain of her youth or the South Africa of her maturity—can be understood not so much as naive and conventional but as sophisticated and even radical from a queer perspective that argues that "identity categories tend to be instruments of regulatory regimes, whether as the normalizing categories of oppressive structures or as the rallying points for a liberatory contestation of that very oppression.[22] In *The Persian Boy,* Renault would develop further and more directly the sex, gender, and identity issues that her letter to the *Ladder* raises so problematically.

Through the body and character of Bagoas, Renault explored the very questions that Judith Butler has posed explicitly when she asked, "And what is sex anyway? Is it natural, anatomical, chromosomal, or hormonal . . . ?"[23] Indeed, Bagoas's physical as well as emotional love for Alexander raises all sorts of matters central to contemporary "queer" theory. His subject position—as narrator of Alexander's story and Renault's text—and his object-position—as Alexander's boy—problematizes not only gender but sex itself. Bagoas's elegant Persian dancing is unreadable as clearly male or female, as either masculine or feminine, as either conscious performance or a "natural"

22. Judith Butler, "Imitation and Gender Insubordination," 13.
23. Butler, *Gender Trouble,* 6.

consequence of his "identity" as the beautiful oriental eunuch. His body, his sex itself, becomes unreadable: He is not a third sex but a sex that is both and neither, a sex that has no name. He is the victim of a brutal castration and the privileged court insider. In his own culture, he would in due course have developed from Darius's toy boy into a harem eunuch; in the world of the Greek camp and later in Greek-influenced Egypt, he is both lover and beloved of the masculine Alexander the Great. Bagoas is first and last both the object of his own narrative (the novel is, after all, entitled *The Persian Boy*) and its subject, the teller of the tale that is at once the second volume of Renault's biography of Alexander—an unusual second installment in that it ends with the death of the ostensible biographical subject/object—and the narrator of his own story, his own life. Indeed throughout her fiction, although nowhere more obviously than in *The Persian Boy,* Renault, like Butler, foregrounds what Elizabeth Grosz has called "an instability at the very heart of sex and bodies."[24]

More specifically and simply, Renault seems to have understood that the status of women was a cultural matter, dependent on place and period. Such awareness figured in her own life as well as in her writing. Often asked why, when she left England, she had not settled in Greece, she indicated that Greece "is a wonderful place to go, but not for a woman to live. . . . It's still to this day a man's country." She explained that she might have been tempted to establish herself in Greece, but it was too repressive of women. "You can't be there for very long without realising," she pointed out, that it was "thought extraordinary if you weren't integrated into a household, as a daughter or as a mother or as a wife." Indeed, "Women just didn't live on their own in Greece in those days [the 1940s and 1950s], and if you went to these little villages, where only the men went to the taverna and if the local whore ever went out, she was painted like a clown almost, because . . . if a man made a mistake and approached a respectable woman, her family would probably have knifed him . . . it was almost like a mask." When asked if she would like to have lived in ancient Greece at a particular time, Renault responded: "I would take very good care to be a man if I were re-incarnated in ancient Greece. . . . I don't think I have the vocation to be a hetaira, and that is the only kind of woman's life in which you would have had any fun or any mental stimulus at all."[25]

24. Elizabeth Grosz, "Experimental Desire: Rethinking Queer Subjectivity," 140.
25. Renault, *Omnibus* interview; Renault, *Kaleidoscope* interview.

Having chosen to write historical novels about the classical world, Renault was exploring on her own terms a universe in which women were marginalized, in which her own ideas, her own female voice, could not speak directly as a woman but only as a (male) artist. Alexias, the first of Renault's characters to tell the story from his own point of view in the first person, is emphatically a male narrator (not Renault, not a woman, not a twentieth-century writer), and he makes very clear that women ought to have little place in his account. They cannot be allowed to voice his narrative, for following the conventions of his culture he insists they are untrustworthy interpreters: "[W]omen, being ignorant of philosophy and logic, and fearing dream diviners more than immortal Zeus, will always suppose that whatever causes them trouble must be wicked" (*Last,* 11–12)—although Renault makes clear through irony that the women who explain the plague by blaming "the country people for bringing in a curse" are in fact correct in that the disease is contagious. Alexias is aware that especially well-born women, wives as opposed to courtesans, should be omitted from his text as a matter of decorum, although he finds this a difficult challenge, giving us a detailed account of his loving stepmother as well as of Thalia, the young woman whom Lysis marries and who, after Lysis's death, becomes Alexias's wife in turn. Of her Alexias finally declares, "But the mother of my sons has deserved better of me, these five and twenty years, than to be talked of at large, and already I have set down more than I ought" (373).

When accused of not writing about women, Renault responded: "I have a bit written about women. Some of my early books when I was writing about contemporary stuff, but I haven't written about them a great deal." In her historical fiction, the focus is on men because "of course it was the men who were doing things. . . . [Y]ou restrict yourself so much if you write about a woman unless you get an exceptional one, like Eurydike, who tried to be queen of Macedon, but that was very unusual. . . ." Julie Abraham has suggested perceptively that "Renault's choice of historical fiction was a choice between female and gay subjects," that "Like Bagoas, she can only tell Alexander's story. Or like Bagoas, she can only tell her own stories, whatever they might be, by telling Alexander's."[26] To tell "Alexander's story," however, *is* to tell her own stories—a tremendous feat—and it is finally a distortion of Renault's achievement to overlook her female characters, to privilege her historical

26. Renault, *Omnibus* interview; Julie Abraham, *Are Girls Necessary? Lesbian Writing and Modern Histories,* 71, 78.

fiction over her modern novels and her male heros over her vivid women, however peripheral they may seem to the central action of her later books.

As early as *Purposes of Love,* Renault rejected any conventional notions of what it might mean to be a woman, to be subsumed by a category. Her wide variety of female characters includes Vivian, Leo, and Hilary, protagonists of early novels, as well as the less central but vital characters found throughout her work—mothers, friends, sisters, daughters, wives, lovers—and an even larger number of women presented only through brief vignettes. Renault's stock female characters—such as the superficial Elsie, the lovelorn Nurse Adrian in *The Charioteer,* and the decorous daughters Simonides trains for the Delian festival—allow her to comment on the nature of female experience under patriarchy, but there are no romantic heroines, and the awkward endings of Renault's first five novels are evidence of the radical nature of her narratives. Without traditional female characters, the marriage plot cannot function, and, as her stories frustrate themselves, the marriages she might offer in the place of other, unimagined conclusions are finally "silly," as she suggests in her afterword to *The Friendly Young Ladies.*

Unorthodox women and unorthodox relationships among them abound in Renault's early novels, no matter how difficult it may be to tell their stories when marriage offers no realistic resolution. Hilary, Renault's most explicitly feminist protagonist, presents a case in point. When she struggles with her own feelings toward Julian and attempts to cope with his conflicted personality, she decides without rancor and with a good deal of insight, "Men were impossible, of any age and of every kind" (*RN,* 175). She understands her position as both woman and physician, confessing to Julian: " 'About the only advantage a female enjoys in this profession is that she isn't exposed to accusations of rape' " (280), while also realizing that whatever her aspirations and achievements, "the hard core for a feminist to bite on had, after all, been . . . that being a woman was a fact about which absolutely nothing could be done" (293). Marriage to Julian at the novel's end thus becomes a suicidal response to her erotic attachment, a union that parallels in its danger the marriage of Lisa and Rupert Clare.

The friendship between Hilary and the woman in whose house she lives is established early in the book when Hilary discovers the thermos of warm coffee Lisa has put in the car, anticipating a late-night call. The deep and unvoiced sympathy between the two women is suggested throughout the novel and emphasized in their similar relationships with men. Passionately in love, Lisa and Rupert have such different interests—hers rural and domestic, his literary and political—that after efforts to live first one sort of life and then the other, they decide to part. At one point they get a divorce, then intentionally annul it by sleeping together before the decree is final. Lisa goes on to have a miscarriage and later a stillborn baby, evidence that the two lovers, despite their desire for each other, cannot make a traditional marriage. Toward the novel's end, Renault recounts Lisa's impossible story, a variation on Hilary's own impossible narrative, a story that Renault can only tell through a technically awkward flash-forward from Hilary's point of view: "Two years later she was to remember the half-prescience which had sprung from the memory of Lisa's exalted face. Lisa, in the end, was to accomplish both her wishes; the child, and the reconciliation of her own and Rupert's irreconcilable lives. After no foothold was left in Europe even for the war reporters, Rupert came home to London, and Lisa to Rupert. No more decisions confronted them." Ironically, "In one of those hotel rooms, about whose recurrence in her story Lisa used to laugh, everything was settled for them while they slept. The little girl, kept in the country for safety (Lisa had rightly guessed the way her own choice would go), was left to resolve in herself two elements so perversely formed to attract but never to combine" (*RN,* 349). Marriage fails to "settle" the problems, which, in this case, are only resolved for Lisa and Rupert in death, while Renault hints here that resolution for the living, as for the Clares' little girl, can only be achieved internally and at least in part by refusing to be ensnared in the sexual conflict.

Thus Renault's sophisticated feminist sensibility, evident throughout her work, complicates rather than resolves the problems her characters face. Her "exceptional" women must continually pit themselves against traditional heterosexuality. Hence Mic objects to Vivian's conventionality when, as he watches her in the candlelight, she wonders only partially in jest, " 'Have you ever thought . . . that civilized people undress in separate rooms? . . . What do you think is the matter with us? Colette says women should never appear in any stage between their frock and their skin. I know at least one who keeps all her make-up under her pillow so as to do her face before her husband wakes up. Would you love me more if I did those things?' " Insisting on her individuality, he responds: " 'Don't talk like that. . . . Don't call yourself Women. It sounds beastly. . . . Rows of them, all pink and bulging. In frilled drawers. . . . You're simply you' " (*PL,* 187–188). In contrast to Vivian here, Renault indicates that her lesbian friend Colonna, who adores the "fairyland" (323) of westerns of the sort Leo writes, "eluded classification" and "accepted her own eccentricities," although "by all the laws of literature . . . [she] ought to have been plain, heavy, humourously passionate and misunderstood, pursuing in recurrent torments of jealousy the reluctant, the inexperienced and the young. She ought to have behaved like someone with a guilty secret" (42).

Instead of conventional heroines, Renault's narratives feature increasingly headstrong and not necessarily admirable women, who play significant if marginal roles in the contemporary fiction and assume more central positions in the Greek novels. Janet Anderson, in *Kind Are Her Answers,* is only the first in a series of fascinating viragoes—wives and mothers who fail their husbands, their children, and themselves. The list includes Mrs. Fleming in *Return to Night* as well as Susan Langton in *North Face* and Mrs. Odell in *The Charioteer.* The historical fiction is rife with polarized mother figures: Alexias's nurse is cruel and petty, while his stepmother, alert to the dynamics of politics and war, is a sensitive woman close to his own age whom against all convention he teaches to read and even to write (*Last,* 204). This "mother" becomes an eroticized figure who attracts Alexias yet keeps her distance; Thalia, who as Lysis's wife stands in for Lysis when Alexias later marries her, becomes the woman who in turn is written out of the text. Theseus's confrontation with matriarchy requires that he forsake his own good mother for "marriage" to the Eleusian queen, whom he must then overthrow, anticipating the tensions in *The Bull from the Sea* between Hippolyta and Phaedra, the good and bad wife who replace Ariadne, who is deserted on Naxos when Theseus discovers her role in the debauchery of the Maenad rites. In the Alexander trilogy, Olympias, the harridan queen, betrays Philip to champion her son, then fails Alexander and finally Macedonia and herself. She in turn is juxtaposed to Sisygambis, Darius's mother, whom Alexander admires and even calls "mother," whose granddaughter, Stateira, becomes Alexander's good wife in contrast to Roxane, the evil wife, who, after her husband's death in *Funeral Games,* kills both Stateira and the unborn heir.

The number and variety of female characters—both admirable and despicable—in this last novel is in large measure possible because of the dissolution of empire, of the Greek society that fostered Alexander and the male virtues that made him "great." With his death, Renault loses not only the central figure, whose presence controlled the first two books in the trilogy, but also the biographical narrative, the aesthetic structure that had shaped all of her novels beginning with *The Charioteer.* The chaos of the late fourth and early third century B.C.E. is reflected in the fragmented plot, shifting focus, and geographical sweep of a novel whose cast of thousands (the Macedonian, Greek, and Persian armies with their various generals, and Alexander's many friends, relations, and enemies) struggle to reconstruct their world and lives in Babylon, Athens, Phrygia, the Himalayas, and Egyptian Alexandria.

This political, social, logistic, racial, and sexual chaos allowed women a significance not previously available to them, and Renault explores their roles in *Funeral Games* through overlapping life stories of the various figures who try to fill the vacuum of power that followed Alexander's death. Among these is Amyntas's daughter, Eurydike, an "exceptional" woman, who, after her father's death, travels from Macedon to marry Philip, Alexander's handsome but dim-witted half brother. Her narrative is a particularly important one for Renault since, as she pointed out, it did not "restrict" her but allowed her at once to tell a woman's story and to say what she wanted to say.

Eurydike is naive and uneducated but also confident and ambitious; with her mother's misplaced encouragement, she attempts to masquerade as a man both literally (to assure her physical safety while on the road) and finally symbolically in her struggle to assume the power behind the throne. When her mother explains to her the political complexity of their mission, the fifteen-year-old girl exclaims: " 'If that is what I must do to avenge my father, then I will. Because he left no son.' " But then, "Kynna was appalled," reflecting in horror, "What have I made? . . . [W]hat have I done?" (*FG*, 126).

Periodically Eurydike's pretense at maleness gives her freedom, but her "mask" backfires at every turn: When they are attacked by robbers in Persia, where their status as royal women would have protected them from such routine violence, her mother is killed and she herself barely escapes. When Eurydike assumes the role of a petty officer in Alexander's former army with which she travels, wedded to Philip in an unconsummated union, she initially exults in the liberation from traditional female constraints: "Now that for the first time she was with an army in the field, all her training and her nature rebelled at being laid aside with slaves and women. Her marriage she had felt as a grotesque necessity, something to be managed, altering nothing of herself; even more, now, she felt women an alien species, imposing no laws upon her" (*FG*, 161). By "women" here, Renault, as in *Purposes of Love*, suggests traditional women, and the reader's sympathies incline towards Eurydike, but the young woman is a fool—both by inexperience and by her impetuous nature. Failing to gain power in a political confrontation later in the novel, Eurydike also fails to understand why she at sixteen cannot equal Alexander's achievements at the same age, while Renault has made clear, in both *Fire from Heaven* and *The Persian Boy*, the long apprenticeship, the privileged Aristotelian education, and the complex assent to power from birth that even such a personally gifted man as Alexander required. Eurydike's ambition comes to seem hubristic, although Renault continues to sympathize with her against her male antagonists right up until her forced suicide.

Eurydike's aspirations are shattered earlier, however, when Renault demonstrates that Eurydike's alienation from "women" as a "species," her denial of her bodily femaleness—rather than her femaleness itself—makes her achievement of power impossible. During a poignant scene at a formal Macedonian assembly in which each orator has the opportunity to gain crucial popular support, Eurydike

> would not, could not admit defeat; she would speak, it was her right; she had won them once and would again. . . . Her hands had clenched, her back and her shoulders tightened; her stomach contracted, achingly. The aching turned to a cramp, a low heavy drag which, with dismay, she tried at first not to recognize. In vain; it was true. Her menses, not due for four days, had started.
>
> She had always counted carefully, always been regular. How could it happen now? It would come on quickly, once begun, and she had not put on a towel.
>
> She had been strung-up this morning; what had she failed to notice in all the stress? Already she felt a warning moisture. If she stood on the rostrum, everyone would see.
>
> The Regent's speech approached its climax. He was talking of Alexander; she hardly heard. She looked at the thousands of faces round her, on the slopes, in the trees. Why, among all these humans made by the gods, was she alone subject to this betrayal, she only who could be cheated by her body at a great turn of fate?
>
> Beside her sat Philip, with his useless gift of a strong man's frame. If she had owned it, it would have carried her up to the rostrum and given her a voice of bronze. Now she must creep from the field without a battle; and even her wellwishers would think, Poor girl!

When Eurydike is finally called upon to speak, Renault writes: "She had come, the morning being fresh, with a himation round her shoulders. Now, carefully, she slipped it down to her elbows, to drape in a curve over her buttocks, as elegant ladies wore it in fresco paintings. Getting to her feet, taking care over her draperies, she said, "I do not wish to address the Macedonians." (*FG,* 195). Eurydike cannot, finally, deny her female body any more than Hilary can, but it is the attempt at denial rather than her womanhood that betrays her; she looks out at the crowd and sees "humans," not "men"—had she seen men, Renault suggests, she might have had a deeper understanding of her predicament. Eurydike's body would, the author implies, have warned her, had she been more in touch with her physical self and less distracted "by all the stress"—Renault herself, after all, never forgot the material reality of the body and never relinquished her female sensibility and experience: It is the author's voice that uses such words as "cramp" and "buttocks"; it is a female voice, noting the "low heavy drag" and the "warning moisture," that writes so accurately of this taboo subject.

In the world of dissolving empire, Renault is able to alternate among various points of view, writing at times from a man's perspective, at other times from a woman's; sometimes from a point of view that is conscious, rational, and lucid, occasionally from one that is interior and confused. Her characteristic literary realism can even give way to the inscription of inner consciousness, as in her account of Olympias's death, one of the most powerful scenes in all of Renault's fiction, whose horror derives in large part from the point of view. Condemned by the Macedonian people for acting "contrary to justice and the law," Alexander's mother is led to "a piece of waste land near the sea":

> Alone in the circle, she stood with her head up while the first stones struck her. Their force made her stagger, and she sank to her knees to prevent an unseemly fall. This offered her head, and soon a big stone struck it. She found herself lying, gazing upwards at the sky. A cloud of great beauty had caught the light from the sinking sun, itself hidden behind the mountain. Her eyes began to swim, their images doubled; she felt her body breaking under the stones, but it was more shock than pain; she would be gone before the real pain had time to start. She looked up at the whirling effulgent cloud, and thought, I brought down the fire from heaven; I have lived with glory. A thunderbolt struck from the sky and all was gone. (*FG*, 257)

Renault's eloquence here depends upon her perspective, upon the point of view of a dying woman whose fading consciousness and blurred vision recapitulate her son's life and Renault's narrative of that life, beginning with the account in *Fire from Heaven.* Alexander is finally understood within the book, however, not by a female character but by Ptolemy's son, who knows him only through his father, the male author who substitutes here for Renault in his efforts to write Alexander's biography. At the end of *Funeral Games,* the younger Ptolemy recapitulates and brings to a close Renault's Greek narratives, with their roots in *The Charioteer,* when he recalls " 'All those great men. When Alexander was alive, they pulled together like a one chariot-team. And when he died, they bolted like chariot-horses when the driver falls' " (*FG,* 270). Alexander is thus memorialized as the great driver, the ideal charioteer, whose recurrent image, despite its source in Plato, is ultimately Renault's own creation, a hallmark of her mature work.

The careful craft and control evident in the shifting perspectives of her last published novel were as much a part of the woman Renault presented to the world as they were of her writing. If the voice in her novels is increasingly masked as other than her own, it is also invariably her own as well. This mask—which both conceals and reveals, which both veils and allows expression—is nowhere more obvious than in the interviews she consented to give beginning in the late 1960s. The initial interviews were to Sue MacGregor, the daughter of an Oxford colleague, then to Cyril Watling, both for radio transmission. These were followed at the end of the 1970s by filmed interviews, first with Roy Sergeant and then, in 1982, a final interview with David Sweetman for BBC television in London. Renault grew increasingly comfortable in these situations, and her interview with Sweetman is particularly remarkable in her openness about her relationship with Julie, but she always appears poised, circumspect, and in command of both her material and her interviewer. The same public persona answers similar questions, offering the same graceful responses over and over, employing identical phrasing, even offering the very same anecdotes. Renault's distilled answers to Watling's questions are so carefully expressed, it would seem that she must have been given the questions ahead of time (or composed them at least in part herself), then written out her responses, which are so formal and considered as to be encapsulated dead ends. Nevertheless, when further polished and elaborated, these answers would become those she offered the public on each occasion; they protected the woman who concluded her interview with Watling by stating modestly, albeit also truthfully, that in her leisure time she occupied herself with "talk with friends," with "the sea, dogs, reading."

Renault was, of course, a much more complicated woman than such details suggest, as her friends certainly knew. Colin Spencer could write accurately of "the layers with which Mary Renault very skillfully covered herself." Such "layers" were not merely a function of having developed various private and public selves; they depended, too, on her awareness of the interpenetration of these selves, especially as represented in her work. Thus her own fictional characters assumed an ongoing existence beyond their texts, as Julie recounted

Mary at work at "Delos" in the 1970s. Photo courtesy of Julie Mullard.

in a revealing anecdote: "People often want to know what happened to Mic and Vivian. Mary used to say she'd write a book called 'Son of Mic,' and we'd make up stories about a lot of her characters and roar with laughter, never thinking that our own lives made up a story. . . ."[27]

Violating the boundaries of their novels, her characters took on an enduring existence in her life; her own life, in turn, reflected in all of her books belonged as much to the aesthetic constructs of her fictional world as it did to her household in South Africa. In terms that equate her with her books, conveying her personal charm as well as her dual role as both creator of and figure in her texts, Spencer would describe meeting her in Greece in 1962: "I certainly fell in love. I longed to paint her, she was, I thought, incredibly handsome, a patrician face, very classical . . . kind and severe at once she had immense serenity and dignity." When he expressed his interest to Mary, however, she drew back: "I must say I was staggered by the idea that you ever thought of painting me. I have always thought the warmest encomium of the

27. Spencer, letter to author, July 21, 1994; Mullard, interview by Sweetman, tape 5, side A.

most indulgent friend upon my face would be something like, 'Of course, Mary's no oil-painting, but. . . .' Come to think of it, I can't even think but *what.* So your kind tribute was much appreciated. Perhaps I should have it lifted, but they say it takes four hours, all of it under a general. . . . I suppose I shall just end by leaving it to weather."[28] Mary's modest and amused response reveals a degree of self-consciousness as well as a disengagement from her own physical self and appearance—she cannot say just "*what*" her face is; she prefers finally to use the distancing pronoun *it* to disassociate herself from her body, as if her face were a building she could leave to "weather" away from her and out of doors.

Yet Mary could also delight in the gaze of others. Julie recalled that Mary relished Robbie Wilson's attentions in the early 1940s, was pleased that "he was physically attracted to her," with "the way he looked at her. He admired her features, her legs and hands and everything about her. And he showed it. He was open to a fault. He would talk about her physical appearance and say how he liked it. I think this did a great deal for Mary, because he himself was attractive. She very much enjoyed it." Mary was especially happy to pose for a camera. The nude photos taken in Sussex in the late thirties hint at the obvious delight she later took in displaying her legs—which she clearly felt were one of her most appealing features—in picture after picture: in knee socks in the late twenties; in trousers, in which she both stands and sits, often as if for a pinup; in a two-piece bathing suit in the 1950s. There are no photos from the war period because film was then unavailable, but Mary bought a camera on the voyage out to Durban and immediately posed with Julie on the deck of the *Cairo,* preserving forever the image of them looking, in Julie's words, "like wild and skinny outcasts."[29]

Before the late 1920s, however, there is no photographic record: no pictures of Mary as a baby; none of her as a little girl, at home or at school; no formal portrait with her sister or parents or relatives in London; no snapshots taken on the rare seaside holiday. The riot of photos after 1948 are yet further evidence of Mary's construction of herself: images that in their very profusion and variety draw attention to the absence of photos before the 1920s; images that often show her looking right into the camera (or, in one instance, into a mirror); and images that depict her talking animatedly with friends, working at her desk, caressing the dogs, relaxing at her beloved house by the sea.

28. Spencer, letter to author, July 21, 1994; Renault to Spencer, June 27, 1965.
29. Mullard, interview by Sweetman, tape 10, side A; Mullard, letter to author, June 14, 1996.

Mary at home in Cape Town in the early 1980s. Photo by Philip de Vos, courtesy of Julie Mullard.

Unfortunately, by 1977 "Delos," the beach cottage whose garden led down to the sand, had come to feel small and cramped. The crowds of young people who flocked to Camps Bay in ever greater numbers throughout the 1970s were encroaching on what had eighteen years earlier seemed a calm and private enclave. Mary's library had also increased considerably since leaving Durban in 1958 just after finishing her second historical novel; by the 1970s, her small study was jammed with "masses of books. . . . There was literally a book behind a book and behind that there were books again." At the end of the year, Mary and Julie moved to a more spacious home. Mary described it enthusiastically as "a very solid cool house, with a balcony to every room, bedrooms included . . . and this wild outside staircase which we adore." Built in a modern bauhaus style, the house perched dramatically on the hillside overlooking the bay below. The required renovations took months—not only redecorating, which both women thoroughly enjoyed, but the removal of walls, the installation of a second bathroom, the tearing up of stones that covered the area that eventually would be refertilized for grass and flowers. Ironically, a year after moving in, they watched their former house burn to the ground. Mary wrote Phyllis Hartnoll, "We got the news in time to drive down and see the roof fall in as the rafters blazed to heaven, and our familiar bedroom windows full of flames. It was a very strange feeling, familiar enough to plenty of people during the war, but odd happening suddenly to a place one has spent almost 20 years in."[30]

With "Delos" left behind and now permanently gone, the new house on Atholl Road would be Mary's home for the rest of her life. It was here that she finished *The Praise Singer,* begun before the move, and here that she wrote all of *Funeral Games.* Then, having finished the Alexander trilogy in early 1981, Renault began research for her last novel. By early 1983 she had begun to write, and by August she felt it was "about 80% done," although she also admitted to Kathleen Abbott that she was feeling tired and daunted by the "knotting up" still to come.[31]

In this final book, Renault returned to the material that had first captured her imagination while a student at St. Hugh's in the 1920s. The vast sweep of her Greek novels had made her an expert on the daily life and grand events that had shaped individuals and their culture for hundreds of years over thousands of miles of physical territory. *The King Must Die* and *The Bull from the Sea* had been set in a mythic past, in a Mediterranean world that stretched south from Attica to Crete and northeast to the island of Lesbos off the coast of Asia Minor. In *The Praise Singer,* Simonides, born on Keos in the Aegean in 556 B.C.E., had told his story over eighty years later in retirement on the eastern coast of Sicily. *The Mask of Apollo* had followed Nikeratos from late fourth-century B.C.E. Athens to Macedon in the north and southwest to Syracuse. The Alexander trilogy, which had begun with his boyhood in Macedon and Thrace in the first half of the fourth century B.C.E., followed him to Kashmir in northern India and followed his body, after his death, west again as far as the northern coast of Egypt, where the elder Ptolemy concluded his biography

30. Mullard, interview by Sweetman, tape 9, side A; Renault to Phyllis Hartnoll, January 1, 1979.

31. Renault to Abbott, quoted in Sweetman, *Mary Renault,* and dated "August 1983," 300–301.

in 286 B.C.E. In "According to Celsus," a short story written in 1976, Renault had recounted an incident that brought together a Greek prostitute and a Jewish carpenter in Alexandria in the early first century C.E. In other words, her historical novels had spanned the Greco-Roman world from the time of the fall of Crete in 1400 B.C.E. into the first years of the Christian era. But her last book was "something new, absolutely new."[32]

In her final narrative, Renault focused on medieval life in early twelfth-century France. Her central characters were crusaders who set out from Flanders and Toulouse to travel overland and by sea via Constantinople to Jerusalem. The action featured both men and women and concerned "the hospices, the injured and dying men and those who tended them," allowing the author to examine the codes of courtly love and chivalry as well as religious beliefs. Renault's story involved the Knights Hospitallers of St. John, an order that included members dedicated to the care of the sick and wounded as well as the fighting knights who participated in the First Crusade. Such a narrative allowed Renault to draw on her knowledge of French, on her geographical and historical understanding of the eastern Mediterranean, and on her own medical experiences. The politics and individual relationships both at court and in armies on the move must have fascinated her as fresh material at the same time that she was working from her understanding of the military experience and noble life about which she had been writing to one degree or another in all of her Greek novels. Such a "new" narrative required a great deal of original research while simultaneously permitting her to return to the romantic world, inspired by Malory and the Song of Roland, which had always compelled her. For several years, Julie reported, "Mary had been collecting material, books and papers on this period and on these subjects," and "in the last three years . . . she read something of that period almost every day."[33]

But by August 1983, as Mary had hinted to Kathleen Abbott, she was not at all well. The cough that had been troubling her for some time was clearly becoming worse, and by late August she developed pneumonia. Despite doses of various antibiotics, the infection persisted and her lungs began to fill with fluid, necessitating periods of hospitalization and aspirations as often as twice weekly by October. Julie knew what the doctors did not need to tell her, that Mary was seriously ill and not improving nor likely to, and when, during a

32. Mullard, interview by Sweetman, tape 6, side A.
33. Mullard, letter to author, February 5, 1997.

bronchoscopy, the surgeon found malignant cells from a mass behind the lungs, Julie was not surprised. As in 1970, she decided not to reveal to Mary what she had suspected for months; indeed, Julie told no one of the seriousness of Mary's condition until early December. At that point, Mary was regularly receiving oxygen and was still at home except for brief intervals in the hospital for tests and treatment, although from August on she had been growing weaker, eating less and less, losing weight, and getting out of bed only with help and for short periods. She now grew increasingly isolated, for talking on the telephone exacerbated her cough, and she did not feel up to visitors. By the end of September, Julie had taken over Mary's correspondence, since she was no longer able to get down the thirty-two steps to her study and to the typewriter that had become over the years an essential link to language. She confessed that the worst part of any illness or injury that kept her from her desk was "that through constantly thinking on the typewriter, I find that I can hardly *think* when I am trying to write an ms. letter. Scribbling with a pencil and rubber I am accustomed to, because I don't have to worry about anyone's reading it but me. Of course I eventually have to get it onto the machine, because it looks different then and has to be frequently re-written." Dictating was no better, she confided to Kathleen, and Julie concurred: "Mary can't dictate. She never can, she just says, ' . . . er. . . .' "[34]

Frustrated by her lack of energy but apparently still unaware of the seriousness of her condition, by November Renault put aside all efforts to work and contented herself with her invariably voracious reading, going through a book or two each day: historical novels, contemporary fiction, detective stories, all of Jane Austen again from the beginning.[35] On December 8, she entered the local nursing home where she could receive constant medication and the necessarily more frequent aspirations; Julie visited several times each day, regularly bringing with her yet more books from the library. Then, just before treatment early on the morning of December 13, Mary suddenly lost consciousness and died.

Following the funeral at St. George's Cathedral in Cape Town, her body was cremated. Julie had at first intended to place the ashes in the crypt, but she soon felt that this was not what Mary would have wanted and brought

34. Renault to Abbott, December 2, 1982; Renault to Abbott, November 24, 1983 (dictated to Julie); Mullard to Abbott, September 28, 1983. Details about the last months of Renault's life come from Mullard, interview by Sweetman, tape 9, sides A and B.

35. Mullard, interview by Sweetman, tape 9, side B; Mullard to Sweetman, December 21, 1983.

them back in their urn to Atholl Road. In 1987 Julie drove a hundred miles east into the Cape mountains and scattered the ashes near Ceres, where she and Mary had often spent holidays. Today, a small bronze plaque on the house reads:

WRITER
MARY RENAULT
BORN
MARY CHALLANS
LIVED AND WORKED HERE
4-9-05—13-12-83

After much deliberation, Julie had destroyed the uncompleted book years earlier, in March 1985. It seems likely that Mary would have approved. The novel had never reached the stage of the final "fair copy" so important to her, and she was invariably careful about her public persona, the author who addressed her interviewers with precision, craft, and grace, the writer whose pseudonym she chose so strategically from the very beginning. A year before her death, having injudiciously strained to touch her toes one morning, she had developed a back pain that prevented her from working at her desk except for short periods. She wrote of her dilemma to Kathleen Abbott: "Perfection of the life or of the work, said Yeats, as if anyone, even he, could hope for perfection in either; but even deciding which of them to get along with is quite a thing sometimes."[36] It is doubtful that, when she was unable to get along with life, Renault would have wished for the publication of unfinished work.

After all, art for Renault was finally anchored in the body, her favorite metaphor, which she employed throughout *The Praise Singer* not only in the contrast between Simonides the active poet and lover and Simonides the aging bard, but in her vivid descriptions of the nature of art and the lot of the artist. Thus Simonides extols the peasant work songs he hears at home in Euboia: "They are simple, these songs, like the beat of the heart or the breath of life; and their sound mates with their meaning as simply as the beasts mate in the spring. They were sung before there were bards or poets, and of them we were all begotten. They are still our kindred, if we know our craft. Pulse and breath set us our bounds, within which is found all mastery. Without pulse

36. Renault to Abbott, December 2, 1982.

and breath the body dies; without their measures the poet. But within their limits are the startled or the tranquil or the eager heart; the breath of ecstasy, or calm, or tears, or terror. What a possession is ours!" (*PS,* 151) As art and the body interpenetrate one another here, this novel about an artist from his own perspective becomes a moving *ave atque vale* that belongs not only to Simonides but quite personally to Mary Renault herself.

bibliography

Selected Works by Mary Renault

Books:

The Bull from the Sea (1962). London: Penguin, 1980.
The Charioteer (1953). New York: Pantheon Books, 1959.
Fire from Heaven. London: Longman Group, 1970.
The Friendly Young Ladies (1944). London: Virago, 1984.
Funeral Games (1981). London: Penguin, 1982.
Kind Are Her Answers. London: Longmans, Green, 1940.
The King Must Die (1958). London: New English Library, 1974.
The Last of the Wine (1956). London: New English Library, 1990.
The Mask of Apollo. London: Longmans, Green, 1966.
The Nature of Alexander (nonfiction). London: Allen Lane, 1975.
North Face. London: Longmans, Green, 1949.
The Persian Boy. London: Longman Group, 1972.
The Praise Singer. London: John Murray, 1979.
Purposes of Love. London: Longmans, Green, 1939.
Return to Night. London: Longmans, Green, 1947.

Shorter Works:

"According to Celsus." In *Women Writing,* ed. Denys Val Baker. London: Sidgewick and Jackson, 1980.

Afterword to *Theseus: A Greek Legend Retold,* by Charles Kingsley. New York: Macmillan, 1964.

"A Man Who Survived Transition." *New York Times Book Review,* August 15, 1965, 1, 20.

"Amazons." *Greek Heritage* 1 (spring 1964): 18–23.

"History in Fiction." *Times Literary Supplement,* March 23, 1973, 315–16.

Introduction to *Sir Nigel,* by Arthur Conan Doyle. London: John Murray, 1975.

"Notes on *The King Must Die.*" In *Afterwords: Novelists on Their Novels,* ed. Thomas McCormack. New York: Harper and Row, 1969.

Interviews:

By Sue MacGregor. *Kaleidoscope.* BBC radio program, broadcast on December 4, 1979. Transcripts and interviews are at St. Hugh's College Library, Oxford.

By Sue MacGregor. *The Woman's Hour.* SABC radio program, broadcast in 1969[?]. Transcripts and interviews are at St. Hugh's College Library, Oxford.

By David Sweetman. *Omnibus.* BBC television program, recorded on January 26–30, 1982, and broadcast on March 14, 1982. Sweetman's audiotapes and transcripts of interviews with Renault and Mullard are at St. Hugh's College Library, Oxford.

By Cyril Watling. *What Life Has Taught Me.* SABC radio program, broadcast in 1965[?]. Transcripts and interviews are at St. Hugh's College Library, Oxford.

Secondary Sources

Abraham, Julie. *Are Girls Necessary? Lesbian Writing and Modern Histories.* London: Routledge, 1996.

Ackroyd, Peter. *Dressing Up, Transvestism and Drag: The History of an Obsession.* New York: Simon and Schuster, 1979.

Adam, Ruth. *A Woman's Place.* London: Chatto and Windus, 1975.

Alexander, Sally. "Becoming a Woman in the 1920s and 1930s." In *Metropolis, London: Histories and Representations since 1800,* ed. David Feldman and Gareth Stedman Jones. London: Routledge, 1989.

Anderson, Margaret C. *Forbidden Fires.* Ed. Mathilda M. Hills. Tallahassee, Fla.: Naiad Press, 1996.

Barale, Michèle Aina. "Below the Belt: (Un)Covering *The Well of Loneliness.*" In *Inside/Out: Lesbian Theories, Gay Theories,* ed. Diana Fuss. New York: Routledge, 1991.

Barker, Rachel. *Conscience, Government, and War: Conscientious Objection in Great Britain, 1939–1945.* London: Routledge and Kegan Paul, 1982.

Bazin, Nancy Topping, and Marilyn Dallman Seymour, eds. *Conversations with Nadine Gordimer.* Jackson: University Press of Mississippi, 1990.

Beard, Mary. "The Classic Paradox." *Times Literary Supplement,* April 23, 1993, 13.

Beauman, Nicola. *A Very Great Profession: The Woman's Novel, 1914–1939.* London: Virago, 1983.

Bergonzi, Bernard. *Reading the Thirties: Texts and Contexts.* London: Macmillan, 1978.

Bertram, Deiter. *Cecil Higgs: Close Up.* Rivonia, South Africa: William Waterman, 1994.

Black, Margaret. *No Room for Tourists.* London: Secker and Warburg, 1965.

Boone, Joseph Allen. *Tradition Counter Tradition: Love and the Form of Fiction.* Chicago: University of Chicago Press, 1987.

Bordo, Susan. *Twilight Zones: The Hidden Life of Cultural Images from Plato to O. J.* Berkeley and Los Angeles: University of California Press, 1997.

———. *Unbearable Weight: Feminism, Western Culture, and the Body.* Berkeley and Los Angeles: University of California Press, 1993.

Braybon, Gail, and Penny Summerfield. *Out of the Cage: Women's Experiences in Two World Wars.* London: Pandora, 1987.

Brennan, Teresa. *The Interpretation of the Flesh: Freud and Femininity.* London: Routledge, 1992.

Brittain, Vera. *Testament of Experience.* London: Gollancz, 1957.

———. *Wartime Chronicle: Vera Brittain's Diary.* Ed. Alan Bishop and Y. Aleksandra Bennett. London: Gollancz, 1989.

Burns, Landon C., Jr. "Men Are Only Men: The Novels of Mary Renault." *Critique* 6 (winter 1963–1964): 102–21.

Butler, Judith. *Bodies That Matter: On the Discursive Limits of "Sex."* New York: Routledge, 1993.

———. *Gender Trouble: Feminism and the Subversion of Identity.* New York: Routledge, 1990.

———. "Imitation and Gender Insubordination." In *Inside/Out: Lesbian Theories, Gay Theories,* ed. Diana Fuss. New York: Routledge, 1991.

Calden, Angus. *The People's War: Britain, 1939–1945.* London: Jonathan Cape, 1969.

Calder, Charles. "Mary Renault." In *Reference Guide to English Literature,* ed. D. L. Kirkpatrick. Vol. 2. London: St. James Press, 1991.

Carlston, Erin G. "Versatile Interests: Reading Bisexuality in *The Friendly Young Ladies.*" In *RePresenting Bisexualities: Subjects and Cultures of Fluid Desire,* ed. Donald Hall and Maria Pramaggiore. New York: New York University Press, 1996.

Carpenter, Humphrey. *OUDS: A Centenary History of the Oxford University Dramatic Society.* Oxford: Oxford University Press, 1985.

Carr, Helen, ed. *From My Guy to Sci-Fi: Genre and Women's Writing in the Postmodern World.* London: Pandora Press, 1989.

Castle, Terry. *The Apparitional Lesbian: Female Homosexuality and Modern Culture.* New York: Columbia University Press, 1993.

Cecil, Mirabel. *Heroines in Love, 1750–1974.* London: Michael Joseph, 1974.

Chandhuri, N., and M. Strobel, eds. *Western Women and Imperialism: Complicity and Resistance.* Bloomington: Indiana University Press, 1992.

Chauncey, George. "From Sexual Inversion to Homosexuality: Medicine and the Changing Conceptualization of Female Deviance." *Salmagundi* 58–59 (fall–winter 1982–1983): 114–46.

Cook, Blanche Weisen. " 'Women Alone Stir My Imagination': Lesbianism and the Cultural Tradition." *Signs* 4, no. 4 (summer 1979): 718–39.

Cotter, Joseph. "Mary Renault." In *Dictionary of Literary Biography Yearbook, 1983,* ed. Mary Bruccoli and Jean W. Ross. Detroit: Gale Research, 1984.

Crosland, Margaret. *Beyond the Lighthouse: English Women Novelists in the Twentieth Century.* London: Constable, 1981.

Cunningham, Valentine. *British Writers of the 1930s.* Oxford: Oxford University Press, 1988.

Cutforth, René. *Later Than We Thought: A Portrait of the Thirties.* Newton Abbot: David and Charles, 1976.

Däumer, Elizabeth D. "Queer Ethics; or, The Challenge of Bisexuality to Lesbian Ethics." *Hypatia* 7, no. 4 (1992): 91–105.

DiBattista, Maria. *First Love: The Affections of Modern Fiction.* Chicago: University of Chicago Press, 1991.

Dick, Bernard F. *The Hellenism of Mary Renault.* Carbondale: Southern Illinois University Press, 1972.

Dollimore, Jonathan. "The Challenge of Sexuality." In *Society and Literature, 1945–1970,* ed. Alan Sinfield. London: Methuen, 1983.

Dover, K. J. *Greek Homosexuality.* Cambridge: Harvard University Press, 1989.

Duberman, Martin, Martha Vicinus, and George Chauncey, eds. *Hidden from*

History: Reclaiming the Gay and Lesbian Past. New York: New American Library, 1989.

Dunn, C. L., ed. *Medical History of the Second World War: Emergency Medical Services.* Vol. 1. London: Her Majesty's Stationary Office, 1952.

DuPlessis, Rachel Blau. *Writing beyond the Ending: Narrative Strategies of Twentieth-Century Women Writers.* Bloomington: Indiana University Press, 1985.

Dworkin, Andrea. "Biological Superiority: The World's Most Dangerous and Deadly Idea." In *Letters from a War Zone: Writings, 1976–1987.* London: Secker and Warburg, 1988.

Edelman, Lee. "Homographesis." *Yale Journal of Criticism* 3, no. 1 (fall 1989): 189–207.

Edwards, Lee R. *Psyche as Hero: Female Heroism and Fictional Form.* Middletown, Conn.: Wesleyan University Press, 1984.

Engelbrecht, Penelope. " 'Lifting Belly Is a Language': The Postmodern Lesbian Subject." *Feminist Studies* 16, no. 1 (1990): 85–114.

Evans, Joan. *Prelude and Fugue: An Autobiography.* London: Museum Press, 1964.

Evens, Tim, ed. *Stand Up and Be Counted.* York: Sessions, 1988.

Evens, Tim, and Stuart Walters. *The Winford Team.* St. Ives: Evens and Walters, 1945.

Faderman, Lillian. *Surpassing the Love of Men: Romantic Friendship and Love between Women from the Renaissance to the Present.* London: Women's Press, 1981.

Farwell, Marilyn. "Toward a Definition of the Lesbian Literary Imagination." *Signs* 14, no. 1 (1988): 100–118.

Fetterley, Judith. *The Resisting Reader: A Feminist Approach to American Fiction.* Bloomington: Indiana University Press, 1978.

Fleishman, Avron. *The English Historical Novel: Walter Scott to Virginia Woolf.* Baltimore: Johns Hopkins Press, 1971.

Fone, Byron R. S. *Hidden Heritage: History and the Gay Imagination.* New York: Irvington, 1981.

Foster, Jeannette H. *Sex Variant Women in Literature: A Historical and Quantitative Survey.* New York: Vantage Press, 1956.

Foucault, Michel. *The History of Sexuality.* Trans. Robert Hurley. 3 vols. New York: Viking Press, 1986.

Freud, Sigmund. *Three Essays on the Theory of Sexuality.* 1905. London: Hogarth Press, 1982.

Fuss, Diana. *Essentially Speaking: Feminism, Nature, and Difference.* New York: Routledge, 1989.

Fuss, Diana, ed. *Inside/Out: Lesbian Theories, Gay Theories.* New York: Routledge, 1991.

Gallop, Jane. *Thinking through the Body.* New York: Columbia University Press, 1988.

Gilbert, Sandra M., and Susan Gubar. *No Man's Land: The Place of the Woman Writer in the Twentieth Century.* 3 vols. New Haven: Yale University Press, 1987–1994.

Glenday, Nonita, and Mary Price. *Clifton High School: 1877–1977.* Bristol: Clifton High School, 1977.

Graves, Robert, and Alan Hodge. *The Long Week-End: A Social History of Great Britain, 1918–1939.* London: Faber and Faber, 1940.

Green, Peter. "The Masks of Mary Renault." *New York Review of Books,* March 8, 1979, 11–14.

Griffin, Gabriele. "*The Chinese Garden*: A Cautionary Tale." In *What Lesbians Do in Books,* ed. Elaine Hobby and Chris White. London: Women's Press, 1991.

Griffin, Penny, ed. *St. Hugh's: One Hundred Years of Women's Education in Oxford.* London: Macmillan, 1986.

Grosz, Elizabeth. "Experimental Desire: Rethinking Queer Subjectivity." In *Supposing the Subject,* ed. Joan Copjec. London: Verso, 1994.

Hall, Donald, and Maria Pramaggiore, eds. *RePresenting Bisexualities: Subjects and Cultures of Fluid Desire.* New York: New York University Press, 1996.

Hall, Radclyffe. *The Unlit Lamp.* London: Cassell, 1924.

———. *The Well of Loneliness.* London: Jonathan Cape, 1928.

Halperin, David. *One Hundred Years of Homosexuality and Other Essays on Greek Love.* New York: Routledge, 1990.

Hamilton, Cicely. *The Englishwoman.* London: Longmans, 1940.

Hartley, Jenny. *Hearts Undefeated: Women's Writing of the Second World War.* London: Virago, 1995.

Hartnoll, Phyllis, ed. *The Oxford Companion to the Theatre.* Rev. ed. London: Oxford University Press, 1967.

Hayes, Denis. *Challenge of Conscience: The Story of the Conscientious Objectors of 1939–1945.* London: Allen and Unwin, 1949.

Heilbrun, Carolyn. "Axiothea's Grief: The Disability of the Female Imagination." In *From Parnassus: Essays in Honor of Jacques Barzun,* ed. Dora B. Weiner and William R. Keylor. New York: Harper and Row, 1976.

———. *Writing a Woman's Life.* New York: Random House, 1988.

Herbert, Kevin. "The Theseus Theme: Some Recent Versions." *Classical Journal* 55 (January 1960): 175–85.

Herdt, Gilbert H. *Guardians of the Flutes: Idioms of Masculinity.* New York: McGraw Hill, 1981.

Higgonet, Margaret R., and Jane Jenson, eds., and Margaret Collins Weitz, contrib. *Behind the Lines: Gender and the Two World Wars.* New Haven: Yale University Press, 1987.

Hobby, Elaine, and Chris White, eds. *What Lesbians Do in Books.* London: Women's Press, 1991.

Hoberman, Ruth. *Gendering Classicism: The Ancient World in Twentieth-Century Women's Historical Fiction.* Albany: State University of New York Press, 1997.

Hollis, Christopher. *Oxford in the Twenties.* London: Heinemann, 1976.

Holtby, Winifred. *Women and a Changing Civilization.* London: Longmans, Green, 1935.

Hughes-Hallett, Lucy. "Quite Contrary." *Sunday Times,* April 11, 1993, sec. 6, p. 6.

Hyde, H. Montgomery. *The Love That Dared Not Speak Its Name: A Candid History of Homosexuality in Britain.* Boston: Little, Brown, 1970.

Hynes, Samuel. *The Auden Generation: Literature and Politics in England in the 1930s.* London: The Bodley Head, 1976.

Isaacs, Gordon, and Brian McKendrick. *Male Homosexuality in South Africa.* Cape Town: Oxford University Press, 1992.

Jacobus, Mary, ed. *Women Writing and Writing about Women.* New York: Barnes and Noble, 1979.

Jagose, Annamarie. *Queer Theory.* Carlton South: Melbourne University Press, 1996.

Jay, Karla, and Joanne Glasgow, eds. *Lesbian Texts and Contexts: Radical Revisions.* New York: New York University Press, 1990.

Jeffreys, Sheila. *The Spinster and Her Enemies: Feminism and Sexuality, 1880–1930.* London: Pandora Press, 1985.

Johnstone, Richard. *The Will to Believe: Novelists of the Nineteen Thirties.* Oxford: Oxford University Press, 1984.

Kenner, Hugh. "Mary Renault and Her Various Personas." *New York Times Book Review,* February 10, 1974, 15.

Kopelson, Kevin. *Love's Litany: The Writing of Modern Homoerotics.* Stanford: Stanford University Press, 1994.

Leonardi, Susan J. *Dangerous by Degrees: Women at Oxford and the Somerville College Novelists.* New Brunswick, N.J.: Rutgers University Press, 1989.

Lewis, Jane. *Women in England, 1870–1950: Sexual Divisions and Social Change.* Brighton: Wheatsheaf, 1984.

Light, Alison. "Family Romances." In *The Progress of Romance: The Politics of Popular Fiction,* ed. Jean Radford. London: Routledge and Kegan Paul, 1986.

———. *Forever England: Femininity, Literature, and Conservatism between the Wars.* London: Routledge, 1991.

Longhurst, Derek, ed. *Gender, Genre, and Narrative Pleasure.* London: Unwin Hyman, 1989.

Longmate, Norman. *How We Lived Then: A History of Everyday Life during the Second World War.* London: Hutchinson, 1971.

Lord, Walter. *The Miracle of Dunkirk.* New York: Viking Press, 1982.

Mackenzie, Compton. *Extraordinary Women.* London: Secker, 1928.

Mantle, Hilary. "Homophobic." *London Review of Books,* May 13, 1993, 18.

Marks, Elaine, and Isabelle de Courtivron, eds. *New French Feminisms: An Anthology.* Amherst: University of Massachusetts Press, 1980.

Marquard, Leo. *The Story of South Africa.* London: Faber and Faber, 1968.

Miller, Nancy K. *Subject to Change: Reading Feminist Writing.* New York: Columbia University Press, 1988.

Moberly, C. A. E., and E. F. Jourdain. *An Adventure.* London: Faber and Faber, 1924.

Moorehead, Caroline. *Troublesome People: Enemies of War, 1916–1986.* London: Hamish Hamilton, 1987.

Nestle, Joan. *The Persistent Desire: A Butch/Femme Reader.* Boston: Alyson, 1992.

Nicholson, Mavis. *What Did You Do in the War, Mummy? Women in World War II.* London: Chatto and Windus, 1995.

O'Rourke, Rebecca. *Reflecting on "The Well of Loneliness."* London: Routledge, 1989.

Ortner, Sherry B. "Is Male to Female as Nature Is to Culture?" In *Woman, Culture, and Society,* ed. Michelle Zimbalist Rosaldo and Louise Lamphere. Stanford: Stanford University Press, 1974.

Partridge, Frances. *A Pacifist's War.* London: Hogarth Press, 1978.

Philips, Deborah, and Ian Haywood. *Brave New Causes: Women in British Postwar Fictions.* London: Leicester University Press, 1998.

Price, Frederick W. *Diseases of the Heart.* London: Oxford University Press, 1927.

———. *A Textbook of the Practice of Medicine.* London: Oxford University Press, 1929.

Radicalesbians. "The Woman-Identified Woman." In *Feminism in Our Time: The Essential Writings, World War II to the Present,* ed. Miriam Schneir. New York: Vintage Books, 1994.

Rich, Adrienne. "Compulsory Homosexuality and Lesbian Existence." In *Blood, Bread, and Poetry: Selected Prose, 1979–1985.* New York: Norton, 1986.

Robb-Smith, A. H. T. *A Short History of the Radcliffe Infirmary.* Oxford: Church Army Press, 1970.

Roof, Judith. *A Lure of Knowledge: Lesbian Sexuality and Theory.* New York: Columbia University Press, 1991.

Rosaldo, Michelle Zimbalist. "Woman, Culture, and Society: A Theoretical Overview." In *Woman, Culture, and Society,* ed. Michelle Zimbalist Rosaldo and Louise Lamphere. Stanford: Stanford University Press, 1974.

Rothblum, Esther D. "Transforming Lesbian Sexuality." *Psychology of Women Quarterly* 18 (1994): 627–41.

Rothblum, Esther D., and Kathleen A. Brehony, eds. *Boston Marriages: Romantic but Asexual Relationships among Contemporary Lesbians.* Amherst: University of Massachusetts Press, 1993.

Rule, Jane. *Lesbian Images.* Garden City: Doubleday, 1975.

Russ, Joanna. *How to Suppress Women's Writing.* Austin: University of Texas Press, 1983.

Schneir, Miriam, ed. *Feminism in Our Time: The Essential Writings, World War II to the Present.* New York: Vintage Books, 1994.

Sedgwick, Eve Kosofsky. *Epistemology of the Closet.* Berkeley and Los Angeles: California University Press, 1990.

Selby, John. *A Short History of South Africa.* London: George Allen and Unwin, 1973.

Selby-Green, Jenny. *The History of the Radcliffe Infirmary.* Banbury: Image Publications, 1990.

Showalter, Elaine. *A Literature of Their Own: British Women Novelists from Brontë to Lessing.* London: Virago, 1978.

———. *The New Feminist Criticism: Essays on Women, Literature, Theory.* New York: Pantheon, 1985.

Siltanen, Janet, and Michelle Stanworth. "The Politics of Private Woman and Public Man." In *Women and the Public Sphere: A Critique of Sociology and Politics.* London: Hutchinson, 1984.

Sinfield, Alan, ed. *Society and Literature: 1945–1970.* London: Methuen, 1983.

Spencer, Colin. *Homosexuality in History.* New York: Harcourt, Brace, 1995.

Stallybrass, Peter, and Allon White. *The Politics and Poetics of Transgression.* Ithaca: Cornell University Press, 1986.

Stambolian, George, and Elaine Marks, eds. *Homosexuality and French Literature: Cultural Contexts, Critical Texts.* Ithaca: Cornell University Press, 1979.

Stark, Felix, ed. *Durban: From Its Beginnings to Its Silver Jubilee of City Status.* Johannesburg: Felstar Publishing, 1960.

Stimpson, Catharine. "Zero Degree Deviancy: The Lesbian Novel in English." *Critical Inquiry* 8, no. 2 (winter 1981): 363–79.

Summers, Claude J. " 'The Plain of Truth': Mary Renault's *The Charioteer.*" In *Gay Fictions: Wilde to Stonewall, Studies in a Male Homosexual Literary Tradition.* New York: Continuum, 1990.

Sweetman, David. *Mary Renault: A Biography.* London: Chatto and Windus, 1993.

Tanner, Tony. *Adultery in the Novel: Contract and Transgression.* Baltimore: Johns Hopkins University Press, 1979.

Todd, Janet. *Women's Friendship in Literature.* New York: Columbia University Press, 1980.

Tyler, Carole-Anne. "Boys Will Be Girls: The Politics of Gay Drag." In *Inside/Out: Lesbian Theories, Gay Theories,* ed. Diana Fuss. London: Routledge, 1991.

Weeks, Jeffrey. *Coming Out: Homosexual Politics in Britain from the Nineteenth Century to the Present.* London: Quartet, 1977.

———. "Questions of Identity." In *The Cultural Construction of Sexuality,* ed. Pat Caplan. London: Routledge, 1987.

———. *Sex, Politics, and Society: The Regulation of Sexuality since 1800.* London: Longman, 1981.

Wilde, Oscar. *The Ballad of Reading Gaol.* 1898. London: Phoenix, 1996.

Wilson, Robert. "Review of Books." *St. Mary's Hospital Gazette,* 1939, 61–62.

Wilton, Tamsin. *Lesbian Studies: Setting an Agenda.* London: Routledge, 1995.

Winkler, John J. *The Constraints of Desire: The Anthropology of Sex and Gender in Ancient Greece.* New York: Routledge, 1990.

Winnifrith, T. J. "Mary Renault." In *Great Writers of the English Language: Novelists and Prose Writers,* ed. James Vinson. London: Macmillan, 1979.

Winterson, Jeanette. *Art Objects: Essays on Ecstacy and Effrontery.* London: Jonathan Cape, 1995.

Wolfe, Peter. *Mary Renault.* New York: Twayne, 1969.

Woolf, Virginia. *A Room of One's Own.* New York: Harcourt, Brace and World, 1929.

Worrall, Clifford. "A Soft Answer: A Short Autobiography of Clifford Worrall, 1915–1992." Typescript in the possession of Tim Evens.

Yukman, Lidia. "Loving Dora: Rereading Freud through H. D.'s *Her.*" In *RePresenting Bisexualities: Subjects and Cultures of Fluid Desire,* ed. Donald Hall and Maria Pramaggiore. New York: New York University Press, 1996.

Zimmerman, Bonnie. "Exiting from Patriarchy: The Lesbian Novel of Development." In *The Voyage In,* ed. Elizabeth Able, Marianne Hirsch, and Elizabeth Langland. Hanover: University of New England Press, 1983.

Index